The Jacobite Rebellion

by

Hilary Kemp

with artwork by

Alan Kemp

ALMARK PUBLISHING CO. LTD., LONDON

First Published 1975.

ISBN 0 85524 239 6

Printed in Great Britain by
Pan Litho Ltd.,
Pan House,
172-176 The Highway,
London E1 9DD.
for the publishers, Almark Publishing Co. Ltd.,
49 Malden Way, New Malden,
Surrey KT3 6EA, England.

Contents

1   Preparations for Rebellion   5

2   The Failure of the 'Fifteen   40

3   The 'Forty-Five   78

4   The Collapse of a Dream   116

Author's Acknowledgements

I should like to express my gratitude to the following people: to the staff of the National Library of Scotland for permitting me to see items from the Blaikie Collection of Jacobite material and for their co-operation in the supply of photocopies; to Dr. Rosalind K. Marshall, Assistant Keeper of the Scottish National Portrait Gallery for her considerable and patient assistance in the collation of illustrative material, for her help in locating private owners of exhibits and arranging the supply of photographic material; to Messrs. Scott of Edinburgh and Annan of Glasgow for their photographs, and the Trustees of the Scottish National Portrait Gallery for permission to reproduce works in the Gallery's Collection. My thanks go also to the library staff of the Society of Antiquaries of Scotland for their assistance, and the Council of the National Museum of Antiquities of Scotland for permission to reproduce the painting of Marshal Wade. I am grateful to the staff of the Scottish Record Office and the Northumberland County Record Office for their help. I would like to thank The Right Hon. the Earl of Mar and Kellie for his permission to reproduce the Kneller portrait of his ancester John Erskine, 6th Earl of Mar, and His Grace the Duke of Atholl for allowing me to reproduce the pen drawing of William Murray, Marquis of Tullibardine. I am also obliged to W. Drummond Moray, Esq., of Crieff for his kind permission to reproduce the Abercairney portrait of George Keith, 10th Earl Marischal. I am grateful to Bill Wake, Curator of the John Joicey Museum, Newcastle upon Tyne for permission to photograph weapons in the Museum's collection; to the Newcastle upon Tyne Society of Antiquaries for permission to photograph the Earl of Derwentwater's death mask and the Highland pipes, and to Bob Mayo, Snr., of Photomayo, Newcastle, for his colour photographs. My thanks also to Richard Holt of Stirling University for the "Chevalier de Johnstone" and for taking me to Sheriffmuir. Finally, I would like to acknowledge the debt I owe to my husband for all the original artwork.

Author's Note

The original spelling of the name, Stuart, as used by the royal family was 'Stewart', taken from the office of Lord High Stewart of Scotland which was hereditary in the family nearly two centuries before the succession of Robert II to the throne. This spelling continued for several reigns but increasing communication with France rendered the 'w' obsolete because that letter does not appear in the French language. Instead 'u' was used and the name was spelt as Stuard or Stuart. Mary Queen of Scots, educated in France, adopted and helped popularize the French spelling.

1 Preparations for Rebellion

Introduction

'Jacobite' is a term which came into use after King James II of England was deposed in 1688 and means 'supporter of James' from the Latin word for his name, *Jacobus*. As a descriptive term, it assumed other implications. In particular it was associated with Roman Catholicism, Divine Right and the Scottish interest in the House of Stuart. But it was never solely a religious movement, nor was it purely a Scottish phenomenon. Jacobites were known to exist in large numbers in Ireland, the West Country and in London. In the 1715 and 1745 rebellions, Roman Catholics and Protestants often fought together on the same side. Jacobitism was a widespread and vague concept, but as an armed movement it was heavily dependent upon the support of the Scottish Highlanders whose social and political conditions and emotional attachment combined to produce in them the strongest reason for attempting the restoration of the Stuarts. After the death of James II in exile in 1701, Jacobite hopes centred on his son who was also called James. The same expression was used for the supporters of his grandson, the legendary Bonnie Prince Charlie.

The Background

On June 10, 1688, Mary of Modena, second wife of the Roman Catholic monarch King James II of England and VII of Scotland, gave birth to a healthy male heir, the first of their progeny to survive beyond infancy. The birth of James Francis Edward Stuart created the threat of a continuing Roman Catholic dynasty in England. The prospect was thought sufficiently odious to call for the implementation of the contingency plans known to history as the Glorious Revolution of 1688. The Dutch invasion brought the unglamorous champions of liberty, William and Mary, to save a Protestant nation from the conspiracies of a Roman Catholic Monarch. James II was forced to flee to France with his wife and baby son, leaving behind him an exaggerated reputation for religious fanaticism and a more accurate title to arbitrary rule.

The new King and Queen, William and Mary, died without issue. But near the end of William's reign, an Act of Settlement provided that he should be succeeded by his Protestant sister-in-law, Anne. Mary and Anne were the offspring of the deposed king's first marriage. They were both staunch Protestants, whose attitude to their father's dethronement was influenced more by their religious faith rather than by filial affection. Anne was thus half-sister to the boy being reared in the exiled court in France, but she was not to be succeeded by him. The Act of Settlement provided that she should be succeeded by her nearest Protestant relation, the Electress Sophia of Hanover and her heirs. (Sophia's mother had been the daughter of James I and VI). At the time of its completion, the Act of Settlement applied only to the English throne. Although England and Scotland had been ruled jointly since the accession of James I of England and VI of Scotland, the northern kingdom was still independent. It had a separate parliament and a people who were at liberty to offer their crown to whom they chose. Although the offer of the crown to William and Mary was made in England on February 13, 1689, it was not until some three months later that a similar offer came from Scotland. A Convention in Edinburgh framed its own conditions for acceptance by the new king and queen and was in no way bound by law or treaty to accept the same rulers as England. In 1703, during Anne's reign, Scottish independence was strongly asserted when the Scottish Parliament passed an Act of Security releasing it from any obligation to accept as successor to Anne the person designated by the English parliament. With each restatement of the Scottish position, the fear grew that someday a movement might develop in Scotland to bring back one of the exiled Stuarts to occupy the vacant Scottish throne.

The deposed king James II died in France in 1701 and the Jacobites regarded his son, James Francis Edward Stuart, by then 13 years old, as the legitimate king of England and Scotland James III and VIII. William III had always been aware of the danger to England if the Scots seriously pressed for their independence. The prospect of a hostile northern neighbour with a Catholic king sympathetic towards the France of Louis XIV was a nightmare he did not care to see realized. A union of the two countries therefore became a matter of vital importance to his peace of mind. The Act of Union, first discussed in his reign, became fact in the reign of Queen Anne in 1707. On May 1, the new Parliament of Great Britain came into being and the two countries were linked under a common flag, common seal, common coinage and a monarchy that was to descend to the Hanoverians. The Union was pushed through the Scottish parliament against stiff opposition. Far from uniting the sympathies of the two peoples concerned, the Union more than any other single event of the period succeeded in uniting all Scotsmen in their hatred of England. In all strata of Scottish society, the consequences of the legislative union were dreaded. It was believed in all sincerity that it would be the ruin of Scotland, that its name would be removed from the map and that it would become a mere province of England.

> 'Fareweel to a' our Scottish fame
> Fareweel our ancient glory;
> Fareweel e'en to the Scottish name
> Sae fam'd in martial story.
> Now Sark rins ower the Solway sands,
> And Tweed rins to the Ocean,
> To mark where England's province stands
> Such a parcel of rogues in a nation.'[1]

The deep cultural and religious divisions in Scottish society were momentarily healed as Scotsmen came together in a mood of indignation at the loss of their independent parliament. At this point the possibility of a

---

1. *The Jacobite Relics of Scotland; Being The Songs, Airs and Legends of the Adherents to the House of Stuart.* Collected and Illustrated by James Hogg. Edinburgh, MDCCCXIX, 2 vols. Vol.1 Pp. 56-7. v.i.

Stuart restoration assumed an additional attraction beyond mere sentiment. It became linked with a desire to reverse the decision to establish the Union and, although the method was never made clear, it was felt that a Stuart king in London would have messianic powers to restore to the Scots their ancient rights and privileges. This consideration weighed heavily with those who took up arms for the Stuarts in the 'Fifteen and was still a motivating force as late as the 'Forty-five.

The emotional ties which might at one time have linked the Stuart royal family with the land of its Scottish ancestors had been severely strained by the mounting indifference of successive Stuart monarchs to the welfare of the Scottish people. None of them were Scottish chauvinists and, by 1715, the Scots had little reason to adore them. James II visited Scotland only twice in his lifetime and on neither occasion did he succeed in forging any special links with the community. Scotland was a poor country, sparsely populated and imperfectly understood south of the border. Geographically, it was divided between Highlands and Lowlands and the most important social factor was the strength of animosity between the people of the two regions. The average eighteenth-century Englishman's view of the Highlander's way of life was limited by an almost total ignorance. He heard of tribal government and clan wars and concluded, quite erroneously, that the Highlanders were savages. Geographically the Highlands were then taken to be:

'...... the Mountainous Parts of Scotland not defined or described by any precise Limits or Boundaries of Counties of Shires but are Tracts of Mountains in extent of Land, more than one half of the Kingdom of Scotland; and are for the most part on the West Ocean, extending from Dumbarton to the North End of the Island of Great Britain near 200 Miles in length, and from about 40 to 80 Miles in breadth. All the Islands on the West and North West Seas are called Highlands as well from their Mountainous Situation, as from the Habits, Customs, Manners and Language of their Inhabitants.'

The Lowlands were seen as:
'... all that part of Scotland on the South of Forth and Clyde and on the East side of the Kingdom from the Firth of Edinburgh to Caithness near the Orkneys is a Tract of Low Country from 4 to 20 Miles in breadth.'

The people living in isolated enclaves beyond the Highland Line (an imaginary line running roughly north-east across Scotland from Dumbarton to the Moray Firth) scraped a living from the barren land. They relied on the clan structure for protection and existed largely beyond the pale of government interference. In the opinion of their Lowland neighbours, the Highlanders did not even have a Scottish identity, but were referred to as 'the Irish' because of their Gaelic tongue. In addition to the language barrier, the Highland and Lowland communities were separated by considerable differences in social organization. The fundamental basis of Highland society was the clan. In Gaelic, 'clann' meant children, and the chief of the clan, as father of his blood relatives, commanded their absolute loyalty in return for protecting their interests. One of the few English travellers to penetrate beyond the Highland Line in the early eighteenth century observed that 'the ordinary Highlanders esteem it the most sublime degree of virtue to love their chief and pay him a blind obedience, although it be in opposition to the government, the laws of the kingdom, or even the laws of God. He is their idol; and as they profess to know no king but him . . . so will they say, they ought to do whatever he commands without enquiry'.[2] In 1724 General George Wade was sent by George I into the Highlands 'narrowly to inspect the present situation of the Highlanders, their Customs,

2. Captain Burt, *Letters from a Gentleman in the North of Scotland to his Friends in London*. London, 1815. P. 84.

Manners and State of the Country'. Wade's observations on Highland life might, with equal accuracy, have applied to any period in Highland history in the previous two centuries.

'Their Notions of Virtue and Vice are very different from the more civilized part of Mankind. They think it a most Sublime Virtue to pay a Servile and Abject Obedience to the Commands of their Chieftans, altho' in opposition to their Sovereign, and the laws of the Kingdom, and to encourage this, their Fidelity, they are treated by their Chiefs with great Familiarity, they partake with them in their Diversions, and shake them by the Hand wherever they meet them.

The Virtue next to this, in esteem amongst them, is the Love they bear to that particular Branch of which they are a part, and in a Second Degree to the whole Clan, or Name, by assisting each other (right or wrong) against any other Clan with whom they are at Variance, and great Barbarities are often committed by One, to revenge the Quarrels of Another. They have still a more extensive adherence one to another as Highlanders in opposition to the People who Inhabit the Low Countries, whom they hold in the utmost Contempt, imagining them inferior to themselves in Courage, Resolution and the use of Arms . . . .

The Highlanders are divided into Tribes or Clans, under Lairds, or Chieftans (as they are called in the Laws of Scotland), each Tribe or Clan is subdivided into little Branches sprung from the Main Stock, who have also Chieftans over them, and from these are still smaller Branches of Fifty or Sixty Men, who deduce their Original from them, and on whom they rely as their Protectors and Defenders. The Arms they make use of in War, are a Musket, a Broad Sword and a Target, a Pistol and a Durk or Dagger, hanging by their side, with a Powder Horn and Pouch for their Ammunition. They form themselves into Bodies of unequal Numbers according to the Strength of their Clan or Tribe which is Commanded by their Respective Superior or Chieftan.'

With their fierce loyalties and cult of military virtue, the Highlanders were marked off from the rest of society by distinctions of language, dress and social organization. They thought of themselves as a separate nation with a unique culture that owed nothing to the rest of society. The clan system was a powerful force and one which the exiled Stuarts succeeded, in part, in harnessing to their cause. Those who bore the royal name in the Highlands might be expected to support Jacobite intrigues out of a sense of familial obligation. Others caught in the complicated network of clan loyalties regarded the Stuart cause as equally sacrosanct. But where the Jacobite Highlander was prepared to be blindly obedient to the House of Stuart, others of his countrymen tended to be more critical.

The major deterrent to the restoration of the Stuarts continued to be the Roman Catholic religion, as indeed, it was the chief reason for their expulsion. If James II had not been inexorably opposed to the idea of his son falling under Protestant influence, a peaceful restoration might have been arranged. In 1696 William III put forward proposals to recognize the young James Francis Edward Stuart as his heir in return for an undertaking from the boy's father to desist from Jacobite intrigue while William lived. In this way William would have been able to live out his reign peacefully free of Stuart machinations to unseat him. James did not respond kindly to the schemes of his successor and was not disposed to barter with a usurper, much less countenancing the inexpiable sin of bargaining with his son's immortal soul. James's religious devotion was no more acceptable to most of his Scots subjects than it had been to the English. Indeed, there were many in what James liked to call his 'antient kingdom' who frankly detested him and to whom 'Popery' was anathema. The Lowland Presbyterians had loudly applauded the anti-papal riots that disrupted James II's last troubled months in power. James's sucession had been opposed on religious ground in the first instance and Protestants in both countries were quite happy to see him in exile. In the pretensions of his son, they saw only an unwelcome revival of the issues of Popery and Absolutism.

The Scottish nation was thus by no means heart and soul united in favour of Jacobitism. The movement received an enormous fillip from the animosity generated by the Union. In 1708, a year after its negotiation and seven years after the death of the exiled James II, the 19-year-old Stuart heir was summoned from France by a dissatisfied and revengeful nation of Scots, in the hope that, given adequate armed support, he would be able to redress the country's many grievances. The expedition was abortive. James set off at the head of a powerful fleet and some 6,000 men for the Firth of Forth but, owing to bad navigation, worse weather and the interference of English men-of-war, the boy destined to become the 'Old Pretender' was unable to make a landing. The opportunity was lost and so strong a mood of national co-operation in Scotland never occurred again.

When Queen Anne died on August 1, 1714, a dynasty, which had lasted for 343 years in Scottish history, came to an end. Her death had been preceded by the death of the Electress Sophia of Hanover and, consequently, the crown passed in accordance with the Act of Settlement to Sophia's eldest son, George Louis. George I appeared to Scots and English alike a parvenu king, a 'wee, wee, German lairdie' in the words of the Jacobite ballad. His disregard for all things English, including the language, made him a particularly unattractive sovereign in London. For a brief interval in 1715, continuing Scottish resentment

George I, son of the Electress Sophia of Hanover, became king of Great Britain and Ireland in 1714. He succeeded Queen Anne and reigned until 1727.

over the Union and English aversion to the Hanoverian monarch united in a mutual interest in the 'king over the water'. In general, the Whig party in England opposed Jacobitism utterly, whereas the Tory party was prepared to investigate its possibilities. Immediately prior to the death of Queen Anne, the ascendancy of the Tory faction created a situation that had looked promising for the Jacobites. A little more energy from them, combined with a positive declaration from the aspirant James III to abjure Catholicism, and the Act of Settlement might have been set aside in favour of a Stuart. But like his father before him, James Francis allowed an opportunity for peaceful restoration to founder on the ground of religious conscience. The occasion for a Jacobite coup provided by Queen Anne's death was allowed to pass unexploited. To the great disappointment of Jacobite sympathizers everywhere, the Elector of Hanover was installed in England without incident. George had already shown favour to the Whigs prior to his landing and, following his arrival, he did not hide his preference. The animosity shown by the new king towards those whom he considered to be his political enemies ultimately made the job of raising a Jacobite rebellion easier than it might otherwise have been. Discarded servants were stung into retaliation and formed the nucleus of the insurgents. Prominent Tories, who had been implicated in abortive schemes to bring James to England on the death of the Queen, were forced to join their exiled Prince in France. The association with Jacobitism cost the Tory party its credibility in Hanoverian England and resulted in its downfall.

After the flight of James II in 1688, and before the vacant throne was filled by William and Mary, the free Parliament, which met during the interregnum, known as the Convention, agreed in principle that before the throne was filled the 'rights, laws and liberties of the nation' should be rendered immune from the sort of attack they had sustained under the arbitrary hand of the departed king. A Declaration of Rights was read out to the new incumbents before they took the throne. This document, which later became embodied in a Bill of Rights passed by Parliament, aimed at limiting the power of the monarchy and, in fact, curtailed privileges in specific ways. James's practice of suspending laws without the consent of Parliament was now outlawed. The king's maintenance of a standing army was made illegal and free elections were demanded. But the importance of the Act lay less in the specific ways in which royal power was limited than in Parliament's implicit decision to take over the sovereignty of the government from the Crown. This was the real starting point of constitutional monarchy in England. The constitution, as it was settled after the 'Glorious Revolution of 1688', enshrined the principle that the monarchs of England would be subject to the elected representatives of the people. This parliamentary title to the throne was emphasized as never before by the accession of George I. General misgivings about the choice, manifest in all strata of society, gave way eventually to the realization that the personal inadequacies of a king whose powers had been curtailed was not the serious matter it once had been, A far-sighted attitude to national institutions began to take precedence over an immediate prejudice against the new king. Jacobitism foundered upon this sort of thinking. Supporters of the Stuart claimant, who championed the natural law of primogeniture, were also identified with the superseded principles of Divine Right and Absolutism. This destructive element at the heart of the movement meant that the longer it lasted, the more backward-looking it was bound to appear. This retrograde aspect was further intensified by the adherence of the loyal Highland chiefs who were clearly the last-ditch supporters of a disappearing way of life. The rebellion of 1715, therefore, gained some advantage from being more closely related in time to the events it sought to upset. But the 'Forty-five, which has survived in history as the major effort, took place some 57 years after the expulsion of the Stuart king.

A Shaky Start

Originally, the 1715 rebellion in Scotland was planned to operate in conjunction with similar risings in the south-west of England and the northern counties. The Jacobites never intended that the main emphasis should fall on Scotland or that the rebellion there should be self-supporting. The Earl of Mar, who became the commander-in-chief of the Jacobite forces in Scotland, encouraged recruitment on the ground that France would supply substantial support in the way of money, arms and personnel. Louis XIV's policy was to give his unofficial support to any Jacobite intrigue which might seriously disrupt the internal peace of his nation's enemy, England. But the death of the French king, some five days before the rebellion officially began in Braemar, precipitated a change in French policy and the considerable preparations which had been made to support the Scottish rising were abandoned. Twelve ships loaded with men and ammunition were prevented from sailing from French ports and only a few small vessels were able to get away. This meant, from the outset, the rebels' expectations were not realized. In his *Journal* the Jacobite leader was later to recall that 'however incredible it may appear, ... we never receiv'd from Abroad the least supply of Arms or Ammunition of any kind; Tho it was notorious in itself and well known, both to Friends and Enemies, that this was what from the Beginning we mainly wanted'.[3] The disappointment was one from which the Jacobites did not easily recover. The situation was aggravated by their unwillingness to concentrate on the slender resources that were available in the vain hope that these might yet be supplemented from abroad.

A handful of the most prominent members of the disgraced Tory party, of whom the Duke of Ormonde and Viscount Bolingbroke were the most significant, became satellites of the exiled court in France. Bolingbroke became James's Secretary of State and applied himself to the task of securing French support for a proposed rebellion in which Scotland was only to play a subsidiary part. The main action was envisaged for the south-west of England. James was to land in Devon whereupon the entire county was expected to rise in his defence, possibly with the support of the army whose loyalty to King George was considered shaky. But before this plan could be implemented, government arrests in England in September and the strengthening of key cities rendered it abortive. James continued to harbour the hope well into October, 1715 that a landing in the west country might trigger off a national uprising, but in fact government vigilance had prematurely wrecked his chances of success. In Scotland, Jacobite intelligence of events in the south was so deficient that the rebel press boldly published the news that King George had found it necessary to flee the capital. Devoid of its essential features — the certainty of French assistance and a successful enterprise in the south-west — the emphasis of the 'Fifteen necessarily fell on the Scottish rebellion which got off to a shaky start.

The prospect of taking up arms for the Stuarts provoked a mixed reaction in Scotland. As well as being divided between Lowlands and Highlands, the country was divided between those who fell under the influence of Jacobite landlords and those who did not. The government in London was well aware that the feudal influence of the Scottish aristocracy over their vassals, tenants and dependants might well prove decisive in the business of raising a rebellion. The government attempted to weaken that influence through an Act for encouraging loyalty in Scotland. Known as the Clan Act, it aimed at giving security of tenure to the tenants of rebel landlords who, acting in disobedience to their superiors, might be spared the fate of destitution by holding their tenures direct from the Crown. Sir Walter Scott suggested that the Jacobite landlords were not renowned for their far-sightedness and valued political principles only in so far as they related to their conception of national honour and the maintenance of privilege. However, it was just these men whom Mar needed to at-

3. Mar's Journal. Extracts reproduced in *History of the Late Rebellion* by the Rev. Mr. Robert Patten. London, 1717.

John Erskine, Earl of Mar (1675-1732), headed the 1715 uprising in Scotland. A skilled diplomat, Mar had held ministerial posts under Queen Anne, but he proved to be indecisive in military affairs.

tract to his enterprise because of their influence and the numbers they could command into the field.

In Scotland the rebellion began officially with the raising of the old Scottish standard at Braemar situated on Mar's estates at Deeside, on September 6, 1715. The enterprise got off to a very shaky start, being in fact sprung upon a surprised nation from an unexpected quarter. The history of the 'Fifteen in its embryonic stage was closely allied to the personal fortunes of John Erskine, 6th Earl of Mar, the 40-year-old self-appointed commander of the pretended James VIII's forces in Scotland. Although Mar was himself chieftain of the Erskine clan and, as such, the representative of an ancient Scottish family renowned for its fidelity to the Stuarts, he was by no means universally respected among the Jacobites of his native land. He was known to contemporaries as 'Bobbing John', possibly because of a nervous head movement, but more probably, because of his facility in changing political horses. He was regarded as

altogether too versatile to be entirely trustworthy. In 1707 he had been a supporter of the Act of Union, a biographical detail not likely to be overlooked by Scottish Jacobites. After the dissolution of the Scottish Parliament, he had taken a seat in the House of Lords where he reversed his view on the Union. He had held ministerial posts in the Tory administration of Queen Anne's reign and became vaguely implicated in the abortive plans for a coup d'état on the Queen's demise. Once George I was obviously installed in London, however, Mar decided to swim with the tide and quickly offered his services to the new king, only to find himself rebuffed. Discarded by the king and unable to drag himself clear of the taint of intrigue, Mar began to fear for his safety. In the London of August 1715, it was dangerous to be even remotely connected with Jacobitism. Mar decided to flee to Scotland where he might vindicate himself against the Hanoverian king by organizing a Scottish revolt. According to Peter Rae, Whig historian and implacable enemy of Jacobitism, 'the Earl of Mar, then at London, not finding how to form his own Interest at Court had resolved on those wicked and traitorous Measures he afterwards followed; and in order to raise and carry on the Rebellion had by some means or other received from abroad, no less than the Sum of one hundred thousand Pounds Sterling . . fearing lest his traitorous designs against his lawful sovereign Prince, to whom he had so early and solemnly promised Fidelity, might possibly be discovered, and he himself secured by the Government, he resolved to make a sudden Tour into Scotland . . . in order to make some speedy Advances in this his pernicious and bloody Undertaking'. On August 1 or 2, 1715 Mar, disguised in plain clothes, embarked with Major-General Hamilton, Colonel Hay and two servants on board a collier in the Thames bound for Newcastle. In Newcastle he hired a vessel which took him to Fife. He was met by friends to whom he made his intentions known and who were apprised of his coming. He then travelled overland to reach his estates at Braemar canvassing support along the way. On August 18, he passed the River Tay, about two miles from Perth, with a body of 40 horse on his way north and next day he issued letters to known Jacobite sympathizers inviting them to meet him at Braemar, where he arrived on the 20th.

By his precipitate action, Mar put a great strain on his relationship with those prominent servants of the Jacobite Prince, such as Secretary of State Bolingbroke, who were working in the Pretender's interest in France to co-ordinate plans for a rising. Although Mar spoke much of being entrusted with the direction of the Pretender's affairs and brandished weighty-looking documents on all occasions, his authority was in fact precarious and his commission was thought to be spurious. It was not until the rebellion was well under way that he was able to offer irrefutable evidence of a royal appointment to command. The sudden eruption of events in Scotland undoubtedly forced James's hand and committed him in name, if nothing else, to open revolt before his own plans had reached fruition. There can be little doubt that if King George had been prepared to accept Mar's offer of service, then the direction of the 'Fifteen in Scotland would have fallen into other hands. But Mar was not alone in being motivated by frustrated ambition. According to the contemporary Jacobite historian Robert Patten, 'many of the Gentlemen concerned . . . had not only offer'd their Services to the King, but had taken Oaths to continue faithfull to him and had in particular abjur'd the Interest of the Pretender'.[4] At the source of the rebellion there was an undercurrent of private animosity against King George as well as a reservoir of Stuart loyalty. By his peremptory action, Mar ensured that the rebellion would be a highly impromptu affair, and there is evidence to suggest that the aspirant James III and VIII or, the Chevalier

de St. George as he was now known, would have checked its untimely birth had he been able to intervene in time.

On August 26, the Earl of Mar held a tinchel, or hunting party, on his estates and so furnished himself with an excuse for assembling a company of noblemen and Highland chiefs, whose real purpose was to foment a rebellion. According to Rae, 'there appeared the Marquis of Huntley, eldest Son to the Duke of Gordon; the Marquis of Tullibardine, eldest Son to the Duke of Athol; the Earls of Nithsdale, Marischal, Traquair, Errol, Southesk, Carnwath, Seaforth, Linlithgow, and several others; the Viscounts of Kilsyth, Kenmore, Kingston and Stormount; the Lords Rollo, Duffus, Drummond, Strathallan, Ogilvie and Nairn, with a good many Gentlemen of Interest in the Highlands, amongst whom were the two Generals, Hamilton and Gordon, Glenderule, Auldbair, Auchterhouse, Glengary, and others from the Clans'.[5] Having assembled likely supporters, Mar assumed the role of propagandist. Whether at this particular meeting or a similar one held later, he exercised his ingenuity and considerable oratorical skill to raise the political temperature of his listeners and bring their simmering discontents to boiling point. He began by breaking down their resistance to him with an eloquent apology for his part in the negotiation of the Union, declaring that now 'his Eyes were open'd, and he could see his Error, and would therefore do what lay in his Power to make them again a free People'. He followed up by playing upon the prejudices of his guests, deploring the enslaving power of the Union for the Scots and denigrating the 'Prince of Hanover' as a careless monarch with small regard for the welfare or religious liberties of his people. He assured his listeners that the Chevalier de St. George was the only rightful king and he beguiled them with a blanket promise that the Stuart heir would 'hear their Grievances and would redress their Wrongs'. Finally, he completely disarmed his

4. In *History of the Late Rebellion*, London, 1717 P. 3.

5. This is the standard list of those present given by Rae in *The History of the Rebellion Rais'd against His Majesty King George I by the Friends of the Popish Pretender*. Second Edition, London M.DCC.XLVI, p. 189. In a footnote, however, Rae says 'I doubt if some of them were there'.

audience with an inspiring declaration that, for his own part, he was resolved to set up his standard and determined to hazard his life in the cause, adding for good measure that there was a certainty of 'powerful assistance from France'. The Jacobite leaders were powerless to resist such an impassioned appeal aimed so skilfully at their prejudices. They expressed themselves in favour of an enterprise which would translate their feelings into deeds. Each of them then disappeared to the area of his own particular influence to prepare his vassals for war. Meanwhile, the Earl of Mar set about assembling his own followers.

For the average clansman, the decision whether or not to take up arms for the Stuart claimant was seldom an independent one. He did as he was told and obeyed his clan chief or feudal superior despite the safeguards of the Clan Act. Among the Highland clans, the hierarchical situation was complicated by a confused system of land tenure. The clan system was essentially patriarchal. A chief with his subsidiary chieftains supervised the welfare of the family. Often, however, a family or members of a family subsisted on land which was not owned by the chief and they owed allegiance to their landlord as feudal superior and legal owner of the land, as well as to their family superior. Where these two loyalties conflicted, the clansman was caught between the duty to his family and the legal imperatives of his situation. Either way his personal inclination was of small consequence. Most Highland chiefs deplored the encroachment of a legal system of land ownership upon their ancient patterns of patriarchal rights. They would have liked nothing better than to shake off the fetters of legality and enjoy the privileges of hereditary ownership unmolested. To the north-east of the Braes of Mar was Kildrummy, where some tenants of the Earl of Mar showed themselves reluctant to 'come out'. Their landlord, using methods of persuasion less subtle than those he had only recently demonstrated, wrote to his baillie instructing him to burn the homes of those who continued to be unco-operative. For these unfortunate tenants and others like them, who were brought to James's standard in a similar way, there was little to be gained by coming out and even less if they stayed at home.

By the time the standard was raised on September 6, 1715, Mar had by his side the nucleus of a Jacobite army. After James Francis Edward Stuart had been declared King of Scotland, England, France and Ireland,[6] the standard was raised. Immediately, an incident occurred which filled the assembled crowd with foreboding and introduced a faintly comic note into the proceedings which was frequently to be heard again thereafter. 'Tis reported', says Rae, 'that when this Standard was first erected, the Ball on the Top of it fell off, which the superstitious Highlanders were very much concern'd at, taking it as an Omen of the Bad Success of the Cause, for which they were then appearing'. The curtain was thus unsteadily raised on covert Jacobite activity in Scotland. The open declaration of James's title to the throne was a process repeated in other parts of the country by prominent Jacobites. James was proclaimed king at Aberdeen by the Earl Marischal, at Dunkeld by the Marquis of Tullibardine, at Castle Gordon by the Marquis of Huntly and at Brechin, Montrose, Dundee and Inverness. Mar's intentions, which had been under suspicion in London since his dramatic disappearance from government circles in early August, were now made abundantly clear.

The Capture of Perth

The measures taken by the government to guard against rebellion in Scotland were neither as prompt nor as effective as those implemented to quash the proposed revolt in the south-west. The Lords Lieutenants of the shires received orders to raise the militia, and the key cities of Edinburgh and Glasgow were

6. The mysterious reference to France in James's list of pretensions must surely have irritated the French allies upon whom James depended so much for the realization of his ambitions.

14

strengthened by their armed volunteers. The merchants of the two main cities and Dumfries, who did not want to see their country's commerce disrupted by a rebellion which might interfere with the favourable trading conditions enjoyed since the Union, were quick to show their allegiance to King George by raising armed defence volunteers. In Edinburgh these men formed themselves into regiments under the name of the Associate Volunteers of Edinburgh and soon set about raising subscriptions for the purchase of arms in the event of their being harassed by the Jacobites. Glasgow also raised a good regiment of volunteers, as well as funds to defend the cause of the King and uninterrupted trade. Dumfries raised from its inhabitants seven volunteer companies of 60 men each and, in general, the common people of Scotland whose only constraint was their conscience, supported the Protestant line of succession and showed themselves willing to arm in its defence. In addition to the volunteers, five regiments of dragoons and three regiments of foot were brought to Stirling and three regular regiments recalled from Ireland arrived in Edinburgh on August 24. On August 27, Major-General Wightman occupied the government stronghold at Stirling Castle which commanded access to the bridge of the Firth of Forth and passage into southern Scotland. However, when the Duke of Argyll arrived on September 16 at the government camp established in Stirling park, with his commission as General of His Majesty's army in Scotland, he was to find that, some ten days after the rebellion had officially begun, there were fewer than 2,000 government troops between the assembling Jacobite army and the border.

Despite the dubiety of his authority and status, the Earl of Mar was beginning to draw the promised support to James's standard. Ebenezer Whittel, one time personal servant to the Earl was later to testify before the Lord Provost of Edinburgh that Mar had gathered together about 500 of his own men '300 whereof, being well-armed, went to Castletoun alongst with the Earl of Mar, Lieutenant General Hamilton . . . and that the remaining 200 went away, 'till they should be provided with better Arms, and then were to follow'. Whittel went on to declare that 'at Castletoun they proclaimed the Pretender and set up a Standard with an J.R. 3 and 8 Figures'. According to the same source, the procession moved on to Kirkmichael where it was joined by 300 horse under the command of Lord Drummond and the Earl of Linlithgow, and the following day a further injection of support came in the shape of 500 of the Duke of Atholl's men, all foot, led by the Marquis of Tullibardine, the Duke's eldest son.

If Mar needed a reminder that the rebellion he had provoked was likely to become a civil war, then it was present in miniature in the internecine struggles within the Murray family. John Murray, 2nd Marquis and 1st Duke of Atholl was regarded as one of the most powerful lords in Scotland and his loss to the Jacobite side was rightly seen as highly detrimental to the cause. His son, the Marquis of Tullibardine with brothers Lord Charles and Lord George Murray together with their uncle, Lord Nairn, however, all took side with Mar. The Marquis described by Sinclair as 'a modest good-natured younge gentleman' endeavoured to bring over the Athollmen to the Jacobite side in opposition to his father's wishes. Whatever the reason for the Duke's minority stand, the Master of Sinclair in his *Memoirs of the Insurrection in Scotland in 1715* suggested that he was not wooed by the Jacobites in a fashion equal to his importance. Always Mar's severest critic, Sinclair suggested that Mar, for his own ends, 'did not want he should joyn' for fear of being outshone by an abler administrator', the Duke, being in Sinclair's view 'of that consequence that he'd (have) done more in one day in raiseing the Highlands than Mar did in two months'. The Murrays were not the only family divided by the 'Fifteen. There were also Gordons and Campbells ranged on both sides and, among specifically "whig" clans, were the Frasers, Grants, Rosses and Monroes. The government army was to form its Highland Companies from among those clans well disposed to the government.

Mar continued to travel south at a leisurely pace, collecting recruits and proclaiming James king along the way. Meanwhile, the Jacobites were about to secure their first victory of the campaign under the direction of Colonel John Hay, Mar's brother-in-law and titular Earl of Inverness. At Perth, members of the Whig party, who had been alarmed by the arrival of exaggerated reports of Mar's success, began to disarm their Tory citizens as a precaution against insurrection. They also applied for outside help and received from the Duke of Atholl a body of 200 Highlanders whose function was to dampen the aspirations of any would-be rebels in the town. But when the loyalty of the Highlanders was investigated, it was found to be shaky. The Tories of the town quickly exploited the possibility of the Highlanders' defection by issuing an urgent message to Colonel Hay, who was then busy collecting recruits in Fife, asking him to come to Perth at once with all the force he could muster. On Hay's arrival it was planned to organize a revolt and hand over the town to the rebels. Hay no sooner appeared on the other side of the Tay outside the town with a cavalcade of horse than the Tory burghers fulfilled their promise. With the passive support of the Highlanders, they delivered the town into the hands of the invaders. Mar's part in the whole venture seems to have been limited to acknowledgement of its success, since it was apparently executed without his knowledge.

The capture of Perth only eight days after the rising began, although scarcely a military achievement, at least struck an early note of success which helped to dispel previous doubts and misgivings. Furthermore, the

location of the town, poised between Highlands and Lowlands, provided an ideal centre for rallying the various Jacobite contingents. Mar arrived there on September 28. By then his following had been swollen by the addition of a large number of Campbells, the Perthshire vassals of the Earl of Breadalbane, under the direction of the lairds of Glenlyon and Glendarule. The old Earl himself, summoned to appear in Edinburgh and swear an oath of allegiance to King George in accordance with the Act for Encouraging Loyalty in Scotland, found a convenient way around the problem by having his doctor and minister submit a plea of infirmity on his behalf. It was reported from Taymouth on September 19 that 'John, Earl of Broadalbine, an old infirm Man of Fourscore Years of Age, is much troubled with Coughs, Rheums, Defluctions and other Maladies and Infirmities which usually attend old Age; that he is much subject to the Gravel and Stitches, and that at this present, and for sometime by-gone, he complains of Pains in his Back and Kidneys; and the Stitches in his Sides have been so violent, that, notwithstanding of his great Age, there was a Necessity for blooding him, which has not yet removed them, and he is so ill that he cannot travel from this to Edinburgh without apparent Danger of his Health and Life'. The next day this decrepit old man showed a remarkable alacrity in rushing off to join Mar and his own followers who were for King James. Estimates vary as to the numbers Mar commanded on arrival at Perth. It may have been as many as 5,000 combined foot and horse, but whatever the exact figure, the setting up of headquarters at Perth was undertaken in a mood of bounding optimism.

From the Jacobite point of view, one of the more startling omissions from the 'Fifteen campaign in Scotland was its apparent lack of hard centre. There seems to be very little evidence of that vital pivotal alliance of individuals at the heart of affairs that is normally considered indispensable to successful revolution. Perhaps this lack of vitality is partially explicable in terms of geography. The Scottish Jacobites began their rebellion prematurely, in isolation and some 470 miles from the seat of government. They were also a good deal farther from the court of their exiled Prince, the real centre of their affairs. Part of the deficiency is also attibutable to personality. Although the Earl of Mar was by no means the utter incompetent as described by Sinclair, it was unfortunate that his particular talents lay quite outside the field of military affairs. He was a diplomat used to the responsibility of high office, but he was not a soldier. He was himself aware of his limited capabilities as commander-in-chief and had severe reservations about his ability to cope with the demands of an army which was increasing daily. The person most obviously suited to assume the responsibilities that Mar found so onerous was James Fitzjames, Duke of Berwick and half-brother to the Old Pretender (the illegitimate son of James II and Arabella Churchill). He was universally regarded as an extremely able soldier and the person most likely to steer the 'Fifteen towards a successful conclusion. Mar, indeed, continually anticipated his arrival and began to see his own duty merely as that of a stopgap. Like other expectations from France, however, the Duke failed to appear. His absence created that impression of vacuum at the centre of Jacobite affairs in Scotland which was only filled by the arrival of the Pretender himself late in December. Meanwhile, the absence of a resolute leader and the presence of a fiercely independent spirit among the Lowland lords and Highland chiefs combined to undermine the army's potential efficiency.

Throughout the rest of September and October, the Jacobite army continued to receive massive injections of volunteers, but a marked absence of discipline in the camp imposed unseen restrictions upon its potential fighting strength. A force of 500 Highlanders under Brigadier William Mackintosh of Borlum arrived at the beginning of October; an estimated 500 horse and 2,000 foot under the Marquis of Huntly came shortly after; and these were joined by 300 horse and 500 foot under the Earl Marischal.[7] For Alexander Gordon, 5th Marquis of Huntly, the decision whether or not to come out had been a difficult one to make. He was a Roman Catholic with a predisposition towards a restoration of the Stuarts, but having married into a Whig family, his allegiance was divided and his performance during the rebellion reflected his uncertainties. George Keith, 10th Earl Marischal, had been involved in the secret negotiations to bring James to Scotland in 1708 and was to survive the 'Fifteen and serve the Stuarts for a long time afterwards. Of Brigadier Mackintosh, more will be heard later. By mid-October, the estimated strength of the Jacobite following at Perth was given by Rae as 12,600 and by Sinclair as 6,600. The first figure is probably too high and the second almost certainly too low. It is likely that more than 1,000 horse and 8,000 foot were assembled in and around the camp and that these were yet to be joined by General Alexander Gordon of Auchintoul appointed to the task of gathering the western clans together. It seems that although orders were given out to form into regiments, according to Sinclair 'everyone did as they pleased'. Mar was rather better at addressing himself to the business of Jacobite public relations and was happier with the vague generalities of the rightness and justness of the cause than with the detailed organization of the army. The most important document to emerge at his instigation in the early stages of the rebellion was a 'Manifesto and Declaration by the Noblemen, Gentlemen, and others, who dutifully appear at this Time, in asserting the undoubted Right of their Lawful Sovereign, James the Eighth, by the Grace of God, King of Scotland, England, France and Ireland, defender of the Faith, &c. and for relieving this his ancient Kingdom

7. These figures are given by Rae in *The History of the Rebellion*, Second Edition, London, M.DCC.XLVI, p. 237, but Sinclair disagrees with the figures and suggests that Huntly brought only 160 horse and 1,400 foot and that the Earl Marischal's contribution was 'not then fourscore'. Huntly was originally expected to bring in a massive array of troops and in the deposition of Ebenezer Whittel (referred to above) the number 15,000 is mentioned by him as a possibility.

from the Oppressions and Grievances it lies under'. It was a cautious document. While it rehearsed the argument of James's blood right to the realm, it probably failed to satisfy those extremists who were looking for secession from the Union, because it stated quite clearly that one of the aims of the insurgents was 'sincerely and heartily (to) go into such Measures as shall maintain effectually, and establish a right, firm, and lasting Union betwixt his Majesty's ancient Kingdom of Scotland, and our good Neighbours and Fellow-Subjects of the Kingdom of England'. Like Bonnie Prince Charlie 30 years later, Mar tried to court the good opinion of all factions, and made strenuous efforts not to outlaw himself in the English public conscience. However, a faintly reassuring passage in the Manifesto dealing the the Pretender's religion could only have had the opposite effect to that intended on real objectors. 'Nor have we any Reason to be distrustful of the Goodness of God, the Truth and Purity of our holy Religion, or the known Excellency of his Majesty's Judgment, as not to hope, that in due Time, good Example, and Conversation with our Learned Divines, will remove these Prejudices, which we know his Education in a Popish Country has not rivetted in his Royal discerning Mind'. Recruits were encouraged to appear from every quarter and perhaps, not unreasonably, one of the factors influencing their willingness to do so was the arrangements concerning pay. In an earlier declaration, Mar had stated vaguely that 'The King, intending that his Forces shall be paid from the Time of their setting out, he expects, as he positively orders, that they behave themselves civilly, and commit no Plundering, nor other Disorders, upon the Highest Penalties..' In the later document, the following invitation occurs:

'And we hereby faithfully promise and engage, that every Officer who joins with us in our King and Country's Cause, shall not only enjoy the same Post he now does, but shall be advanc'd and preferr'd according to his Rank and Station, and the Number of Men he brings off with him to us; And each Foot Soldier so joining us shall have 20 Shillings Sterling, and each Trooper or Dragoon, who brings Horse and Accoutrements along with him, 12 Pounds Sterling Gratuity, besides their Pay.'

These munificent arrangements were undoubtedly to secure the services of men already serving in the army and it is thought that some of the Jacobites serving the cause were little more than mercenaries. According to Mar's *Journal,* some 'never thought of quitting the Army' although in Jacobite pay and 'others return'd soon to it'. For the average Jacobite 'volunteer' soldier, vassal or clansmen, Highlander or Lowlander, pay arrangements were erratic and circumscribed by the personal finances of his particular leader. At Perth, Lords Panmure and Southesk were reputed to have dipped into their pockets to the tune of £500 each to satisfy the clamouring discontents of impecunious followers. The problems of discipline occasioned by this catch-as-catch-can arrangement soon became apparent when men began to drift off home at frequent intervals to get 'a fresh supplie of the readie', according to Sinclair. This negligent attitude to detail became the hallmark of the 'Fifteen.

The very last thing that the Highlanders and Lowlanders who were thrown together at Perth resembled was a modern army. A lack of uniformity invaded every aspect of their collective existence. The Highlanders wore native costumes which had as many variations as there were shades of difference in the men's condition, rank and social status. A chieftain with his Breacan-feile (literally, the chequered covering) linen shirt, web stockings, leather pumps, smart shortcoat and feathered bonnet sharply contrasted with the barefoot Highlander humbly devoid of plaid or coat and wearing nothing but a flimsy garment which exposed his thighs, resembling nothing so much as a cut-down nightshirt. Captain Burt, an English officer and one of the few eighteenth-century travellers to penetrate beyond the Highland line and witness the privations of Highland life, recorded with some surprise the discovery of a gentleman reputed to be of some consequence dressed in this primitive but not uncommon fashion. '. . . he was without shoes, stockings, or breeches, in a short coat, with a shirt not much longer, which hung between his thighs, and just hid his nakedness from two daughters about seventeen or eighteen years old, who sat over-against him', records the shocked Captain in his *Letters from a Gentleman in the North of Scotland to his Friend in London.* Beside the variously garbed Highlanders, the Lowland peasantry at least had the advantage of being uniformly covered — albeit in varying degrees of unattractiveness. Highlander and Lowlander spoke different languages and were further discouraged from integrating by the traditional animosity already referred to. Just as the appearance of the men varied, so there was little uniformity in their equipment. The 'Fifteen was very close to being a pitchfork war and, indeed, many of the rustic volunteers owned no other weapon. The Highlanders, however, were usually better equipped. It was part of their national heritage to display a warlike spirit and brandish arms on all occasions when national pride and tribal honour were thought to be at stake. The distinctive weapon was the broadsword, (often erroneously referred to as the claymore, a much larger weapon that had by this time largely fallen into disuse). In addition, many well-equipped Highlanders carried daggers at their belts and dirks in their stockings. Some carried cumbersome barrel-loading muskets or small pairs of steel pistols. Essential to the defence of the Highlander in combat was the target, or round shield of metal studded leather. The target was slung across the back

when it was being carried and held on the left arm in action. Many of the guns brought to Perth were unserviceable. 'There was no methode fallen on, nor was the least care taken to repair those old rustie broken pieces which it seems were carried about more for ornament than use', wrote Sinclair. Nor, apparently, was the least care taken to obtain supplies of gunpowder, which explains why shortages of this vital commodity continually bedevilled the campaign.

The appearance of the horse was as motley as that of the men. An account of Huntly's arrival told of how he was greeted with hoots of laughter and howls of derision when it was discovered that, along with a body of perfectly acceptable mounted gentlemen volunteers, his contingent was found to contain about 50 'great lubberly fellows', wearing bonnets but no boots, riding long-tailed little ponies bridled with rope, the animals sagging under the weight of the men whose bare feet trailed the ground. In the Highlands, horses were kept mainly for ploughing and carrying peat and the other essential commodities of a simple life. Grazing was poor in the mountains and Highland livestock was not renowned for its robustness. In winter, when food was in short supply for humans and animals alike, the cattle, which normally shared the same roof with their owner, were bled to provide the Highlanders with an additive to their staple of oatmeal. This practice reduced the already scrawny beast to a state of miserable weakness. Captain Burt, who witnessed the privations of Highland life observed that the animals became so weak that 'in a morning they cannot rise from the ground, and several of the inhabitants join together to help up each other's cows'. The Highland horses, known as *garrons*, were usually in better condition. They were hardy and nimble, not unlike the modern Shetland pony, but they were scarcely of the quality usually demanded by regular armies in the eighteenth century to make up their cavalry.

Of the heterogenous crowd assembled at Perth, the Highlanders were the least likely to object to campaign conditions. Renowned for their toughness, they displayed an impressive disregard for physical comfort in their daily lives. They thought nothing of sleeping outdoors in all weathers with only their woollen plaid for protection against the elements. The manner of its use on certain occasions, as recorded by Captain Burt, was calculated to strike terror into the heart of an eighteenth-century English valetudinarian gentleman. 'I have been credibly assured', wrote the observer, 'that when the Highlanders are constrained to lie among the hills in cold dry windy weather, they sometimes soak the plaid in some river or bourn; and then holding up a corner of it a little above their heads, they turn themselves round and round till they are enveloped by the whole mantle. They then lay themselves down on the heath, upon the leeward side of some hill, where the wet and the warmth of their bodies make a steam like that of a boiling kettle. The wet, they say, keeps them warm by thickening the stuff, and keeping the wind from penetrating'. Burt himself was rather sceptical about the Highlanders' ability to survive these self-inflicted tortures and went on to say: 'I must confess I should myself have been apt to question this fact, had I not frequently seen them wet from morning to night; and even at the beginning of the rain, not so much as stir a few yards to shelter, but continue in it, without necessity, till they were, as we say, wet through and through. And that is soon effected by the looseness and sponginess of the plaiding; but the bonnet is frequently taken off, and wrung like a dish-clout, and then put on again'. After a lifetime of exposure to cold and damp, one might expect that the average eighteenth-century Highlander could look forward to a rheumatic old age. But, on the contrary, it seems that rheumatism was almost, if not wholly, unknown in the Highlands until the introduction of linen shirts.[8] Any attempt to introduce a self-indulgent note into the harsh strains of Highland life was usually regarded with suspicion if not open contempt. One particular Highland chief, sleeping out with his men in the hills, was reputed to have gathered together a snowball to make himself a pillow for the night. This lapse was interpreted by his followers as evidence of dwindling stamina.

The Highlanders were not unused to daring exploits. Although the last out-and-out clan battle had taken place in the 1600s, the Highlanders' tribal animosities still involved them in minor raids and skirmishes with their neighbours from time to time. Most of their predatory activities at this stage were connected with cattle stealing. Raids launched for this purpose demanded more spirit than organization and, as the weeks wore on in Perth without event, the Highlanders in particular began to resent the period of inactivity forced upon them by Mar's delaying tactics.

Forays for Arms

As the Jacobite army in Scotland continued to increase and multiply, John Campbell, 2nd Duke of Argyll and commander-in-chief of His Majesty's forces in Scotland, could only watch from Stirling in a state of impotent alarm. He sent frantic requests for reinforcements to London emphasizing in his dispatches the dangers of the Scottish situation. Apart from the slender garrison at Stirling and the makeshift arrangements at Glasgow, Edinburgh and Dumfries, active signs of government sympathy were evident in the most northerly shires of Sutherland and Caithness, where the Earl of Sutherland was struggling to raise the clans that were well disposed to the government. But none of this had any real impact upon Argyll's situation at Stirling which remained extremely vulnerable. He faced a Jacobite army not 40 miles away with a fighting strength already three times his own and increasing by the hour. To the west of his position, General Gordon busied himself gathering the Jacobite clans that were yet

8. 'Their shirts were of woollen cloth and as linen was long expensive a considerable time elapsed before linen shirts came into general use. We have heard an old and intelligent Highlander remark that rheumatism was almost, if not wholly, unknown in the Highlands until the introduction of linen shirts.' *A History of the Highlands and of The Highland Clans*, James Browne. Vol. 1., Glasgow, MDCCCXXXIV.

John Campbell, 2nd Duke of Argyll (1678-1743), was the commander-in-chief of His Majesty's forces in Scotland during the 1715 Rebellion.

to come out. To the south there were ominous Jacobite rumblings in Dumfriesshire, Kirkcudbright and Wigtownshire, and the English Jacobites in Northumberland were beginning to stir themselves. Most of the government's regular forces were still preoccupied with the situation in the south-west of England and a request for Dutch auxiliaries had yet to be complied with.

Argyll was not a man to allow the grass to grow under his feet. He took his duty very seriously indeed and his political and military credentials for the post he occupied were impeccable. He had been marked out at an early age as a likely candidate for fame, and the fact that he belonged to the most powerful family in Scotland no doubt helped to smooth his path to success. As a boy 'his disposition leading him to the military line, he could not

be prevailed upon to give much attention to books', said a contemporary biographer. It was a tendency his father found encouraging. He was presented to King William in 1694 and was chosen to command a regiment of foot at the age of 16. When he was 25, Macky said of him: 'Few of his years have a better understanding nor a more manly behaviour. He hath seen most of the courts of Europe, is very handsome in his person, fair complexioned'. He had served with Marlborough as a Brigadier-general at Ramillies, and he commanded 20 battalions at Oudenarde. At Malplaquet, he was reputed to have distinguished himself by extraordinary feats of valour, escaping unhurt but a little ruffled from the fray when 'several musket balls penetrated his clothes, hat and periwig'. As high commissioner to the Scottish parliament, he had devoted himself wholeheartedly to recommending the Union, but by June 1713, disillusioned by the inequities of the alliance, his attitude to the Union, like Mar's, went into reverse and he supported a motion for dissolution of the bond. He continued to be a staunch supporter of the Protestant succession and remained pro-Hanoverian. Only in his view of the Union did he resemble his counterpart on the Jacobite side. In all other respects, he was Mar's polar opposite. Even Argyll's political enemies were forced to concede that 'he was extremely forward in effecting what he aimed at and designed, which he owned and promoted above board, being altogether free of the least share of dissimulation, and his word so sacred, that one might assuredly depend on it. His head ran more upon the camp than the court . . . ' (George Lockhart of Carnwath). The Duke of Argyll was 37 in the year of the rebellion.

On the evening the Duke of Argyll took his leave of King George before setting out for Scotland, an initiative taken by a party of Jacobites, again independent of Mar's authority, had already emphasized the need for swift government action in Scotland. A

Jacobite conspiracy was formed to surprise Edinburgh Castle and secure for the cause the government money, equipment and ammunition stored there. The assault was to take place 'on the Eighth of September', according to Rae, 'betwixt 11 and 12 at Night, by mounting the Walls, on the West side of the Castle, not far from the Sally-Port, by Ladders made of Ropes, provided for that Purpose, by Direction of the Lord Drummond, a Papist'. Lord James Drummond, the architect of the plan, had already been imprisoned as a Jacobite in 1708 and was prepared to risk his life in this venture in the hope that he would be given the governorship of the Castle if he succeeded. There were about 80 or 90 men involved in the attempt, besides the officers, and of the whole about half were Highlanders. It was a risky undertaking and, by way of incentive, the men were promised £100 each after their mission had been successfully accomplished.

The entire success of the operation depended upon whether the Jacobites retained the advantage of surprise, and everything turned upon the maintenance of secrecy. One 'Mr. Arthur, formerly an Ensign in the Castle and afterwards in the Scotch-Guards' had engaged in the conspiracy by bribing members of the castle garrison into lowering ropes from the castle walls on the north side near the Sally Port where the descent was less steep than elsewhere. James Thomson and John Holland, two of the sentries had received eight guineas and four guineas respectively, with the promise of more, for assisting in the operation. The principal traitor was one, William Ainsley, a sergeant who was corrupted by the prospect of preferment to a lieutenancy. The conspirators advanced their project to the eleventh hour without the slightest leakage of information. At last, Mr. Arthur found the burden of a guilty conscience too oppressive to bear alone. He divulged the details of the plan to his brother, who in turn shared the illicit information with his wife. On the evening the attempt was to be made, the lady sent a servant to the Lord Justice Clerk with a warning. In turn, he warned the deputy governor of the Castle, Lieutenant Colonel Stuart. Stuart did not react with the trenchancy demanded of a man in his critical situation. He merely doubled the guard and retired to bed. It was afterwards thought that an explanation for his lethargy might be sought through the implications of his name.

At eleven o'clock, the conspirators assembled at the foot of the castle walls. Some were a little unsteady, after having dissipated a little of their strength and a good deal of the time allocated to co-ordination of the exercise, carousing in a local tavern. The insurgents now perceived with some dismay that a confederate assigned to bring the scaling ladders was not of their party. A few ladders were available but these were found to be about two metres too short for the job. The rebels waited for a while. As they delayed, the advantage of surprise began to shift imperceptibly onto the government side. At last it was decided to begin the assault with what faulty equipment was available. With the assistance of Thomson and Holland, the short ladders were attached to ropes thrown over the side. Just as the ladders were being hauled into position, the change of guard arrived on the ramparts. One of the assisting sentries panicked, fired his gun and called out to those below warning them of the imminent ruin of their plot. Exasperated by the muddled manoeuvres of the Jacobites, he called, 'God damn you all! you have ruined both yourselves and me! Here comes the round I have been telling you of this hour, I can serve you no longer'. At the same moment, his companion let go the ropes and the ladders fell to the ground. The noise created a general alarm both inside and outside the castle walls and a patrol, sent out by the Lord Provost as an extra precaution, came rushing to the scene. It was met by the sad sight of one 'Captain McLean, formerly an Officer of King James the Seventh, sprawling on the Ground and bruis'd by a fall from the Precipice'. Three of his fellow conspirators were also found as well as the jettisoned ladder which had occasioned McLean's accident and some dozen 'firelocks and carbines' thrown away by the rebels in their haste to disperse.

It was an ignominious defeat. Culpable negligence robbed the insurgents of a considerable prize. The difference a successful assault on Edinburgh Castle might have made to the subsequent campaign was not lost upon the relieved Whigs:

'. . if it had succeeded (it) would certainly (have) been of very ill Consequence to his Majesty's Affairs in Scotland; For by that Means the Rebels had not only been Masters of the Castle, the strongest Fort in the Nation, with Abundance of Arms and Ammunition to furnish those who would fight for the Pretender, and vast Sums of Money to pay them, but could also (have) commanded the City of Edinburgh, and kept a Communication betwixt their Friends in the North, and those in the South. And beside, the Royal Army wou'd (have) been hereby depriv'd of Military Stores, which they afterwards found necessary to oppose this Rebellion.'

As it happened, however, some of the arms that escaped capture at Edinburgh did in fact fall into Jacobite hands through the operation of a different plan which restored a little of the lustre to the Jacobites' reputation.

News of a small ship loaded with arms and ammunition lying off the Fifeshire port of Burntisland reached the Jacobite camp on October 2. The arms were being sent from Edinburgh to the Earl of Sutherland and the messenger who brought the intelligence reckoned that the ship had some 3,000 weapons on board destined to equip the Whig clans in the north. The person to whom the news was first communicated was John Sinclair. In his memoirs he records: 'I was transported with the news, tho'. . . not being

altogether so well with my Lord Mar, was at a loss how to behave in it. But on second thoughts, (I) resolved to goe straight to him. . . I found him in bed, and told him my storie'. Mar did not react to the news with great alacrity. This dismayed Sinclair because he knew the ship planned to leave harbour on the midnight tide. Any expedition launched to reach it in time would of necessity need to be clear of Perth at the very latest by five o'clock in the evening. At mid-day, Mar was still deliberating what to do. Eventually he gave his assent to a raid and Sinclair set about supervising the arrangements. To reach the port it would be necessary for Sinclair's raiding party to pass within ten miles of Stirling on both the outward and return journeys. He suggested to the rebel leader the necessity for support troops to cover the return journey and Mar reluctantly detached 500 foot to guard the route.

At five o'clock, Sinclair with 'fourscore horse' and a baggage train left Perth. When the expedition reached Burntisland, it was to find that the ship was no longer at anchor in the harbour but was standing off beyond the entrance. After a guard had been posted in the town, the rest of the party seized some small boats and, with the help of pressed townsmen, endeavoured to haul the ship back to its original mooring in the teeth of a contrary wind. The peril of the exercise was increased and valuable time was wasted and so it was imperative that the final stages be accomplished with expedition. To Sinclair's horror, however, the efficiency of the raid began to disintegrate when it was discovered on returning to the shore that the men detailed to assist in the unloading of the weapons were no longer at their posts but had drifted off into town to look for drink and amusement. Forced to participate in much of the manual work himself, Sinclair made a second dispiriting discovery. It soon became apparent that his informant's account of the ship's contents was grossly inflated. He found to his grief 'but 300 (guns), wanting one; we found a bag of flints and two little barrels of ball, and two or three barrels of pouder, about a hundred pound each, and some cartridge boxes'. The disappointment was offset by an unexpected haul of 25 firelocks and a barrel of powder from another ship accidentally found in the harbour. When the offloading was completed, the stray men were rounded up and between three and four o'clock in the morning the raiders left the town and made for Kinross where the back-up force was waiting. The expedition got back safely to Perth before five o'clock in the evening having 'marched nere to fourtie Scots miles in twentie-four hours'. The fruits of the victory were considerably less than anticipated at the outset but at least the expedition had the distinction of having outwitted Argyll and sabotaged the government's scheme for assisting the loyal clans. The memory of the earlier disgraceful affair at Edinburgh was obliterated by this small success and it stimulated the ambitions of smaller raiding parties sent out to scour Fife for all the weapons they could rake in.

The Jacobites were now forced to face the fact that things might not turn out as well for them as they had imagined at the outset. When the news was received in Scotland of the death of Louis XIV and the abandonment of the French expedition, Mar tried valiantly to convert ruin into profit by assuring everyone that the new regime was likely to prove even more vigorous than the old in assisting the Jacobite cause, but his optimism had a hollow ring to it. Without French supplies and with little evidence of the anticipated English rising, the Jacobites in Scotland began to realize that their chances of victory were far from being a certainty. The men were encouraged to expect the arrival of their king any day and when he failed to appear, a gradual disenchantment began to steal into the camp. So far, however, with little in the way of outright military endeavour, the Earl

of Mar held the country from Fife to Inverness. He had seven or eight counties from which to levy provisions, money and recruits and more than 200 miles of seashore was under his control. On the west side, the Isles of Skye, Lewis and the Hebrides were Jacobite. If the creeping mood of disenchantment was not to prove destructive, Mar had to try something more ambitious than a raid.

Southwards at Last

Mar was reluctant to venture anything while he was without his full complement of recruits. General Gordon had still not arrived and the Earl of Seaforth had yet to come down from the north. Many in the camp disagreed with Mar's hesitant tactics and, while he delayed the Jacobite leader ran the risk of alienating many of his followers, especially the Highlanders, who might simply disperse once boredom had taken the cutting edge off their fighting spirit. Even his procrastinating nature told him that he was running a risk and wasting valuable time if nothing was done to demonstrate Jacobite strength while Argyll remained in a position of extreme weakness. Accordingly, he opted for the least satisfactory of solutions, a compromise. He decided to send a detachment from the main force across the Firth of Forth to establish a disturbing Jacobite presence in Argyll's rear. At a time when it should have been obvious that a straightforward frontal assault on Argyll's position would have brought undoubted victory to the Jacobites, Mar busied himself with a complexity of stratagems bent on surrounding his feeble enemy, and enclosing it in 'a Hose-net', as he put it in a letter at the time. The general aim of the detachment was to rendezvous with the emerging Northumbrian and Lowland Scottish forces. This combined force, operating in conjunction with General Gordon's force in the west and Mar's own army in the north was to complete the cordon Mar schemed to throw around Argyll. The operation involved an unnecessary expenditure of time and effort to secure a paltry prize, but it was a scheme which recommended itself to Mar because it bought him time in which to work out a more dynamic strategy. With the usual lack of concern, the detachment was not provided with detailed orders on how it should conduct itself once the crossing had been made. Plans were left deliberately vague in the hope that the contrivance of the protagonists would supply the deficiency.

The strongest weapon in the Duke of Argyll's arsenal throughout the 'Fifteen was the river bridge at Stirling. Because the navy patrolled the sea routes around Britain and the country to the west of Perth was in the main hostile to the Jacobites and not easy to traverse on foot, any southward advance from Perth was immediately confronted with the problem of how to cross the Firth of Forth. The most convenient passage was under constant government surveillance and other likely crossings were closely watched by English men-of-war in the estuary. On this occasion, the problem was overcome with a degree of ingenuity entirely absent from previous Jacobite manoeuvres. A flotilla of small boats was secretly assembled in various fishing villages on the eastern coast of Fife. From these ports of relative obscurity, a night time crossing was made to the ports of Aberlady and Gullane on the southern shore. In a campaign of undisguisedly paltry operations, this particular undertaking was exalted above others owing to the planning and organization which contributed to its success, ingredients due in large measure to the influence of the expedition's leader, Brigadier William Mackintosh of Borlum (known to contemporaries as Old Borlum). Old Borlum was one of the few Jacobite leaders who brought a potent mixture of a distinguished military reputation and a determination of spirit to bear on the operations of the 'Fifteen. He had seen service in the French army and was acting as clan leader while the hereditary chief

was under-age. Old Borlum had wasted no time in raising the Mackintoshes once he had sniffed rebellion in the air and claimed to be the first to organize his clansmen in 1715. The Forth crossing was not the Brigadier's first exploit of the campaign. In an independent action, he had seized Inverness for King James before coming to the camp at Perth and his contingent of 500 Mackintoshes was reckoned to be the cream of Mar's army. Along with his own men, Mackintosh's detachment included the greater part of Mar's, Nairn's, Lord Charles Murray's and Lord Drummond's regiments. A total of 2,500 men was involved in the operation of whom 1,600 successfully crossed the Forth. A few hundred were driven off course, and the remainder served as decoys. Because Old Borlum took the trouble to calculate the winds and tides correctly, his flotilla remained largely beyond the power of the English men-of-war to pursue. Most of the rebels landed safely on the southern shore whereupon they immediately fell prey to Mar's imprecise directions. With his zeal for improvisation, Old Borlum decided to launch an attack upon Edinburgh. As soon as the alarm was raised in the capital, the Lord Provost ordered the city guard, trained bands and associate volunteers to assume defensive positions and a message was sent to the Duke of Argyll requesting reinforcements. It was an awkward moment for Argyll. He could scarcely afford to deplete his feeble garrison at Stirling any further. On the other hand, he could not stand by and see the spoils of Edinburgh fall into Jacobite hands. With 300 dragoons and 200 infantry, Argyll left the camp at Stirling and made a forced march to Edinburgh, nearly 40 miles away. At ten o'clock on Friday October 14, as Argyll and his men approached the West Port of Edinburgh in the dark, Mackintosh and his men approached from the east. While the Jacobites were coldly received, it was to the 'unspeakable joy of the Loyal Inhabitants' that Argyll arrived in the city in time to create an impasse. The Jacobites advanced as far as Jock's Lodge, less than a mile from the royal palace of Holyroodhouse. Their frosty reception left them in no doubt which way the affections of the citizenry tended. On the other side of the city, the government forces were received by an enthusiastic party of volunteers. After a short council, the Jacobites decided to retire to Leith to take measures to protect themselves from the likely concerted attack from the adversaries who were collecting in the city. They arrived in Leith late at night and took up their position for the night in a square fort, a relic of Cromwell's time, still standing in North Leith. Having barricaded themselves in and fortified the citadel with several pieces of cannon taken from ships in the nearby harbour, the Jacobites sat back and waited for Argyll to make his move. Mackintosh, no doubt regretting the rashness of his initiative, dispatched two letters to the Earl of Mar informing him of recent events and emphasizing the peril of his current situation.

The Jacobites at Leith did not have to wait long for Argyll's appearance. The next morning, Saturday October 15, the Hanoverian commander appeared outside the citadel with his small army and summoned the Jacobite garrison to lay down its arms and surrender upon pain of high treason. The Laird of Kynnachin appeared on the walls to give the Jacobite answer. He said they did not understand the meaning of the word surrender, and hoped they never would. They were determined in the event of engagement neither to give nor take any quarter. In fact the Jacobites were strongly entrenched and Argyll, who had placed his men beyond the range of the Jacobite guns soon realized that he would be courting disaster if he tried to bring them in any closer. The fort was surrounded by a dry moat and any attempt to storm the position would be likely to result in unnecessary casualties among the assailants. Argyll saw that he might lose half his men

without gaining any advantage. Thus, with the purpose of making fuller preparations to achieve his object the next day, he retired to Edinburgh. Old Borlum had no wish to be blockaded in Leith and, as soon as it was dark, the Jacobites slipped quietly out of the fort and made off in the direction of Musselburgh, marching unobserved along the deserted beaches. It had been a chastening experience for Old Borlum and he felt disinclined to come up with any new initiatives. After wandering about indecisively for some time, the detachment pursued the original plan to rendezvous with the border forces, and so the Highlanders began to move south.

The disappearance of the Jacobite contingent from Leith did not put an end to Argyll's ambition of securing it. The royalist leader prepared to go in pursuit of his quarry and, while Argyll was thus preoccupied with the situation to the south-east of Edinburgh, Mar was presented with a golden opportunity to overpower the tiny garrison at Stirling and march his vastly superior army into southern Scotland. But no such stratagem occurred to him and instead of making a determined thrust he toyed with the idea of making a feint in the direction of Stirling with the object of drawing Argyll off Mackintosh's scent by providing him with an urgent reason for returning to base. The arrival of Old Borlum's despondent letters in Perth had cast a shadow over Jacobite affairs. Sinclair recorded that Mar, 'with a most dejected countenance and a sad voice', announced to assembled corps commanders, clan leaders and noblemen the bad news of the detachment's plight. Mar, apparently gave the expedition up for lost and offered the suggestion of a feint only as a desperate remedy not likely to succeed. General Hamilton took up the idea and said that 'a feint towards Stirling might doe good and could doe no harm' and another operation was begun without a detailed plan.

On Sunday, October 16, the Duke of Argyll received news that a Jacobite army was moving from Perth in the direction of Stirling. The next day he left the capital at noon. That night a detachment of Jacobite horse was pushed out to Dunblane, about six miles north of the royalist camp, while the rest of the Jacobite army remained a few miles behind at Ardoch. The horse remained briefly in Dunblane and after a modest display of sabre-rattling retreated the next day, rejoined the foot and the entire force returned to Perth. It seems that at one point it did occur to Mar that he had used a sledgehammer to crack a nut and that a general advance against Argyll might conceivably be made by his unwieldy force, but that idea was soon dispelled by news of reinforcements at Stirling. Argyll, on his return from Edinburgh, quickly took stock of the situation and immediately sealed off Stirling bridge and arranged for the destruction of a second bridge which the rebels might have used had they been in any measure determined to reach the royalist camp. Afterwards, the Jacobites realized what a catastrophic loss of opportunity their feeble initiative represented. Prior to Argyll's return, fewer than 1,000 men remained to garrison Stirling and, by mid-October, Jacobite strength only lacked Gordon's and Seaforth's contingents before reaching its zenith. But bad judgment alone did not cripple the Jacobite cause at this juncture. Once again, the inevitable careless omission turned out to be important. Mar later confessed in a letter to one of his generals that he had 'come away from Perth before our Provisions were ready to go with us, and I found all the Country about Stirling where we were to pass Forth, was entirely exhausted by the Enemy, so there was nothing for us to subsist on there'. If the army had been provided with the necessaries of a deliberate campaign, then the outcome of the exercise might have been more glorious.

Before October was out, a second incident involving a Jacobite expedition again resulted in punctured pride. The situation evolved from the shortages of money which afflicted the army from time to time. Mar had decided to supplement the sources of Jacobite revenue by levying *cess* (land tax on valued rent — the basis of government revenue in Scotland) in the name of King James III and VIII in the shires of Fife, Clackmannan, Kinross and Perth. After the feint, a party of Jacobites was sent off to Dunfermline to collect the money, by force if necessary, from the unwilling townspeople. The strength of the detachment was variously reported as between 300 and 400, with a preponderance of Highland foot. The town lay some 30 miles south of Perth, but the detachment received instructions to make its way there by an indirect route which would take it under the nose of Argyll's garrison at Castle Campbell, only six miles from the main royalist camp. Because the smaller post was manned by rustics, it was felt that the opportunity should not be lost to insult them by marching openly in their sight. This cavalier attitude assumed by the Jacobites unfortunately prevailed long after their arrival in Dumfermline. The tax collectors evidently regarded their mission as something of an unexpected holiday and 'all the gentleman of the horse separated into alehouses and taverns and afterwards most went to bed'. The leaders of the party took inadequate precautions against surprise attack. The infantry was billeted in the local Abbey, a few sentries were posted and then the leaders applied themselves to the more serious business of retiring to enjoy a 'heartie bottle'. At about five o'clock in the morning a company of dragoons from Argyll's camp under Colonel Cathcart, entered the town, dispatched the sentries and took prisoner all those of the Jacobite expedition who were alert enough to stagger out of bed and onto the streets. The infantry lodged in the Abbey did not disclose their whereabouts and made no attempt at all to retrieve the situation, apparently 'not doubting that the number of the enemie was greater in town than they reallie were'. A good deal of energy, however, was expended by others in an unseemly haste to escape which created a confusion of prostrate bodies in the narrow streets of the town. Riderless horses galloped off towards Perth and arrived in the camp as mysterious harbingers of the disaster. Their owners straggled in sporadically throughout the day while the concealed foot remained inert until the danger had passed. They marched back to Perth in an orderly fashion on the next day, hard pressed to devise an excuse for their behaviour equal to their blame for the rout.

The Jacobites then continued to kick their heels in Perth while Mar anxiously scanned the horizon for the last trickle of recruits. It had been hoped that General Gordon's activities in the west might have opened up a south-western route into England for the unified force. But the Duke of Argyll had anticipated the danger and early in the campaign had sent his brother, Lord Islay, to the Campbell's family seat at Inverary with orders to raise the well-disposed clansmen and establish a bulwark against just such a thrust. After a long and desultory siege of Inverary town and castle, Gordon now planned to move the clans east and rendezvous with Mar without having achieved his objective. At about the same time as General Gordon abandoned his operations in the west, William Mackenzie, 5th Earl of Seaforth finally arrived in the Jacobite camp in Perth. News of his approach had enlivened the drooping spirits of the idle Jacobite volunteers, and reports that the leader was approaching with an army of 4,000 men transformed the prevailing air of boredom into one of eager anticipation. But, as usual, the expectation exceeded the performance. When it arrived, Seaforth's army had mysteriously dwindled to 700 Mackenzies, an equal number of Macdonalds, 400 Frasers and 40 'scrub' horses and a few freelance recruits. Jacobite intelligence of local affairs was hopelessly erratic and Mar's ignorance of national issues was almost complete. He was still clinging to the shreds of a belief that the Jacobites in

England would mount a rebellion. He had used the possibility of this prospect to defer action by the Scots for long enough, but with the imminent realization of his dream of a full complement of volunteers, Mar's last excuse for inactivity had now disappeared. At last, preparations were made to evacuate Perth and move the army south into England.

The Southern Army

Although Jacobite plans for a rising in south-western England had collapsed, a pocket of Stuart sympathizers in Northumberland found themselves precipitated into open revolt by a series of accidents. Rae wrote that: 'the rebellious Conspiracy in England was formed at the same Time with that in Scotland; and, that London was the centrical Place where their grand Design was laid down, and where their Jacobite Measures were principally concerted; and from whence a Correspondence and Intelligence was settled with all the Conspirators in the several Parts in Great Britain'. The county of Northumberland perhaps secured its reputation as the last remaining link in the Tories' shattered plan for a series of risings, because of its proximity to the Scottish border and distance from the Hanoverian court. Certainly Northumberland had been visited by Jacobite agents 'riding from place to place as Travellers', according to historian Patten, 'pretending a Curiousity to view the Country, and thereby carrying Intelligence'. Trouble had been brewing in the county for some time, but there were few signs that open revolt was contemplated. The event which transformed a conspiracy into an armed insurrection was the issue of warrants for the arrest of prominent local personalities, James Radcliffe, third Earl of Derwentwater and Thomas Forster, a Northumberland member of parliament.

Derwentwater received notice of the warrant towards the end of September 1715, and immediately consulted his J.P. on the consequences of its enforcement. He could scarcely have been surprised that he had incurred Hanoverian displeasure, because he was an obvious target for suspicion in the North. In fact, he was a cousin of James Francis Edward Stuart (through his mother who was an illegitimate daughter of Charles II). He was also a contemporary of the Old Pretender and had spent his youth at the exiled Stuart court in France. His personal bias towards his cousin and preference for the Roman Catholic faith were well known. Whether he was in fact guilty of conspiring against King George is uncertain, but he did not behave like a guilty man until the agents of his arrest were practically on the doorstep of his seat, Dilston Hall, near Hexham in Northumberland. The young earl was not inclined to sit at home and wait to be taken, so he took to the field with a small retinue of servants and tenants, with considerable reluctance, realizing that he had a lot to lose in the venture.

Similar factors influenced the behaviour of his cousin, Tom Forster, whose zeal to escape his captors far exceeded any interest he had in a Stuart restoration. The rebellion began officially in Northumberland on October 6. Responding to a notice calling on the friends of King James to meet at a place called Greenrig near Hexham, the two renegades met with a following of some 50 to 60 volunteers. Having once come out into the open, this tiny force, which never exceeded more than 300 at its peak, sought a military objective. Naturally enough, the choice fell upon the nearby city of Newcastle where a number of influential Jacobite residents were known to be willing to co-operate in its capitulation. For the next two weeks, the Jacobite army moved restlessly between various towns and villages of Northumberland making threatening noises and waiting for their sympathizers in Newcastle to provide an opening for advance.

What this miniscule force most evidently lacked was any real sense of purpose and the blame for this deficiency redounded upon its leader, 'General' Tom Forster. He received his command more by default than election. The most obvious leader of the force was the Earl of Derwentwater but because his religion was so well known it was feared that if he became the leader, it might confuse a political protest with a Roman Catholic crusade, and thus discourage recruits. At 36, Forster was ten years older than Derwentwater and possessed nothing beyond his maturity and Protestantism to recommend him to the the leadership. In fact, he did not receive his General's commission until some time after he assumed the title. This piece of precocity combined with his lack of ability rendered him suspect, if not ludicrous, in the eyes of more professional soldiers. Derwentwater was always the more popular man. He apparently measured up to Patten's commendation: 'so unbounded that he seemed only to live for others', by serving Forster dutifully and without the least show of resentment at his subordinate position. It was generally assumed that Derwentwater might have brought many more men with him into the field than he actually did had he been prepared to test the affections of his friends and tenants. His lack of proselytising zeal was later interpreted as evidence of his reluctance to 'come out'. In the event, however, he rallied 'all his Servants, mounted some upon his Coach Horses and others upon very good useful Horses and all very well arm'd'. The Earl's younger brother, Charles Radcliffe, was also a member of the contingent.

After the rendezvous with Forster on October 6, the rebels embarked upon an adventure which dissipated their strength. This adventure took the form of a fairly pointless nine-day's odyssey which finally brought them back to their point of departure, exhausted and not massively augmented. They first journeyed to Rothbury in Northumberland and then moved off down the Coquet valley to Warkworth. There, a good deal of local curiosity was generated by Forster when he scared off the local parson so that the Jacobites' own chaplain had to take the Sunday service. With a great sense of occasion, James was proclaimed King of Great Britain and Ireland to the accompaniment of a trumpet. Forster contributed to the bizarre ceremonials by officiating in disguise.

The sense of being about a great business accompanied the itinerant force to Morpeth. On the way, 70 'Scots Horse, or rather Gentlemen from the Borders' joined the cavalcade, but many more volunteers on foot were turned away because there was no means of equipping them. In an effort to give their trifling activities some sense of portent, the Jacobites secured for themselves a trophy in the shape of an unfortunate blacksmith who fell in their way between Felton and Morpeth: '. . . they made him their Prisoner, set him on the bare Horse pinion'd and carry'd him Captive from Place to Place, as the first Fruits of their Warfare'. News of a greater prize, however, soon reached the rebels in Morpeth where it was learned that owing to a daring enterprise initiated by one Lancelot Errington and a tiny band of desperadoes, the castle on Holy Island had fallen into Jacobite hands. However, the great elation which celebrated this success proved sadly premature, when it was subsequently discovered that the Jacobite control had lasted only a day. But the Jacobites still had their sights set upon Newcastle, where little sign of a revolt in their favour had been shown as yet. In the meantime, the army returned to Hexham passing on the way within sight of Dilston Hall, which no doubt looked more alluring to its erstwhile occupants than it had ever done before.

While the Jacobites were thus busily dissipating their advantage of surprise, the Newcastle magistrates were using the time to greater effect. Suspected Jacobite collaborators were imprisoned and bands of armed volunteers were raised. Alderman White apparently displayed particular energy in that he 'mur'd up' all the city gates with stone and lime with the exception of Bridge and Brampton gate where cannon were positioned. The county militia was brought inside the city and members of the gentry loyal to King George equipped their tenants and neighbours with horses and invaded the town for its better protection, 'so that in a short Time, the Town was full of Horses and Men, for his Majesty's Interest' wrote Rae. Clearly, Newcastle was not going to open its gates to the Jacobites and the possibility of making a forced entrance was out of the question for the tiny élitist Jacobite force without an infantry division. The spirits of the rebels at Hexham were horribly deflated when they realized the truth. Far from being a ripe plum about to fall into their lap, the city was in fact up in arms declaring for King George. The final blow to their ambitions was delivered with the news that Newcastle had received regular reinforcements on October 9 and 12. Furthermore, the Northumbrian Jacobites learned with fear that their activities were not so distant from London as to go entirely unperceived. The government had issued orders to Lieutenant-general George Carpenter to assemble Cobham's, Molesworth's and Churchill's regiments of dragoons and Hotham's regiment of foot. He was directed to 'go in Pursuit of the Rebels whithersoever they went'. Accordingly, he left London on October 15 and arrived on October 18 in Newcastle, where he instantly began to prepare an attack on the Jacobites at Hexham. This was scarcely the result the Jacobites had anticipated. Thrown into a panic by the prospect of an engagement they had little counted upon, they began to scour the town and county frantically for all the arms and horses they could lay hands on. While thus preparing, in a mood of thinly disguised terror, for an encounter with the formidable General Carpenter, a happier prospect suddenly loomed on the Jacobite horizon. Details of a Jacobite rising in the south-west of

Scotland reached the tiny force at Hexham together with an invitation to rendezvous. The Lowland Scottish force invited Forster's army to meet it at Rothbury. Only too relieved to be given an opportunity for honourable disengagement, the English Jacobites abandoned their operations in Hexham and went off to meet their allies.

The history and complexion of the Lowland Scottish Jacobite army was not unlike that of its Northumbrian counterpart. It, too, was a force of gentlemen volunteers, mounted, with servants and friends and devoid of infantry. Its leaders, like Derwentwater and Forster, were driven into the field by hostile government pressures. The Act for Encouraging Loyalty in Scotland which received royal assent on August 30 1715, provided for named individuals to appear in Edinburgh and give assurance of their loyalty to the king or else be regarded as rebels. It was this Act that the wily old Earl of Breadalbane managed to circumvent by submitting a catalogue of spurious diseases as testimony of his inability to appear. There were others who, for legitimate reasons, were also unable to attend when called upon. As Sinclair recorded in his *Memoirs,* the Act was counter-productive and contributed significantly to Mar's project in that persons who defaulted on the summons were automatically given rebel status whether they were enthusiastic for the cause or not. The areas of Dumfriesshire, Kirkcudbright and Wigtownshire in the south-west of Scotland were all known to be strongholds of Jacobite opinion and, as a consequence, prominent peers of the districts, William Gordon, 6th Viscount Kenmure, William Maxwell, 5th Earl of Nithsdale and Robert Dalziel, 6th Earl of Carnwath were all named in the Warrant attached to the Act. So far only a passive Jacobite Association had been formed in the area. The failure of these noblemen to comply with the terms of the Act, however, nudged them into open conflict.

Like the Northumbrians, the Lowland Jacobites had an obvious local objective in the town of Dumfries and their aspirations were also concentrated on taking the town by consent rather than assault. On Tuesday, October 11, 1715, a message from the Lord Justice Clerk in Edinburgh arrived with the following letter addressed to the Provost of Dumfries:

Edinburgh, October 8th, 1715

SIR

HAVING good Information that there is a Design framed of rising in Rebellion in the Southern Parts, against his Majesty and the Government, I send this Express to advise you thereof, that you may be upon your Guard: For, by what I can rely upon, their first Attempt is to be suddenly upon your Town. I heartily wish you may escape their intended Visit. I am,

SIR,
Your Well wisher
and humble Servant.
A. D. COCKBURN.

Viscount Kenmure, at the head of some 150 horsemen assembled at Moffat, began his march on Dumfries. It was with some surprise that he learned from an informer, when he was almost within striking distance of the town that it was 'full of People well arm'd who were in readiness to give them a warm Reception'. The prospect of meeting with strong resistance arrested the Jacobites' progress and there was some debate as to whether their honour as well as their ambitions might not be vanquished by a hasty retreat. This dilemma was resolved by an enigmatic pronouncement from Viscount Kenmure who declared that he 'doubted not but there were as brave Gentlemen there as himself, and therefore he would not go to Dumfries that Day'. The expedition retired to Lochmaben where it was allowed to proclaim King James in peace.

At Moffat, George Seton, the young 5th Earl

of Wintoun had joined with his following. Generally considered to be an eccentric, Sir Walter Scott recorded that Wintoun was 'said to be afflicted by a vicissitude of spirits approaching lunacy'. Other less damning pronouncements on his character included the following. 'He is a young gentleman who hath been much abroad in the world, is mighty subject to a particular caprice, natural to his family, hath a good estate, a zealous Protestant not 25 years old'. Wintoun had brought along with him a party of Lothian gentlemen and their servants, numbering about 70 in all. The accumulated force was now divided into two squadrons, one under the mad Earl of Wintoun and the other under the Earl of Carnwath, while Viscount Kenmure retained supreme overall command. The re-organized army moved on to Ecclefechan and then to Langholm where it was joined by the Earl of Nithsdale. The augmented force then pushed on to Hawick and finally it began to move east towards Rothbury in Northumberland to rendezvous with the English Jacobites. Both armies were at their maximum strength of about 300 each when they met. The most convivial evening of the campaign for both forces was spent in Rothbury, carousing in The Three Half Moons and the Old Black Bull.

The next day the combined force moved on to Wooler in Northumberland where it received the welcome news that Brigadier Mackintosh and the Highlanders were journeying south with the object of meeting up with them. Early on the morning of October 22, it was decided to move forward to Kelso north of the border in anticipation of Old Borlum's arrival. Prior to its advance into the town, the English and Lowland Scottish force made some attempt at organization. The men under Lord Viscount Kenmure were found to make up five troops, 'well mann'd but indifferently armed; but many of the Horse small and in mean condition', said Patten. Forster's force likewise consisted of five troops but these were neither as well regulated nor armed as the Scots. The peculiar composition of both armies made it necessary for the troops to be double-officered in order to accommodate all the gentlemen. In addition to these organized troops, both contingents had a considerable following of disorderly volunteers and adventurers, and despite their efforts it must have been a fairly motley crew which drew up to meet Old Borlum at Kelso.

The Highlanders came into the town from the Scottish side with their bagpipes playing, led by the Brigadier. The long march and persistent rain had exhausted their strength and dampened their spirits. Only Old Borlum appeared unwearied, and it did not take him long to realize that the force he had been sent to rally was indeed a pitiful assembly. He took immediate exception to Forster whose blustering incompetence ran directly counter to his own sense of professional pride. Eventually, a system of command was worked out whereby the overall leadership of the combined force rested with Kenmure while it remained north of the border but would pass to Forster when, or indeed if, it moved into England. For Mackintosh, Kenmure's leadership could only have been marginally preferable to Forster's, because the Scottish Viscount was, alas, 'utterly a stranger to all Military Affairs'.

Despite the obvious shortcomings of the amalgamated army, all parties turned out next day in revived spirits to proclaim King James. The Highlanders marched in order to the market place with colours flying, drums beating and bagpipes playing. A review of the situation revealed that the southern army was now about 2,600 strong with much the greatest source of its strength residing in the Highland foot. Its leaders had now to decide how best to employ this strength. Deliberations on this subject received a violent jolt when news came in that General Carpenter had left Newcastle and was moving purposefully in their direction.

Highland chieftains on both sides dressed in a similar
way. The distinguishing badges were usually cock-
ades, ribbons or sprigs of plants of certain colours.
As a result, identification in the heat of battle must
have been extremely difficult.

A grenadier of the Princess of Wales Regiment (2nd Foot) wears the uniform of the English infantry in 1715, which had changed little since Marlborough's day. The Battalion Company Sergeant of Lord Forfar's Regiment (3rd Foot), which was present at Sherriffmuir, wears the cocked hat of the battalion or centre companies. His halberd is a symbol of rank.

This volunteer horseman of a local troop wears clothes which were typical of the horsemen irregulars on both sides during the 1715 rebellion. Troops of volunteer horsemen were raised mainly in Northumberland, Lancashire and the Scottish lowlands. Although this rider is shown on a *garron* (rough pony), many were mounted on high-quality coach horses.

A trooper of the Royal Scots Greys is representative of the cavalrymen of the Hanoverian army, as they would have looked at Sherriffmuir. The artillery gunner could well have been an ex-gunner of Marlborough's wars, because the Crown had no standing force of artillery in 1715. Batteries were raised when required and they were operated by civilians.

These drawings of Highland peasants were made from actual clothing in the Scottish Museum of Antiquities. The clothes were discovered on skeletons of men who lived in the early 1700s. These skeletons were buried in peat bogs. Although one outfit was found in Caithness and the other on Arnish Moor, Lewis, the fabric in each case is of the same coarse weave and colour.

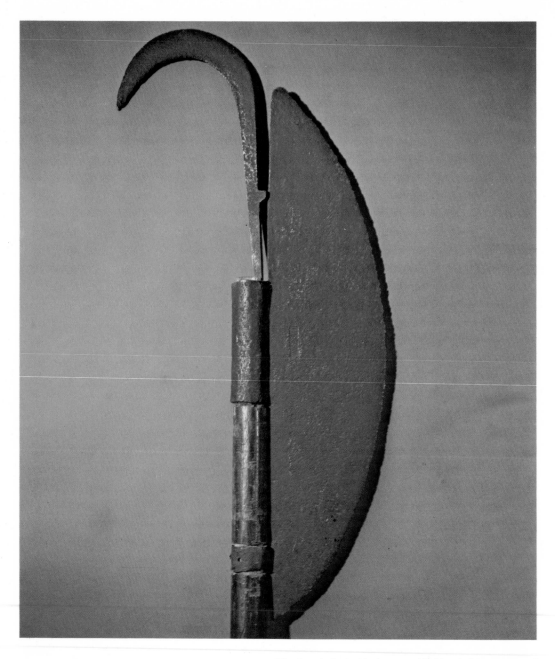

The head of a Lochaber axe. Highland clansmen used this weapon to terrible effect. Patterns of head varied. This one had a fairly shallow cutting blade and a hook for pulling horsemen out of the saddle.

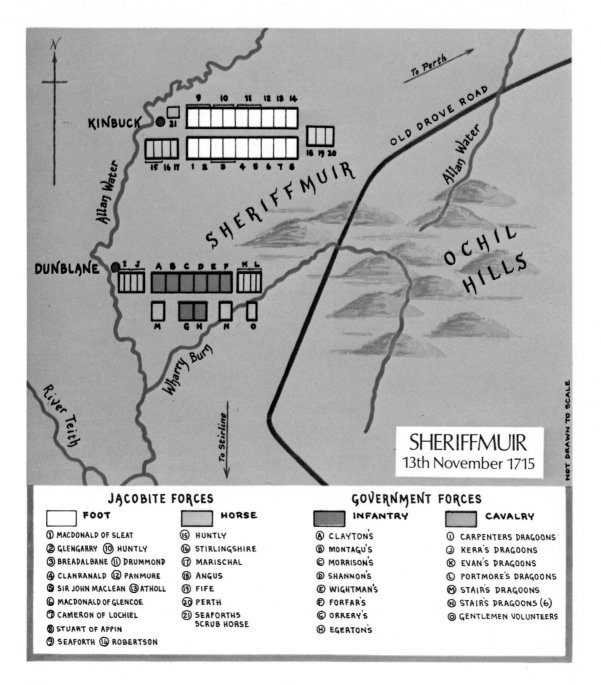

SHERIFFMUIR
13th November 1715

JACOBITE FORCES

FOOT **HORSE**

① MACDONALD OF SLEAT
② GLENGARRY ⑩ HUNTLY
③ BREADALBANE ⑪ DRUMMOND
④ CLANRANALD ⑫ PANMURE
⑤ SIR JOHN MACLEAN ⑬ ATHOLL
⑥ MACDONALD OF GLENCOE
⑦ CAMERON OF LOCHIEL
⑧ STUART OF APPIN
⑨ SEAFORTH ⑭ ROBERTSON

⑮ HUNTLY
⑯ STIRLINGSHIRE
⑰ MARISCHAL
⑱ ANGUS
⑲ FIFE
⑳ PERTH
㉑ SEAFORTHS
SCRUB HORSE

GOVERNMENT FORCES

INFANTRY **CAVALRY**

Ⓐ CLAYTON'S
Ⓑ MONTAGU'S
Ⓒ MORRISON'S
Ⓓ SHANNON'S
Ⓔ WIGHTMAN'S
Ⓕ FORFAR'S
Ⓖ ORRERY'S
Ⓗ EGERTON'S

Ⓘ CARPENTERS DRAGOONS
Ⓙ KERR'S DRAGOONS
Ⓚ EVAN'S DRAGOONS
Ⓛ PORTMORE'S DRAGOONS
Ⓜ STAIRS DRAGOONS
Ⓝ STAIR'S DRAGOONS (6)
Ⓞ GENTLEMEN VOLUNTEERS

This map illustrates the positions of the rival armies
at Sherriffmuir (see pages 44-49).

2 The Failure of the 'Fifteen

Argyll Prepares for Action

Meanwhile, in Perth, the main army prepared to evacuate the town. Preparations were made to fortify Perth against attack while the army was away so that it might retain its status as a Jacobite stronghold to impress King James when, or indeed if, he came. Unaccountably, the fortifications were the responsibility of 'a French fellow who had been a footman . . . . and taken up the trade of being a danceing and fenceing master in the North'. With such an unlikely training it was scarcely surprising that he ' made the strangest line that every was made'. A review of equipment revealed the existence of 11 field pieces in the camp, six of brass and five of iron. In a fleeting mood of industry and enterprise, carriages were made for the guns, although unfortunately there was 'neither pouder nor ball' to accompany them. Clan regiments were assembled with the utmost difficulty, because each civilian leader insisted on having a regiment under him no matter how small. The same situation prevailed with the troops of horse. The Jacobite army had by now reached unwieldy proportions. There were about 9,000 men in the camp with a high percentage of Highlanders. With the prospect of amalgamating with General Gordon on the outward journey, the rebels could look forward to their last influxion of support before descending upon their enemies.

All that was needed now was some incisive plan of campaign from the Major-General. Mar had received his proper commission early in October when it became clear that the Duke of Berwick would not be released from his duties in France to lead the Scottish rising. It was an asset to Mar's precarious position to be able at last to speak with the King's authority, but the existence of a commission had little material effect upon the military situation. It appears from letters Mar wrote to other Jacobite leaders at this time that beyond a vague aim to get out of Perth and move south, he had no grand strategy. Furthermore, he was in a state of deplorable ignorance about events in the south. He wrote to Viscount Kenmure on October 21: 'I long extremely to hear from you . . . . since I have not had the least Accounts almost of your Motions since I sent the Detachment over (i.e. Borlum's detachment) . . . I know so little of the Situation of your Affairs, that I must leave to your self what is fit for you to do'. Kenmure, with his ignorance of military matters, must have been dismayed by the lack of direction. On the same day, Mar wrote to Forster reiterating his ignorance. 'I have now writ to Lord Kenmure but it is ten to one if it comes to his Hands. I know not what he is doing, where he is, or what Way he intends to dispose of his People, whether he is to march into England, or towards Stirling, to wait my passing Forth; and in the Ignorance I am in of your Affairs besouth the River, I scarce know what to advise him'.[1] Mar's tone scarcely bears that stamp of ruthless determination normally considered an indispensable part of revolutionary fervour. But it is worth remembering that Mar's forté was elaborate intrigue. George Lockhart of Carnwath recorded in his memoirs that Mar's great talent 'lay in the cunning management of his designs and projects in which it was hard to find him out, when he aimed to be incognito'. Perhaps he was employing his talent to maximum effect at this time, and had laid some deep plot against the government which palled through no fault of his own. Without doubt, Mar's operations were hindered by the uncertainties which hedged his communication with the Stuart claimant. The presence of a royal figurehead was just the catalyst the amorphous Jacobite army needed and Mar was in a continual state of suspense concerning the arrival of the Chevalier.

A system of signals for making contact with the King's ship had been devised.

'A White Flag on any of the Topmast-heads, pulled up and down for several Times, and the Answer from the Shore, a white Cloath shown on the nearest Eminence.
Upon the signal, a Boat to be sent off, and the Word from the Boat, Lochaber
The Answer from the Ship, Lochyeal
The People who make the Signal, to know of Horses and Carriages.
If any Ship be seen chased, Boats to be immediately sent off.'

Although Mar thought the King would land in Dumbarton on the west coast, he had no certain intelligence and was obliged to post look-outs on the east coast as well. On October 8, he wrote 'Tho' I judge the Place above mentioned (Dumbarton) the most probable for the King's landing, yet I am by no Means sure of it, nor is it fit even this Probability should be known; . . . . . . I have sent a Party of Horse this Morning to Angus to watch the Coasts there, and I have wrote to Lord Huntly to send back a Hundred Horse for that Use to the Shire of Banff. This is taking all the Methods I can think of to make his landing safe, and we must leave the rest to Providence, which, I hope, will conduct him to us without Danger'. Mar was evidently concerned at the time that his precautions might be too late, but a month later he was still waiting for James. 'I hope my stay here shall be very short, and you may depend upon its being no longer than it necessarily must', Mar wrote to Forster in the third week of October. But while he waited, the Duke of Argyll was receiving reinforcements.

The arrival of reinforcements at Stirling enabled Argyll to put a guard on his rear and protect himself against the possibility of attack by the southern Jacobite army. By the time matters came to a head in Scotland, it was mid-November and Argyll could muster eight battalions of infantry and five regiments of dragoons. His strength had doubled and his force amounted to nearly 4,000. Mar's aim of increasing his army to its maximum strength had in no way consolidated his advantage.

---

1. The complete letters appear in Patten's *History of the Late Rebellion*, London, 1717, Pp. 74-81. The letters reached Forster and Kenmure by sea. Duplicates sent by land were intercepted and their contents made known to the government.

Numbers had increased on both sides and their relative strengths were the same as before. Furthermore, the Jacobites had not used the intervening time to maximise their potential. The men were as ill-trained after two months in the army as they had been on arrival. Argyll's army was much smaller but it was made up of regulars, well drilled, disciplined and equipped. None of the aberrations which blighted the Jacobites' prospects afflicted the government force which was at least properly provisioned and paid. The quality of the government cavalry was consistent and more than a match for the variety of mounted gentlemen that made up the Jacobite horse. It exercised a psychological advantage over the rebels as yet unknown to it, in that the Highlanders in the rebel ranks had a very real, although superstitious, fear of cavalry. Argyll was reliably informed on local and national issues and he was aware that further reinforcements were on their way. On the other hand, the Jacobites were clinging to the impossible dream of foreign aid. They searched the horizon for some encouraging sign but remained blind to real opportunities close at hand. By the time they left Perth, on November 10, 1715, the optimum conditions for an overthrow of the government forces in Scotland had passed. The Jacobites suffered from a miserable failure to face the facts of their situation. What was fabulous was taken for truth and what was obvious was persistently ignored. Indiscretion might certainly have served their cause better than any of Mar's deep plots, a lesson not lost upon Bonnie Prince Charlie when he made his own bold attempt to overthrow the government some 30 years later. Meanwhile, in 1715, while the Jacobites in Scotland waited on the affairs of others, their own fortunes began to fall imperceptibly into decline. When it could wait no longer, the army left Perth and went forth to grapple with an enemy whose identity was in fact uncertain, because, when it left Perth, the army was not looking for a fight with Argyll. It was off in pursuit of yet another illusion. The county of Lancashire was reputed to be a stronghold of Jacobite feeling in England and Mar apparently believed that he had only to show himself there to have the population flocking to his standard. It was in pursuit of this expectation that the army began to move south. But the Duke of Argyll received intelligence of Mar's plans as soon as they emerged and his own course was clear. He must try to scotch the attempt.

The same consideration which influenced Mar's decision eventually entered the calculations of the leaders of the secondary force farther south. The prospect of attracting substantial support in Lancashire seemed to invite a march into England. Left very much to its own devices, the smaller Jacobite army was weakened by divisions which were never more apparent than in the behaviour of its leaders. Personal animosities and conflicting national loyalties of the composite Scottish-English force prevailed over the need to demonstrate unified support for the house of Stuart, and frequent bickering interfered with pressing strategic business. When General Carpenter was little more than a day's march away, the border force was still dithering over its future course. Three possibilities suggested themselves initially. The army could go north and join the main force; it could launch an independent attack upon Stirling; or it could turn and face its pursuer. None of these courses was followed. Instead, the Jacobites marched south-west to Jedburgh which had no strategic importance at all and was a satisfactory destination only because it was unclassifiable in terms of either advance or retreat.

At this stage, young Lord Wintoun, demonstrating that his wits were not so far impaired as some contemporaries imagined, suggested the army make its objective a rendezvous with General Gordon and the western clans. A march through the south-west of Scotland presented no problem to the Lowland lords of the party who knew the terrain. It was sane enough advice, but the proposal was rejected. In the meantime, the army worked off its frustrated desire for action in a second abortive attempt on Dumfries. A detachment of 400 horse under the Earl of Carnwath was ordered to 'block up' Dumfries until such time as the rest of the border force could come to its assistance. While Carnwath was away, further deliberations took place on the long term prospects of the army and whether its future lay in England or Scotland. Eventually, the lure of Lancashire and the proximity of the Border proved too much for the English contingent. 'The English Gentlemen were positive for an Attempt upon their own Country . . . and urged the Advantages of a speedy March into England with such Vehemence that they turn'd the Scale . . So the Design of continuing in Scotland was quitted'.[2] The decision may have satisfied the inclinations of the Northumbrians, but it was abhorrent to the Highlanders. They had already begun to show signs of restlessness, suspecting that their destiny lay in a 'foreign land', and now they came close to mutiny en masse once their worst fears were realized. With uncanny percipience, 500 went off with the parting shot that they would rather surrender themselves prisoners than go forward to certain destruction. The Earl of Wintoun, sharing their gloomy view, also went off with a good part of his Lowland troop, but then, displaying the changeability of spirits for which he was renowned, he returned shortly afterwards to the main body.

On November 1, 1715, the border Jacobites crossed the River Esk and entered England, spending their first night at Brampton, near Carlisle in Cumberland. In accordance with the terms worked out earlier, General Forster now assumed overall command of the combined force. Conveniently enough, his spurious title was finally authorized when a commission was delivered into his hands from Mar. The army, which he was now officially empowered to direct, had just covered 100 miles in five days and was tired, divided and confused. The remnant of Highland foot was especially jaded and the army commanders deemed it expedient from this point on to offer the Highlanders the inducement of sixpence a day to secure their loyalty in the undoubted trials, hardships and dangers which lay ahead.

Meanwhile in Perth on November 9, the Jacobites held a Council of War to agree on a strategy for moving south. The difficulty of crossing the Forth was the major consideration. A plan was devised whereby the crossing was to be made well to the west of Stirling by the main body, while a diversionary party, 3,000 strong divided into three bodies of 1,000 men each, made three simultaneous sham attacks on targets in the vicinity of Stirling bridge to draw off Argyll's troops. It was a good plan, but it was in Argyll's hands the following day. His response was immediate. Before the Jacobites could implement any part of their elaborate strategy, he planned to intercept them. The weather was turning very cold and Argyll feared that the river might freeze over, in which event the Jacobites would be able to cross at several points and he would be powerless to prevent them. It was imperative that the Jacobites be intercepted before reaching the banks of the Forth. Argyll sent for the troops that were quartered in Glasgow, Kilsyth and Falkirk to supplement his own eight battalions of foot and five regiments of dragoons. On November 11, at night, arrangements were made for the Lord Lieutenant of the County and the shire militia to guard the town. Early next morning, the Duke of Argyll marched out of Stirling, towards Dunblane. By the evening of November 12, he had made his dispositions. It was a bitterly cold night, but no tents were pitched. Privates and officers alike slept in arms at their positions, quietly awaiting the approach of the enemy.

2. Patten Op. Cit. P. 71.

A Pyrrhic Victory at Sheriffmuir

Leaving Colonel Balfour and three battalions to hold Perth, the Earl of Mar at last led the Jacobite army out of the town on Thursday, November 10. It was a case of 'the blind leading the blind', according to Sinclair. Most of the men were in a state of 'not knowing whither we were goeing or what we were to doe', he said. The tactics developed to meet the exigencies of the Forth crossing had not produced so far their logical corollary, a long-term strategy. However, it was sufficient for the Highlanders in the army to be on the move at long last. The route followed was substantially the same as that taken on the occasion of the feint towards Stirling. On the first day out, the army was met by General Gordon with a following of approximately 2,500 clansmen and the augmented force camped that night at Auchterarder, about nine miles from Perth. At a review held the next morning, a dispiriting discovery was made. The entire Fraser clan had deserted in the night and 200 of the Marquis of Huntly's best men had disappeared. In addition to this setback, squabbles broke out over the disposition of the squadrons of horse and the rest of the day was spent in trying to devise an order of battle and order of marching, which would be acceptable to all parties. It was not a promising beginning.

On Saturday, November 12, after these initial problems had been solved, the army was able to resume its advance. Orders were given to General Gordon and Brigadier Ogilvy to take eight squadrons of horse and nine battalions of the clans and march on Dunblane. Mar was in complete ignorance of Argyll's manoeuvres and anticipated no problems in securing the town. The main body of the army, after another review, was to follow Gordon's advance guard and the whole force would rendezvous in the town. At three o'clock in the afternoon, as the advance guard was approaching its destination, a Jacobite quarter-master, who had gone on ahead to make provision for the arrival of the army, was spotted returning from Dunblane in an agitated condition. He had with him a young boy who breathlessly recounted the circumstances of Argyll's passage through the town. General Gordon immediately detached half a dozen horse to reconnoitre the position and sent an urgent message to the main body which was about two miles behind.

The Earl of Mar was evidently quite confident that his plans were still safe. He had gone off to Drummond Castle, a little to the north-west, on some personal business, and was not with the army when the storm broke. In Mar's absence, General Hamilton took what measures he thought necessary to cope with the emergency. The army was hastily drawn up in order. When Mar returned, his confidence was a little shaken but because no subsequent news came from General Gordon, it was considered that all was well. It was decided, therefore, to move the main body on, to join up with the advance guard. Meanwhile, Gordon's scouts had so far failed to pinpoint Argyll's exact position and it was thought inadvisable for the advance guard to penetrate any farther into potentially hostile territory in the fading light of evening. The tiny hamlet of Kinbuck on the banks of Allan Water was picked out for a billet. The men and horses of the advance guard were no sooner squeezed into their cramped quarters than news reached them of the imminent arrival of the main force. The Master of Sinclair who had been with the horse of the advance guard was immediately interrogated by Mar as to the latest intelligence. Sinclair rightly believed the enemy to be posted to the north-east of Dunblane, but his information was treated, he said, 'with ane air of neglect, as if he had a mind to accuse us of fear, and said he'd lay anie monie that it was not true. Afterwards he called for Generall Gordon, who came alonge with Huntlie. And when the Generall told him the same he said, He knew the contrarie; and to this there was no answer

44

to be made'. Mar's procrustean efforts to adapt the circumstances to suit his own interpretation fooled no one but himself. He had certainly not planned for an engagement so early in the campaign and was evidently disturbed by the prospect. Why he should have continued to prevaricate with such a vast superiority of numbers over his adversary, is a mystery.

The rival armies spent the night of November 12 not more than two miles apart. Argyll had chosen the rising ground above Dunblane to make his dispositions because it seemed the likeliest vantage point from which to view the approach of his enemies. The ground which lay between the hostile armies was known as Sheriffmuir, a stretch of barren moorland that received its name from having been used as a rendezvous by the militia of the sheriffdom of Monteith. The ground was undulating, containing pockets of marshland and swamp. It had a general tendency to rise in Argyll's direction but the slope was not so steep as to make it a hill. It recommended itself to Argyll as an area in which his cavalry might be deployed to some advantage. Before dawn on November 13, the freezing government troops had their distribution of ammunition augmented from 24 rounds each to 30, in preparation for an engagement. At six o'clock, stiff and aching from the cramped conditions of their quarters in Kinbuck, the Jacobites assembled on the moor and drew up in two lines, facing towards Dunblane.

The Jacobites were deployed in a simple two-line formation with nine or ten battalions of foot in the front line flanked on either side by horse, and a similar number of battalions in the second line protected by Seaforth's 'scrub' horse on the right. The battalions of the first line consisted chiefly of Highlanders, ranged in their clan ranks according to social status, with common clansmen in the rear and more exalted persons in the front. General Gordon had the overall command of the front line foot. Subordinate leaders included Alexander Macdonald of Glengarry, Macdonald of Clanranald, Brigadier Ogilvy of Boyne, and Sir John Maclean. Among others, there were Camerons and Stewarts of Appin in addition to the numerous Macdonalds of the front line, eager to share the brunt of the attack.

At this point, it is perhaps necessary to point out that the Highlander as a fighting man in no way conformed to the orthodox eighteenth-century view of the soldier. The Highlanders had a very distinctive way of fighting and regular troops used to regular warfare discovered in a Highland charge something that was quite unique. Although the following description of the Highlanders' fighting tactics was written by a participant in the 'Forty-five, the technique was the same then as it had been in 1715.

'Their manner of fighting is adapted for brave but undisciplined men. They advance with rapidity, discharge their pieces when within musket-length of the enemy, and then, throwing them down, draw their swords and holding a dirk in their left hand with their target, they dart with fury on the enemy through the smoke of their fire. When within reach of the enemy's bayonets, bending their left knee, they, by their attitude, cover their bodies with their targets, that receive the thrusts of the bayonets, which they contrive to parry, while at the same time they raise their sword-arm, and strike their adversary. Having once got within the bayonets, and into the ranks of the enemy, the soldiers have no longer any means of defending themselves, the fate of the battle is decided in an instant, and the carnage follows; the Highlanders bringing down two men at a time, one with their dirk, in the left hand, and another with the sword.'[3]

The strength of a Highland attack lay in its impetuosity. A regular army relied on discipline

3. *Memoirs of The Rebellion in 1715 and 1716* by The Chevalier de Johnstone. Third Edition with Additional Notes &c., London, 1822, Pp. 113-4.

and training for success. The outcome of the battle would provide vindication of the principles of one or the other.

While the Jacobites were lining up on the moor, the Duke of Argyll was surveying their activities from a hill about two miles away. From what he could see of the 'dark cloud-like masses of the clans as they wheeled into order', no decision had yet been made on the matter of giving battle. The clans were facing towards Dunblane and indeed Argyll interpreted the move correctly as one indicating uncertainty. The Jacobites were in a dilemma, still wondering whether it might not be possible to press on with their original intent regardless of Argyll's presence. Could they not proceed towards the higher reaches of the Forth without offering battle, leaving Argyll to make of their decision what he would? Characteristically, at the moment of crisis the results of careless planning reduced their prospects of success. It was now discovered that the territory which lay ahead was virtually unknown to members of the expedition. No attempt at reconnaisance had been made before they set out. It appeared that the River Teith lay in their path and as this was in flood it represented as great an obstacle to their progress as the Forth itself. Moreover, for the second time, boundaries were placed on their initiative by inadequate provisioning. The rudimentary Jacobite commissariat had miscalculated the army's requirements, Although an estimated 12 days' provisions had been brought from Perth, after three days campaigning there were thought to be sufficient supplies for another day's march only. From six o'clock to eleven, the two Jacobite lines waited for a decision on their future. The peers, commanders of corps and clan leaders were called to a conference on a piece of rising ground between the lines. After a rousing speech Mar put it to them, to fight or not to fight, and with the exception of Huntly, the leaders were unanimously in favour of a fight. As the decision was communicated to

the men, it ran like fire down the lines and a mood of feverish excitement was kindled in the ranks. From the Highlanders came loud huzzas and there was much lively tossing of bonnets in the air. The lines quickly wheeled to face the moor and Argyll watching from the hill was left in no doubt as to the consequence. Returning at full gallop to the government camp, he ordered the drummers to beat 'the General', the call to arms for all the troops.

Argyll had only about 3,500 men with him and he had deployed them so as to have their right flank protected by a stretch of marshland generally thought to be impassable. What he knew of the activities of the clans led him to believe that a sizeable body of the Highlanders might attempt to gain the high ground to the right of his position, so that they might descend in their impetuous fashion upon the right flank of his army. This manoeuvre would have been impossible if the weather had complemented Argyll's calculations about the boggy ground. But, the previous night's severe frost had so hardened the morass that it had become quite capable of allowing an attack on that side. At the last minute, Argyll decided to alter his dispositions and move forward to meet the Jacobite threat. If there was an air of hovering uncertainty on the Jacobite side, all was not efficiency and expedition in the government ranks. It took the royal troops almost an hour to prepare for the manoeuvre and it was almost twelve o'clock before they began to move. Argyll was aiming at a simple two-line formation with six battalions of foot in the front line supported by Carpenter's and Kerr's dragoons on the left and Evans's and Portmore's (the Scots Greys) on the right and two battalions of foot in the second line flanked on either side by Stair's dragoons. But he had scarcely formed the right wing, which was under his own immediate command, when a general discharge of firearms from the other side heralded the commencement of the action.

The faltering movements of both sides gave the start of the battle an air of accidental encounter. Undulations in the ground obstructed the view of participants on both sides and no clear impression of the strength of one force could be gathered by the other. As the rival armies were approaching each other from opposite sides of the same hill, the scene was set for a surprise encounter on the summit, which was in effect what happened. Mar had broken the two Jacobite lines into two columns each for the march and these columns were proceeding piecemeal to the rising ground. The first to move were the foot of the front line, the Highlanders, and they were bounding up the hill long before the last column was ready to move off. What they encountered when they came to the top of the ridge was the disorderly left wing of Argyll's force which was still reassembling. In an instant it became clear that the rival armies were not properly opposed — they were out of alignment. What had been the front line of the Jacobite army, when it first formed up early in the morning, was now to be the right wing in battle and it was clear to the first arrivals on the ridge that their right would far outflank Argyll's left and vice versa. This disconcerting discovery caused a temporary halt in proceedings, but General Gordon not wanting to lose the advantage of surprise gave the order 'to attack the enemie before they were formed'. General Whetham, who commanded the left of the government line, found his wing at a disastrous disadvantage because of the faulty alignment of the two armies. Instead of facing the right wing of the rebel force, his hastily assembling wing found itself opposed to the centre of the Jacobite line and thus massively outflanked to the left. 'The Left Wing of the Duke's small Army fell in with the Centre of theirs, which consisted, especially of the first Line, of the Flower of the rebel Army'.[4] Within four minutes, the doubly disadvantaged government left wing was to feel the full force of a Highland attack.

'The order to attack being given, the tuo thousand Highlandmen . . . run towards the ennemie in a disorderlie manner, always fireing some dropeing shots, which drew upon them a generall salvo from the ennemie, which begun at their left, opposite to us, and run to their right. No sooner that begun, the Highlandmen threw themselves flat on their bellies; and when it slackned, they started to their feet. Most threw away their fuzies, and drawing their suords, pierced them everie where with ane incredible vigour and rapiditie, in four minutes' time from their receiving the order to attack' (Sinclair)

In characteristic fashion, the Highlanders had advanced flinging aside their plaids to free their arms for action and screaming their individual clan slogans. In his *Journal,* Mar later recorded some histrionics of his own, claiming to have advanced towards the enemy waving his hat in encouragement to the clans who had followed after, animated by his loud huzza. The clan leaders were in fact conspicuously brave. The first fire of the enemy fell on them and in the opening seconds of the action the captain of Clanranald fell. The superstitious Macdonalds faltered, considering his loss to be a bad augury, but Glengarry leaping into the breach urged them on with the cry 'Revenge, revenge! today for revenge and tomorrow for mourning'. The government soldiers were paralysed by the bizarre and terrifying assault of the Highlanders. They 'behaved gallantly, and made all the Resistance they could make, but being unacquainted with this Savage Way of Fighting, against which all the Rules of War had made no Provision, they were forced to give way, fell in among the Horse, and help'd the Enemy to put them in Confusion; so a total Rout of that Wing of the royal Army ensued'.[5] Survivors of the onslaught on the government side ran all the way back to Stirling with the Highlanders and Mar with some of the Jacobite horse in pursuit.

4. *The Life of the Most Illustrious Prince John, Duke of Argyle and Greenwich,* by Robert Campbell, London, 1745.

5. Campbell. Op. Cit.

Meanwhile, on the right of the government lines, where Argyll commanded, little impression had been made by a Jacobite attack launched at about the same time as the successful onslaught just described. The exact composition of the Jacobite army on this left wing remains shrouded in doubt and mystery. Cavalry directed to support the left flank had been misplaced and may or may not have been in position when the fighting was at its thickest on this wing. The nineteenth-century Jacobite historian, Robert Chambers, evidently thought that it was. 'The Duke, afraid of being out-flanked by the cavalry of the enemy, quickly determined upon making a charge with his own cavalry. Accordingly, commanding Colonel Cathcart to lead a powerful squadron circuitously through the frozen morass, and, at once attacking that part of the hostile army in front and side, beat it back a considerable way at the point of the sword, and confounded the two lines of which it consisted'.[6] A frontal attack by Argyll's foot supported by the dragoons weakened the Highlanders but met with tough resistance. 'The Highlanders . . . begun the Action with a great deal of Fury; and their second Fire, levell'd particularly at the Dragoons (the weight whereof fell most upon Evans's, which made that brave Corpse [sic] to reel a little) was as good, perhaps, as ever came from any disciplined Troops'.[7] But Cathcart's flanking movement soon tipped the balance in Argyll's favour. The rebels found themselves outflanked by superior cavalry on their left and raked by the constant fire of the regular platoons of foot to the front. They began to retreat slowly down the hill towards Allan Water, disputing every inch of ground along the way so that a retreat of three miles occupied as many hours. At as many as ten different places, the Jacobites tried to rally and but for Argyll's incessant exertions, they would have succeeded. Argyll's conscience was evidently pricking him during these proceedings. One of the more harrowing

aspects of the battle of Sheriffmuir was that rival officers were known to each other and carried memories of happier days together, not easily obliterated by an instant feigned hostility. Friends, and even relatives found themselves freakishly paired as adversaries in the field. Argyll, to his credit, found the prescriptions of internecine warfare too horrible to enjoy his duty. He himself offered quarter to those he recognized and tried vicariously to save the lives of others. 'On seeing his troopers dash in upon a great huddled band of Lowland foot, whom they cut down almost without resistance, he could not help exclaiming, with the national feeling for a moment predominating over the political, and every other, "Oh, spare the poor Bluebonnets!".'[8]

The left of both armies was now in full flight. The Duke of Argyll was so preoccupied with his repugnant duties on the right that he had lost all track of the progress of his other wing. As soon as he heard of the disaster, he regrouped his own fatigued men and, together with three battallions of foot from the centre commanded by General Wightman, he prepared to reconnoitre the situation. The rout of the government left had created a gap in the field which had been filled by Jacobites as yet inactive in the struggle: 'crossing the Field of Battle, in Number then about 4,000 Men (they) marched up to the Top of that Part of the Hill, called the Stony Hill of Kippendavie, where they stood without attempting any Thing, with their Swords drawn for near four Hours Space . .' (Rae). Jacobite combatants returning from the rout of the government left could see quite clearly that their men were still in possession of the field. Argyll approached from the opposite direction and made the same observation. He 'halted and form'd the few Men he had, which were scarce a Thousand; the Grays on the Right, Evans's on the Left, the Squadron of Stairs next them, and the Foot in the Center. With these he advanced towards the Enemy,

6. *History of the Rebellions in Scotland under The Viscount of Dundee and The Earl of Mar in 1689 and 1715* by Robert Chambers, Edinburgh, 1829, P. 258.

7. Rae's *History of the Rebellion*, London, M.DCC.XLVI, P. 305.

8. Chambers. Op. Cit. P. 359.

who were about 4000, form'd on the Top of the Hill, a little to the Southward of the Place where they formed at first, and fronting towards him: And being come to the Foot of the Hill, and having the convenience of some old Enclosures or Fold-Dykes, about Breast high, there they posted themselves . . . where they stood a considerable Time expecting the Enemy to attack them'. But nothing happened. There was some feigned aggression from a party of Jacobite horse. They advanced to within a few hundred yards of Argyll's position and then quietly retreated. With the approach of evening, the tension began to evaporate. Combatants on both sides became aware of cold and hunger and fatigue. The rival armies gradually melted away, the Jacobites to the north and the Hanoverians to the south. The battle of Sheriffmuir was over.

Next day, Monday November 14, 1715, at daybreak Argyll returned to the field with a patrol. He wanted to view the preparations of the Jacobites for a second round, but to his immense relief he found the enemy gone. The government troops were allowed to pick over the battlefield unmolested. Major-General Wightman was later to record that; 'The Enemy behaved like civil Gentlemen, and let us do what we pleased'. Argyll returned to Dunblane and then marched the army back to Stirling taking with him 'fourteen of the Enemy's Colours and Standards, amongst whom was the Royal Standard, call'd the Restoration, . .'; he also took some prisoners and captured six pieces of Jacobite cannon, which like his own, appeared to have served little purpose in the action. On November 15, Mar returned to Perth to see to the urgent business of provisions. Two days later, the army was recalled to the city, having achieved nothing and sustained losses in the battle variously reported as between 60 and 700.

Each side was subsequently to claim the victory for itself at Sheriffmuir. Because the action was indecisive, it was open to various interpretations and Mar chose to see it as a triumph for the Jacobites. No amount of trumpet blowing, however, could eradicate the unpleasant fact that the Jacobite army had been prevented from implementing its plan to move south by an opponent scarce a third its own strength. A week later, Mar wrote to James offering him an excuse for the army's premature return to base. The night before the battle, 'the armie had lyen without cover', he said, 'and wee had no provisions there, which obliged me to march the armie back two milles that night, which was the nearest place where I could get any quarters. Next day I found the armie reduced to a small number, more by the Highlanders going home than by any loss wee sustained, which was but very small; so that and want of provisions obliged me yet to retire, first to Auchterarder and then here to Perth'.[9] The Jacobites were back where they started in deteriorating circumstances. It was a Pyrrhic victory indeed, and a Jacobite ballad subsequently became popular.

'There's some say that we wan,
Some say that they wan
And some say that nane wan at a', man;
But one thing I'm sure,
That at Sheriffmuir,
A battle there was, that I saw, man
And we ran, and they ran,
And they ran, and we ran,
And we ran, and they ran awa', man.'[10]

Defeat in Lancashire
The letter sent by the Earl of Mar to the Old Pretender after Sheriffmuir spoke not only of the rebels' situation in Scotland, but commented also on the fate of the Jacobites in the secondary force farther south, which had last been heard of in Brampton. After a night's rest in the town, this force had set off next day, Wednesday November 2, 1715, for Penrith with the object of taking a south-westerly route into Lancashire. To secure support for this scheme, members of the English

9. Historical Manuscripts Commission. *Report on the Manuscripts of the Earl of Mar and Kellie Preserved at Alloa House*. London, H.M.S.O., 1904.

10. *The Jacobite Relics of Scotland; Being The Songs, Airs and Legends of the Adherents to the House of Stuart*. Collected and Illustrated by James Hogg. Second Series, Edinburgh, MDCCCXXI, Vol, 2,. P. 1.

contingent had offered assurances of reliable backing in Lancashire, some claiming to be in possession of letters from Lancastrians testifying to the existence of allies in the county, numbering 20,000. Thus, with the impression that they were about to blaze a glorious trail through friendly territory, the Jacobites of the border force continued their journey into England, leaving General Carpenter to follow after them in his own time.

Next day many of the men encountered their first opposition since the beginning of the rebellion. The threat was a potentially serious one which diminished in the actuality. As they proceeded towards Penrith, the Jacobites were warned that the sheriff of the county, with a *posse comitatus* (a force of county men) reckoned to be some 14,000 strong, was preparing to bar their way. The Jacobites advanced with trepidation to meet their adversaries, who in turn were just as anxious, not knowing what to expect from a rebel army. A reconnaisance party sent out from the town returned with alarming details of the rebel's efficiency. The party had watched the Jacobites emerging from a nearby wood and draw up on the common in preparation for an ordered approach towards the town. The mere prospect of such an organized advance threw the informal gathering into a panic. The posse dwindled to a mere handful and, to the immense relief of all concerned, the Jacobites were allowed to enter Penrith at about 3 o'clock in the afternoon without a blow being struck. The rebels did nothing to antagonize the local people beyond helping themselves to the excise and other public money. An investigation into the availability of arms and horses at nearby Lowther Hall, the seat of the Viscount Lonsdale, however, led to rumours of vandalism, and the Jacobites were accused of defacing statues and despoiling the gardens of the stately home after their searches proved fruitless. They stayed in Penrith only one night, after which they set off for Appleby in Westmorland.

It must have seemed remarkable to the Jacobites that their adventures had not so far been accompanied by any noticeable increase in their numbers. On the contrary, they were suffering minor desertions continually. A mood of fatalism began to settle over the expedition. Blind hope began to take its toll of disappointment when rosy expectations failed to materialize. A chance still remained that business would pick up in Lancashire but the auspices had not so far been particularly encouraging.

On November 3, the Jacobites reached Appleby, where they remained for two days without experiencing any significant rise in their fortunes. They resumed their southward advance on November 5 and proceeded to Kendal. A journalist described their entry into the town as a miserable and dispiriting affair. An advance guard of Highlanders came in on horseback, each wearing a plaid, with his shield slung across his back, a sword by his side and a gun and a case of pistols. Brigadier Mackintosh was observed to look 'with a grim countenance'. About an hour later, the rest of the army appeared. It was raining hard and the weather had been bad for days. Travelling was difficult and discomfort endemic. Low morale was reflected in the solemnity of the occasion. No swords were drawn. The drums were silent and the colours furled. A mere six Highland bagpipes announced the arrival of the Jacobite army at Kendal.[11]

The rebels were becoming accustomed to the pangs of disappointment and at Kendal they found once again that their presence was regarded as more irritating than inspirational. They received no co-operation from the local people in the business of augmenting their small supply of equipment. The Mayor stubbornly refused to disclose the whereabouts of the militia arms and the rebels were thus forced to exact some grudging labour from the local gunsmiths in an effort to refurbish the defective pieces they had brought with them. The response to the proclamation of King

11. According to Peter Clarke, an attorney's clerk in Kendal at the time.

James was muted. While the Jacobites in general were made to feel unwelcome, Forster in particular was singled out for special reproach. He had the misfortune to run into his godmother, a certain Madam Bellingham, who happened to be staying in the town. She was frankly unimpressed by the arrival of her upstart godson at the head of a rebellious army and refused to acknowledge him. Unfortunately, the estranged pair bumped into one another by accident in the lady's lodgings, whereupon she took the initiative and promptly delivered Forster 'two or three boxes on the eare', calling him at the same time a rebel and a 'Popish tool', all of which the General is reputed to have taken 'patiently'.

Without further incident, and still deprived of the cache of arms, the Jacobites left Kendal on Sunday November 6, at eight o'clock in the morning, adding significantly to their unpopularity by leaving debts behind them. They departed in much the same manner as they arrived, without drums or colours and with Brigadier Mackintosh looking as grim as before. There was small reason for any of that party to appear elated. A mere handful of recruits had by then joined them and their journey was assuming a doggedness of purpose unrelieved by hope. They were in desperate need of a tonic when at last some stimulating news reached them as they proceeded to Lancaster. The army was met en route by an emissary who informed them that the people of Lancashire were preparing to offer their support. That day King James was being proclaimed in Manchester and the citizens were busy raising a troop of 50 men at their own expense. It was perhaps not an extravagant gesture, but it was interpreted by the Jacobites as the prelude to greater things. Three rousing huzzas of relief went up from the Highlanders and the army proceeded with lighter step towards Lancaster. At about one o'clock the Jacobites entered the city and marched to the market cross to proclaim the sovereignty of King James.

While they waited for the anticipated deluge of supporters, the Jacobites busied themselves with the usual collection of revenue and search for weapons. There were found to be six cannon worth taking, as well as other perquisites in the way of claret and a quantity of brandy, not strictly necessary to the campaign. Little evidence beyond a trickle of friends to their standard gave support to their revitalized hopes. Nevertheless at this stage, 'they resolv'd on a March for Preston, designing to proceed and possess themselves of Warrington-Bridge, and of the Town of Manchester, where they had Assurances of great Numbers to join them; and, by this Means they made no Doubt of securing the great and rich Town of Liverpool, which would be cut off from any Relief, if they were once possess'd of Warrington-Bridge' (Rae). Forster did not relate this ambitious programme to any counter-measures being taken by the Hanoverian government. He received intelligence at Lancaster that General Carpenter had doubled back and was doggedly following the Jacobites' cold trail, but the General was still a long way off in Durham and Forster was blissfully ignorant of what lay ahead. In fact, the government had already planned measures to arrest the invaders' progress. Forster's strategy, which seemed to be operating in a vacuum, was about to lead him into a trap. Major General Wills, stationed in Cheshire, had been ordered to assemble as many regular men as he could conveniently muster and advance without delay to meet the invaders, and if possible, to seize Warrington-Bridge and reach Preston before them. Accordingly, he had called up the regiments quartered in Shropshire, Worcestershire, Staffordshire and Cheshire and these were ordered to assemble at Warrington on November 10.

Meanwhile, as the Jacobites prepared to leave Lancaster, they began at last to receive that infusion of support so long withheld. The prevalence of Roman Catholicism and High

Church Torysim in Lancashire was the original base from which the great hopes for the county's Jacobite militancy had grown. It was now found that most of the new recruits were gentlemen volunteers with servants and friends, and practically all were Roman Catholics. When it came to the point, the High Church party dependables, according to Patten, did not care for 'venturing their Carcasses any farther than the Tavern'. The exclusive religious complexion of the new adherents gave the Presbyterian Scots an uneasy time, but nevertheless it was a revitalized army that left Lancaster for Preston on November 9. The weather made travelling difficult. It was especially arduous for the foot to make headway along roads that were made impassable by rain and mud. Consequently, they fell a long way behind the horse and were forced to spend the night at Garstang, half way between Lancaster and Preston. The horse entered Preston in the evening of the 9th and were naively cheered to learn that two troops of government dragoons posted in the town had hastily retreated on learning of their approach. They took the retreat to be a sign of the government's infirmity. The foot arrived in Preston the next day, and marched straight to the market cross to hear the proclamation. The Lancashire gentlemen and Roman Catholics continued to turn out in force and, as their numbers increased, the Jacobites saw their horizons widening. What they did not know was that Wills was already in Manchester, just 30 miles away.

The Jacobites in Preston were preparing to march on Manchester when they received the shattering news that General Wills had advanced as far as Wigan and was currently on his way, accompanied by six cavalry regiments and Preston's regiment of foot, to attack them. Forster had already given the order to evacuate Preston and was preparing to lead the Jacobites out on Saturday, November 12, when he suddenly found that his false paradise was about to be brutally invaded. He was still without the dimmest notion of what lay ahead and his surprise was complete. That the Jacobite leader should have been so little concerned to keep himself informed of current anti-invasion measures seems to demonstrate a negligence amounting almost to insanity. Robert Patten, who was there in Preston, explained:

'All this while they had not the least Intimation of the Forces that were preparing to oppose them, much less of the near approach of the King's Army: And as it is a Question often asked, and which very few can answer, viz. How they came to be so utterly void of Intelligence at that time, as to be so ignorant of the March of the King's Forces, and to know nothing of them 'till they were within sight of Preston, and ready almost to fall on them? It may be very proper to give a plain and direct Answer to it, which will in short be this, viz. That in all their Marches Mr. Forster spared neither Pains nor Cost to be acquainted with all General Carpenter's Motions, of which he had constant and particular Accounts every day, and sometimes twice a Day; but the Lancashire Gentlemen gave him such Assurances that no Force could come near them by Forty Miles but they could inform him thereof, this made him perfectly easy on that side, relying entirely on the Intelligence he expected from them.'

Forster was satisfied that the vigilance of the 'Lancashire gentlemen' was insurance enough against surprise.

The two days which had elapsed since the army's arrival in Preston had been spent in relaxation and amusement. No attempt had been made to fortify the town against invasion and the prospect of having to defend it at a moment's notice gave rise to panic. Forster burdened with the necessity of inventing a scratch strategy found his ingenuity taxed to the limit. The government army had left

Wigan at daybreak and at one o'clock in the afternoon, the compact force arrived at the Ribble bridge, about a mile from Preston. Forster was busy investigating the possibility of defending this vital pass to the town when he ran into Wills's vanguard. Stung into taking immediate action, the project of defending the bridge was abandoned and Forster withdrew all his men inside Preston 'and having given the Alarm, the Rebels applied themselves resolutely to their Business, in casting up Trenches, barricading the Streets, and posting their Men in the Streets, By-lanes and Houses, to the greatest advantage for all Events'[12]. It was a makeshift strategy but there was no time to lose in second thoughts. Barriers were erected at points of access to the town with fall-back positions farther inside. The first barricade, below the Parish Church was commanded by Borlum. It had an advance barricade in front of it and was supported by mounted gentlemen volunteers drawn up in the churchyard under Lords Derwentwater, Kenmure, Wintoun and Nithsdale. The second barricade, on the Left flank of the first was under the command of Lord Charles Murray. The third held by Colonel Mackintosh of Mackintosh was on the exit road to Lancaster and had a fall-back position nearer the Mitre Inn, Forster's headquarters. The fourth and last defensive position was at Fishergate, commanded by Major Miller and Captain Douglas. As the minutes ticked away before the action began many of the latest Jacobite recruits managed to find a back door out of Preston and, before long, the fighting force was reduced to its original nucleus of about 2,000.

When Wills's main body arrived at the Ribble bridge, it was surprised to find the pass undefended. Suspecting a trap, Wills pushed his men cautiously towards the town, casting about him for signs of an ambush. When he finally realized that the rebels were barricaded inside the town, he began to deploy his men in preparation for a two-pronged attack which would dam the Jacobites up in their claustrophobic position. Forster had retreated like a snail into his shell and the Jacobites suffered from all the disadvantages of having the venue for the forthcoming battle forced upon them. Nevertheless, certain unforeseen benefits accrued from their leader's shyness that made the Jacobites not unhopeful of success. Wills' army was smaller than that of the Jacobites and his chief strength lay in his cavalry. Clearly, the narrow streets of Preston offered no arena for its effective deployment, while the same environment gave the Jacobites enough cover to ensure than any attacking force would come off worse under fire than they the defenders. Last-minute preparations were made in the town. The Earl of Derwentwater, stripped for action, supervised the digging of trenches, proffering cash incentives to his men for faster work. At two o'clock, everyone froze. The first attack came from the eastern side of town, near Old Borlum's position. Some 200 of Wills's men, led by Brigadier Honeywood, advanced from the direction of the Wigan road. They were met by a decimating fusillade from the windows of nearby houses, from cellars and doorways as well as from the barricades. Within ten minutes, 120 of them lay dead. More might have fallen but for the erratic fire of the volunteer gunners on the Jacobite side whose marksmanship was so unpredictable as to inflict more damage on nearby buildings than on the enemy. Nevertheless, the government troops were effectively repulsed and those who survived the initial attack quickly retreated.

At the opposite end of town, two hours later, Brigadier Dormer led the government troops into a similar attack upon Colonel Mackintosh's position, and once again the sharpshooters in the Jacobite army proved more than a match for government orthodoxy. Dormer tried twice to dislodge the Jacobites and both times he was repulsed. Meanwhile, Lord Charles Murray commanding the position next to Old Borlum's withstood an equally ferocious attack in spite

---

12. Rae's *History of the Rebellion*, P. 319.

of being undermanned. By evening, the Jacobites had inflicted three major defeats on the royal army. However, a tactical error had allowed some of Honeywood's men to occupy two large houses situated on the outskirts of town near Borlum's and Murray's positions. The Highlanders who had originally occupied these buildings had been withdrawn and their places were quickly taken by the enemy. As darkness began to settle over the besieged town, sporadic firing could be heard from the occupied quarter. Otherwise, the king's army camped quietly in the fields around Preston, and General Forster whose performance in the battle had not been conspicuously brave was able to enjoy a peaceful night's rest, despite the threatening implications of his army's enclosed position. 'There were several Houses and Barns set on fire by both Parties, both for covering themselves among the Smoak and dislodging Men; so that if the Wind had blown almost from any Quarter that Town had been burnt to the Ground, and the Rebels had been burnt to Ashes in it'[13].

The next morning, the Jacobites turned out unharmed to review their situation. A worrying shortage of gunpowder threatened to impair their power of resistance, but otherwise they were confident for another round of fighting. The date was auspicious. It was Sunday, November 13, 1715, and while the Jacobites deliberated in Preston, their Scottish counterparts were lining up near Sheriffmuir. But, at the moment the Highlanders at Sheriffmuir were flinging their bonnets in the air, the rebels in Preston were suddenly and unexpectedly forced to contemplate a future of stygian gloom. General Carpenter had finally caught up with them. ' . . about Noon, General Carpenter arrived, with the Regiments of Cobham, Molesworth, and Churchill, and a good many Country Gentlemen . . . . As soon as he was come up, General Wills acquainted him with what he had done, shew'd him the Dispositions he had made, and then offered to resign the Com-

mand to him, as his superior Officer'[14]. With one or two exceptions, Carpenter was satisfied with the measures that had been taken and happy to relinquish his superior claim to Wills. He was, however, surprised to discover that 'no Troops were posted at the End of Fisher-gate-Street, to block up that Part of the Town, and that for want of it, several of the Rebels had escaped there and more rid off that Way, even before his Face'. This was the site of the one Jacobite barricade that had escaped attack in the previous day's fighting and Carpenter was in no mood, after his exhausting trek, to allow it to become an avenue of escape for his quarry. The town was surrounded on all sides.

Despite the new odds, the Highlanders, cooped up inside Preston were all for making a desperate sortie and dying sword in hand. They knew with the prescience of warriors that they could look for no clemency from Carpenter. Forster, however, was not touched by such immoderate proposals and searching, as always for the golden mean he began to plot with his closest advisers to find a way out of his nightmarish predicament. Eventually, he began to flatter himself that he could extract good terms for surrender from the King's general. 'The common Men were one and all against capitulating, and were terribly enrag'd when they were told of it, declaring that they would force their Way out and make a Retreat'. wrote Patten. The frail courtesies, which alone had bound the border force together, now cracked to reveal an ugly undercurrent of seething mistrust in the final negotiations. The lowland Scots and the English treated separately and secretly with General Wills to secure advantageous terms. Colonel Oxburgh, the English negotiator, infected by Forster's fatuous optimism went boldly to Wills's tent to parley, but found his reception lacked the warmth he had expected. Wills pointed out coldly that the Jacobites had killed a number of his Majesty's subjects and should anticipate a similar fate for themselves.

13. Patten's *History of the Late Rebellion*.

14. Rae. Op. Cit. P. 320.

Oxburgh could only plead for the lives of the rebels. Wills was prepared to relinquish a fraction of his advantage but he made his final position clear. He would not bargain with rebels, but he was prepared to restrain the government troops from cutting the Jacobites to pieces, if they would 'lay down their arms and surrender at Discretion'. He gave them an hour to think it over. Before the time was up, Mr. Dalziel, brother of the Earl of Carnwath was sent out to inquire what terms Wills would allow to his countrymen in particular. The answer was the same. In other words, there were no terms. The Jacobites were to surrender unconditionally. They were to have recourse to 'The King's Mercy', but there was little leaven in that empty prospect. The Scottish negotiator asked for more time, but his request was denied. At three o'clock on the afternoon of the 13th, a government drummer beating a *chamade* (call to parley) proclaimed the arrival of Wills's deputy for an answer. Meanwhile, Preston had been the scene of bitter activity among the Jacobite factions. Fighting broke out on the issue of surrender: '. . . it was astonishing to see the Confusion the Town was in, threat'ning, yea killing one another, but for naming a Surrender'. Forster, who had been barely tolerated by the Highlanders before, now went in fear of his life and only very narrowly escaped assassination. The unseemly confusion in Preston delayed immediate and dignified surrender. 'The Colonel alighted at the Sign of the Mitre, where the chief of the Rebel Officers were got together, and told them he came to receive their positive Answer. 'Twas told him, There were Disputes betwixt the English and Scots, that would obstruct the Yielding, which Others were willing to submit to; but if the General would grant them a Cessation of Arms 'till the next Morning at Seven, they should be able to settle the Matter . . .'15. A dissentient note was struck by a Jacobite sniper who expressed his disgust at the peremptory dealings of his masters by

shooting the royal drummer off his horse. After this event, it was deemed expedient to take the Earl of Derwentwater and Brigadier Mackintosh as hostages against a last desperate revolt.

On the morning of November 14, 'about seven o'clock' according to Rae, 'Mr. Forster sent out to acquaint General Wills that they were willing to give themselves up Prisoners at Discretion, as he had demanded. But Mackintosh being by when the Message was brought, said he could not answer that the Scots would surrender in that Manner, for that the Scots were People of desperate Fortunes . . .'16. Wills was in no mood to tolerate Mackintosh's bombast. 'Go back to your People again', he said icily to the Brigadier, 'and I will attack the Town, and the Consequence will be, I will not spare one Man of you'17. Mackintosh did go back and was forced to concede that, under the circumstances, the Highlanders had no choice but to surrender with the rest.

'The Rebels having thus submitted to the King's Mercy, Colonel Cotton was sent in to take possession of the Town, and to order the King's Troops to march and disarm the Rebels, which was done accordingly. The Generals entered the Town in Form at the Head of the Troops, which came in at the End next Lancaster; and Brigadier Honeywood with the remaining Troops entered at the opposite End of the Town, with Sound of Trumpets, and Beat of Drums, both Parties meeting at the Market-place, where the Highlanders stood, drawn up with their Arms'18. The clamour of a royal victory must have made especially sad music to the Highlanders' ears. While they stood in stunned silence, the Lords, gentlemen volunteers and officers were disarmed and taken off to various places of confinement in the town. Next, it was their turn to lay down their arms and be escorted under guard to their prison in the nearby church. What the Highlanders were thinking at this moment is a matter for conjecture, but it must surely have crossed the mind of not a

15. Patten.

16. Rae. P. 323.

17. Wills's deposition at the Earl of Wintoun's trial. Patten, Ibid. Pp. 117-8.

18. Rae. P. 323.

few that they had made a useless sacrifice of their political hopes and probably their lives in a town in Lancashire, as remote in their minds from the Stuart cause as the Highland hills were distant from Preston's walls. As events turned out, they were able to repent their lost cause at leisure, because the Highlanders remained incarcerated in the church for a month, subsisting during that time on nothing but bread and water. They were driven to the extremity of tearing the linings from the seats of the pews to protect themselves from the bitter cold.

So, the Earl of Mar was able to report in his letter to James on November 24, 'I had certain accounts yesterday of those who had appeared in arms besouth Forth and in the North of England, all being made prisoners at Preston in Lancashire, which I'm afraid will putt a stop to any more risings in that countrey at this time'. He was right. The Jacobite rebellion in England was over, and the colours of King James III and VIII, which were to have flown triumphantly over Lancashire, were found unceremoniously stuffed into the pocket of an escaping Jacobite officer. The losses in battle had been small on the rebel side; about 17 had been killed and 25 wounded. Government losses were in the region of 200. But the wound inflicted on Jacobite morale by the abrupt, and many felt dishonourable, surrender was more damaging than any decimation of the army in a full-scale bloody engagement might have been. The feeling died hard among the Jacobite rank and file that they had been betrayed by mendacious leaders. Later, at Tyburn, a Mr. John Hall articulated the grievance of many of the rebels when he declared, 'Mr. Wills may not impose upon the world as if he and his troops had conquered us, and gained the victory; for the truth is after we had conquered them our superiors thought fit to capitulate and ruin us'. By dissociating themselves from the decisions of collaborators, the crushed Jacobites rescued a figleaf of respectability from the shameful ruin of their cause. It was a small enough covering, because it must have been apparent that Forster's strategy had left the Jacobites with few alternatives. Walled up as they were, surrender or annihilation would have come sooner or later. Forster's behaviour was described in a lament:

' "Adzounds!" cried Foster, "never fear,
"For Brunswick's army is not near;
"And if they dare come, our valour we'll show,
"And give them a total overthrow."
But Derwentwater soon he found
That they were all enclos'd around.
"Alack!" he cried, "for this cowardly strife,
"How many brave men shall lose their life!"

Old Mackintosh he shook his head,
When he saw his Highland lads lie dead;
And he wept-not for the loss of those,
But for the success of their proud foes.
Then Mackintosh unto Will's he came,
Saying, "I have been a soldier in my time,
"And ere a Scot of mine shall yield,
"We'll all lie dead upon the field".

"Then go your ways," he made reply;
"Either surrender, or you shall die.
"Go back to your own men in the town;
"What can you do when left alone?
Mackintosh is a gallant soldier,
With his musket over his shoulder.
"Every true man point his rapier;
"But, damn you, Foster, you are a traitor!"

Lord Derwentwater to Foster said,
"Thou hast ruin'd the cause, and all betray'd.
"For thou didst vow to stand our friend,
"But hast prov'd traitor in the end.
"Thou brought us from our own country;
"We left our homes, and came with thee;
"But thou art a rogue and a traitor both,
"And hast broke thy honour and thy oath".[9]

9 *The Jacobite Relics of Scotland Being The Songs, Airs and Legends of the Adherents to the House of Stuart*. Collected and Illustrated by James Hogg. Second Series, Edinburgh MDCCCXXI, Vol. 2, Pp. 102-4. An Excellent New Song on the Rebellion, verses 3,4,5 & 6.

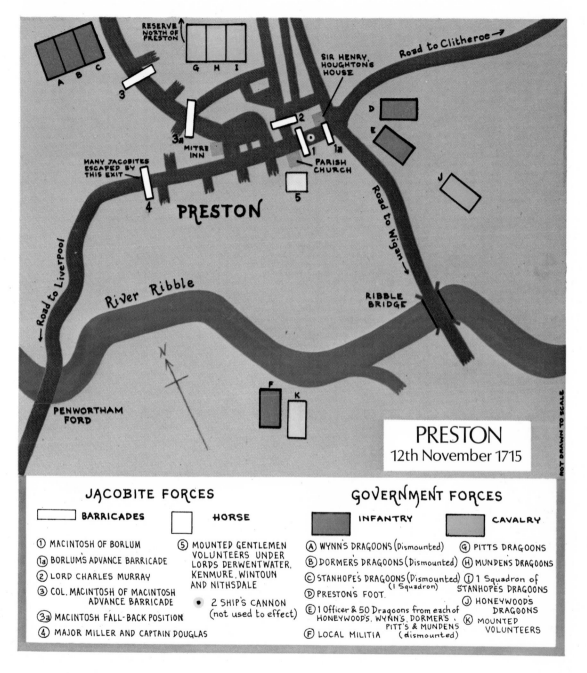

JACOBITE FORCES

☐ **BARRICADES**   ☐ **HORSE**

① MACINTOSH OF BORLUM

①ₐ BORLUM'S ADVANCE BARRICADE

② LORD CHARLES MURRAY

③ COL. MACINTOSH OF MACINTOSH ADVANCE BARRICADE

③ₐ MACINTOSH FALL-BACK POSITION

④ MAJOR MILLER AND CAPTAIN DOUGLAS

⑤ MOUNTED GENTLEMEN VOLUNTEERS UNDER LORDS DERWENTWATER, KENMURE, WINTOUN AND NITHSDALE

⦿ 2 SHIP'S CANNON (not used to effect)

GOVERNMENT FORCES

☐ **INFANTRY**   ☐ **CAVALRY**

Ⓐ WYNN'S DRAGOONS (Dismounted)

Ⓑ DORMER'S DRAGOONS (Dismounted)

Ⓒ STANHOPE'S DRAGOONS (Dismounted) (1 Squadron)

Ⓓ PRESTON'S FOOT.

Ⓔ 1 Officer & 50 Dragoons from each of HONEYWOOD'S, WYNN'S, DORMER'S, PITT'S & MUNDENS (dismounted)

Ⓕ LOCAL MILITIA

Ⓖ PITTS DRAGOONS

Ⓗ MUNDENS DRAGOONS

Ⓘ 1 Squadron of STANHOPES DRAGOONS

Ⓙ HONEYWOOD'S DRAGOONS

Ⓚ MOUNTED VOLUNTEERS

This map illustrates the positions of the rival armies at Preston (see pages 52-56).

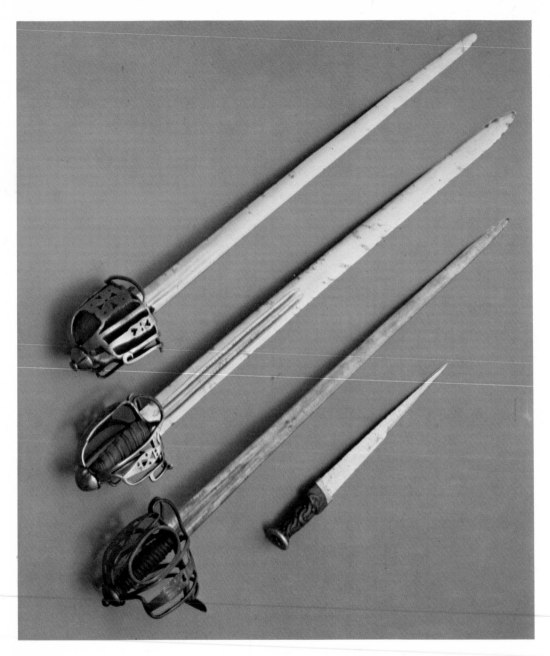

These Highland broadswords show the variations in the basket hilts. Most blades were between 86 and 93 centimetres (34 and 36 inches) long. The dirk was carried in a sheath and held in the left hand in battle.

The basket hilts of three Highland broadswords.
These steel weapons have wooden grips covered
with fish skin and bound with wire. The broadsword
is often wrongly called a claymore, a much earlier and
larger weapon.

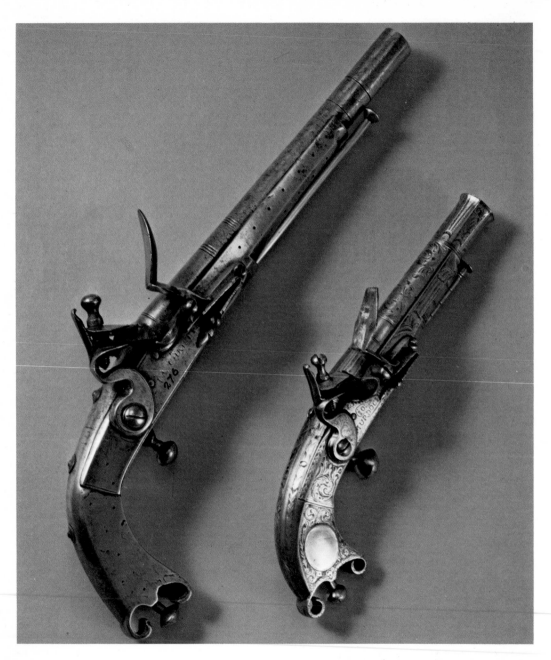

These all-steel Highland pistols were known as
Ram's horn pistols because of the shapes of the
butts. After firing, they were often used as clubs.
They were carried high on the left side from a strap.

This target, or Highland shield, is about 47 cm (18 inches) in diameter and is leather covered. Some were covered by animal skin and they were often decorated with metal studs. The dirk shows comparative sizes.

This rare type of Scottish Highland small pipe contrasts with later pipes made from tartan cloth. The chanter is plain and open with a leading note **G** to **A**. Three drones are pitched to **A, E, A**.

A wax impression of the head of the Earl of Derwentwater made after he was beheaded on February
24, 1716, for his part in the 1715 uprising. He was 27
at the time of his execution.

These Scottish powder flasks date from the first half of the 1700s. They are made from horn and the largest has a leather shot pouch attached to it. Most firearms carried by Highlanders were of inferior quality. Some were so broken that they were unserviceable for anything other than clubs.

This portrait shows James Francis Edward Stuart (1688-1766), who was also known as the Old Pretender or the Chevalier de St George. He was taken to France as an infant and, when his father died in 1701, he was recognized by France as the legitimate king of England. However, all his attempts to win the throne of England were all unsuccessful.

The Arrival of the Pretender

For the Jacobite survivors of the two main engagements of the rebellion, Sheriffmuir and Preston, the residual feeling of bitterness was the same. Both armies were left with the conviction that they had been betrayed by faulty leaders. In Perth, the Earl of Mar was losing his slender grasp on Scottish affairs because of his pusillanimous dealings. A rebel stated, 'the Councils which were followed immediately after the Fight were so foolish and so weak as evidently disgusted us all!'[20] Mar was beginning to find himself a victim of the Highlanders' free spirit. 'Amongst many good Qualities the Highlanders have one unlucky custom not easy to be reform'd', he noted, 'which is, that generally after an Action they return Home'. When nothing happened to rivet their attention in Perth men drifted off daily. Feelings of despair and disgust needed only the catalyst of bad news to harden into revolt. When the news came in of the southern army's defeat at Preston, the celebrations which were to have marked its triumph had to be hastily called off. The defeat at Preston made up three reverses sustained by the Jacobites on November 13, 1715, because, in addition to the two main encounters on that day, government forces had recaptured Inverness. Before long, capitulation was openly discussed in the camp and, by the end of the month, individuals in the army were making overtures to the Duke of Argyll for separate surrender treaties. It was clear that the indecisive action at Sheriffmuir had terminated the activities of the Scottish Jacobites as effectively as the complete surrender at Preston had concluded the campaign in England. Rae predicted of Sheriffmuir, that 'by this Battle the Heart of the Rebellion was broke' and events were to prove him right. Therefore, it came as something of a surprise to the last stalwarts of a broken-down revolt to learn that their tardy Prince was at last on his way. On December 9, Mar wrote to the voyaging Chevalier; 'Wee are all here in the utmost anxiety and pain till we know of your Majesties safe arrival. I have done what was in my power in the situation wee are in to make it safe, and I wish it had been in my power to do more. I hope in God Providence will protect you, and bring you safe to your longing people'.[21] At a time when the rebellion wore its most deathly aspect, the aspirant James III and VIII arrived in Scotland to lead the 'Fifteen.

Without making any announcement to the effect, Mar had in fact mentally abandoned the rebellion long before the Chevalier's arrival. A few days after Sheriffmuir, the Jacobite army was reduced to half its maximum strength. The initiative taken by individual deserters was later endorsed by the Earl of Seaforth when he withdrew with 300 horse and two battalions of foot, ostensibly to relieve Inverness but, in reality, to quit the cause. A few days later, the Marquis of Huntly, whose loyalty had always been in doubt, withdrew with his personal following. In his *Journal*, Mar recorded that 'a month before the Chevalier landed, the Resolution was taken of abandoning Perth as soon as the enemy should march against it'. This, at least, was consistent with the lack-lustre and defeatist course so far followed. Mar had needed the absolute assurance of overwhelming numerical superiority before venturing out of Perth and running the risk of an encounter with Argyll. It was, therefore, unlikely that he would have opted for any course other than retreat at a time when his own army was in decline while that of his adversary was increasing daily. Now that the regular troops were no longer needed to suppress the Jacobites in the Midlands or guard against revolt in the south, they were free to concentrate in Scotland, and Argyll's puny force quickly felt the benefit. For the first time, towards the end of December, Argyll achieved the same superiority over the Jacobites as the rebels had boasted that they had over him prior to Sheriffmuir. The 6,000

20. *A True Account of the Proceedings at Perth; the Debates in the Secret Council there; with the Reasons and Causes of the suddain breaking up of the Rebellion*. Written by a Rebel. London, 1716. Formerly attributed to Sinclair, but now more generally attributed to Defoe Reprinted in *Scottish History from Contemporary Writers. The Chevalier de St. George and the Jacobite Movements of 1701-1720*. Ed. by C. Sanford Terry. London, 1901.

21. Historical Manuscripts Commission. The manuscripts of the Earl of Mar and Kellie preserved at Alloa House.

Dutch auxiliaries had arrived and Mar had already written limply to the Chevalier: 'I see not how wee can oppose them even for this winter when they have got the Dutch troops to England, and will power in more troops from thence upon us every way'. A great deal of blind faith had been invested in the ability of 'the King' to bring a revival of hope to the rebellion but it was not anticipated that this miracle would be achieved by personality alone. The hallmark of the true Jacobite was a reverence for the person of the Stuart claimant that fell little short of idolatry. But, at this desperate juncture, practical considerations had a way of obtruding themselves onto finer feelings. James would be welcomed not merely for himself but for the quantities of arms, ammunition, men and money he was expected to bring with him from France. Thus, the remnant of the army learned with the utmost disappointment that James had landed at Peterhead on December 22, 1715 with nothing more in the way of practical assistance than a handful of friends.

'. . after a Voyage of 7 Days, he (James) arrived the 22d of December, 1715. And being come on Shore with a Retinue of Six Gentlemen only, the Ship immediately returned for France with the News of his safe Arrival; and Lieutenant Cameron was sent Express to Perth, where he arriv'd on the 26th, with the acceptable Tidings to the Earl of Mar, who presently mounted with the Earl Marischal, General Hamilton, and 20 or 30 Persons of Quality on Horseback, and set out from thence, with a Guard of Horse, to go and attend him. The Pretender and his five Companions having lodged one Night, in the Habit of Sea-Officers, at Peterhead, and another at Newburgh, a House of the Earl of Marischal, on the 24th they passed incognito thro' Aberdeen, with two Baggage Horses, and at Night came to Fetteresso, the principal Seat of the Earl of Marischal, where he stay'd till the 27th,

when the Earl of Mar, Marischal and Hamilton, came up to wait on him. Having dress'd and discovered himself, they all kiss'd his Hand, and own'd him as King.[22]

The Pretender had been obliged to scurry about the bye-roads of France incognito, in order to evade arrest and effect an escape from Dunkirk. Neither the Regent Orléans, who was acting for the heir to the French throne, Louis XV, nor the English Ambassador in Paris approved of James's aspirations. Strenuous efforts had been made to thwart his plans. James's melancholy and courtly disposition made him unsuited to the role of private adventurer and it was with a profound sense of relief that he arrived intact in his ancient kingdom. After having risked a good deal in terms of personal safety to accomplish the mission, he was naturally disappointed to discover that the rebellion, which had borne all the marks of success when he set out, was now in something of a ruined state. In direct contrast to the expectations of his supporters, James himself now contributed to the general air of decay surrounding the rising by collapsing almost immediately after his arrival, with an ague.

While James was laid up, the Earl of Mar, who had been elevated by royal decree to a Dukedom, attempted to stifle the curiosity of the mob with the following communication to commend the King to the masses.

Glames, 5 Jan. 1716.
'I met the King at Fetteresso on Tuesday Sen'night . . . . . The King design'd to have gone to Dundee to Day, but there is such a fall of Snow, that he is forced to put it off till to-morrow, it be practicable then; and from thence he designs to go to Scoon. There was no haste in his being there sooner, for nothing can be done this Season, else he had not been so long by the Way. People everywhere, as we have come along, are excessively fond to see him, and express

22. Rae's *History of the Rebellion*, Second Edition. Pp. 351-2.

that Duty they ought, without any Compliments to him; and to do him nothing but Justice, set aside his being a Prince, he is really the finest Gentlemen I ever Knew; He has a very good Presence, and resembles King Charles a great deal. His Presence however is not the best of him: He has fine Parts, and despatches all his Business himself with the greatest Exactness. I never saw any Body write so finely. He is Affable to a great Degree, without losing that Majesty he ought to have, and has the sweetest Temper in the World . . . .[23]

As the recent recipient of a Stuart favour, Mar, no doubt felt himself justified in thinking the Chevalier 'Affable', but his was undoubtedly a minority view. The anonymous author of *A True Account of the Proceedings at Perth,* approached nearer the general impression when he ascribed to the Prince a heavy countenance and dejected spirit.

'. . his Person is tall and thin, seeming to encline to be lean rather than to fill as he grows in Years. His Countenance is pale and perhaps he look'd more pale by Reason he had three Fits of an Ague . . . . . yet he seems to be Sanguine in his Constitution, and has something of a Vivacity in his Eye that perhaps would have been more visible if he had not been under dejected Circumstances and surrounded with Discouragement . . . . . His Speech was Grave, and not very clearly expressing his Thoughts, nor overmuch to the Purpose; but his Words were few; his Behaviour and Temper seem'd always composed; what he was in his Diversions we know nothing of, for here was no room for those Things, it was no Time for Mirth, neither can I say that I ever saw him Smile: . . . . . I must not conceal that when we saw the Person who we called our King, we found ourselves not at all animated by his Presence, and if he was disappointed in us, we were tenfold more so in him . . .'

James had prepared a Declaration before leaving France in which he told his pseudo-subjects of Scotland: 'We are come to take Our Part in all the Dangers and Difficulties to which any of Our Subjects, from the greatest down to the meanest, may be exposed'. He explained that his mission was to relieve the Scots 'from the Hardships they groan under on Account of the late unhappy Union; and to restore the Kingdom to its ancient, free, and independent State'. However, it would take more than goodwill to translate brave words into deeds, and as soon as he was recovered from his illness, James prepared to review the army. Passing through Brechin, Glamis and Dundee, the Chevalier came to Scone, on January 8. Scone was the location of one of the ancient palaces of the kings of Scotland and only two miles from Perth. James decided to make his headquaters there. The day after his arrival at Scone, on January 9, he made a public entry into Perth to review the army.

James, who had seen service in the French army at Malplaquet, knew that the basic tenets of army life were uniformity and discipline. He was therefore rather amazed by the fact that the Jacobite force was composed of so many separate elements. He had grasped the basic principles of clan structure and asked first to see ' those little kings with their armies'. The warlike mien of the Highlanders apparently impressed him greatly, but, on inquiring how many such troops were in arms for him, he was disagreeably surprised to learn of their diminished numbers. Nevertheless, he issued a proclamation naming January 23, 1716, as the date upon which he was to be crowned at Scone.

On the day that James reviewed his dwindling army, George I addressed Parliament. He expressed the hope that 'this open and flagrant Attempt in Favour of Popery' would abolish 'all other Distinctions among us, but of such as are zealous Assertors of the Liberties of their Country, the present Establishment, and the Protestant Religion'. In reply,

23. The entire letter appears in Patten's *History of the Late Rebellion,* London 1717, Pp. 221-2.

both Houses readily promised 'to grant such early and effectual Supplies' as would enable his Majesty 'to put an End to this unnatural Rebellion'. The Duke of Argyll, who had been nothing less than George I's saviour in Scotland, now suffered a quite unmerited loss of reputation in government circles, because his generous nature had prompted him to cast a favourable eye over the applications of individual rebels for terms. It was felt in London that Argyll was too full of the milk of human kindness to press the government's advantage now that he had an army of crushing dimensions at his disposal. General William Cadogan, an officer who was not inhibited by earlier associations with the Highlands, was sent to Stirling ostensibly to assist Argyll, but in fact to supersede him. Under the joint direction of the two commanders, feelers were put out in the third week of January 1716 to investigate the possibilities of launching a successful attack on Perth.

The weather was very cold and Argyll wanted to be sure that his men would be able to endure the two or three nights under canvas which the 35-mile journey in thick snow would demand. The activities of the government's reconnaisance parties left the rebels in Perth in no doubt about the imminence of attack. James's coronation arrangements were put in abeyance and all hands turned to the fortification of the city. It will be remembered that the Earl, (now the Jacobite Duke) of Mar was working on plans of quite a different order. He had no intention of putting up a stout resistance against Argyll, but appreciated the fact that any disclosure of his covert schemes for withdrawal and secession might, at this critical juncture, incite riots of disapproval in the army. Pruned of all its irresolute members, the army consisted predominantly of Highlanders. It now represented the hardcore Jacobite enthusiasts whose only interest was in furthering the cause of Prince James and vindicating the dubious reputation they had brought with them from Sheriffmuir.

There was no mention of capitulation or retreat. On the contrary, 'there was nothing to be seen, but the planting of Guns, marking out Breast-works and Trenches, digging up Stones in the Streets, and laying them with Sand, to prevent the Effects of a Bombardment; and in a word, all possible Preparations were made, as if they had really intended to defend the Place'.[24] James, whose military experience leant some weight to his opinion, was genuinely in favour of venturing a battle in Perth's defence, although in the words of Robert Chambers: 'Before he had been three days at Perth he became completely aware, to use a vernacular phrase, that he was in a scrape'. The fact was, however, that Mar had prevaricated long enough to manipulate Argyll into a position of crowning invincibility. The Jacobite leader had at last managed to shuffle off his embarrassing advantage. At Stirling, an army between 8,000 and 9,000 strong, equipped with more than one train of artillery, was poised to attack the reduced Jacobite force of less than 4,000 combined foot and horse. Of this total force, according to Mar 'for want of Arms and for other Reasons, not above, 2,500 (could) be rely'd upon as good fighting Men'. At last, with some justification, Mar could say privately: 'all this puts us into an absolute Necessity of leaving Perth and retiring Northwards'. But Mar knew that even this sadly truncated Jacobite army would never accept a public announcement to this effect. Therefore, he contributed to the illusion that the offensive would continue, to ensure that when the blow fell, it would be disguised as the bludgeon of cruel necessity.

On January 28, 1716, a message arrived at Perth from Stirling with information that 'Argyll would March the next Day, That all was in readiness, the Carriages provided, and the Horses for the Baggage come in, and that General Cadogan was already advanc'd with the first Line of the Army to Dumblane, 2000 Men being employed to remove the Snow'. To

24. Rae. Op. Cit. P. 364.

halt the royal advance, the Jacobites adopted a scorched earth policy towards the areas of Auchterarder, Muthill, Blackford, Dunning and Crieff where all the homes of the villagers were burned down to deny shelter to the on-coming army. This act of unfeeling brutality was a disastrous stop-gap so far as the Jacobites' public relations were concerned. It introduced a barbarous note into a campaign which had so far been remarkable for its lack of gratuitous violence. Many of the dispossessed villagers turned out into the snow died as a consequence of exposure. This did little to recommend King James's cause to the masses, and gave substance to the myth propagated by Hanoverians that the Highlanders were savages. Nor did it assist in the process of carving out a future course for the army. A permanent 'show' Council now sat in Perth to discuss Jacobite tactics. Many of the members were still unaware that the whole exercise was merely academic, and the chief topic of debate was not whether to stand and fight, but how to do it. After an all-night sitting on January 29-30, a general air of uncertainty began to take hold of proceedings and this doubt quickly percolated down to the men who began to sniff treachery. Military organization and command had never been rigorously enforced in the Jacobite army, but a complete breakdown in discipline now occurred. Riots broke out in the streets of Perth between the pro- and anti-war factions. Mar recorded: 'We carried this so high that some of our Number ruffled the great Men in the open Streets, call'd them Cowards, and told them they betray'd the Ch--------- instead of advising him'. An intimate of Mar's questioned a mutinous Highlander: 'Why, what would you have us do', and received a rapid fire of equally pertinent questions in reply. 'What did you call us to take Arms for? Was it to run away? What did the Ch-------- come hither for? Was it to see his People butcher'd by Hangmen and not strike a Stroke for their Lives? Let us Die like Men and not like Dogs'. The army that barely maintained its unity for the sake of its king was now threatened with schism. The Highlanders, as always, the most fiercely loyal to the House of Stuart, began to hatch their own plots. An Aberdeenshire gentlemen declared 'That the Loyal Clans should take the Ch-------- from them and that if he was willing to Die like a Prince, he should find there were Ten Thousand Gentlemen in Scotland that were not afraid to Die with him'. These were brave words, but it was now much too late to breathe new life into the limp carcass of the rebellion. The ghost of Preston stalked the corridors of Perth and members of Mar's coterie feared they would suffer the same fate as their southern counterparts if they stayed to defend Perth. When the moment was propitious, Mar put all his weight behind a motion for withdrawal In an address to the Council he dramatically unveiled, for the first time, the real issues that were at stake in Perth. The question was not one of battle or retreat, he told them, but of the cause itself and whether it could be prosecuted any further. Mar put his case succinctly. None of the rosy expectations with which the rebellion had set out had been realized. There would be no English rising and no substantial aid from France. The Scots must face the fact that they were now completely alone in the enterprise and facing impossible odds. On January 31, 1716, the Duke of Argyll advanced to within eight miles of Perth. At about ten o'clock on the same day, the Jacobites quietly abandoned it, marching out over the frozen River Tay towards Dundee.

Escapes and Executions

The 'Fifteen, in Scotland, now began to shuffle towards its ignominious end, nudged on by shabby intrigues and the underhand dealings of its leaders. Although members of the War Council in Perth had agreed to Mar's recommendations for the entire abandonment of the project, the ordinary men saw the retreat merely as a postponement of their inevitable collision with Argyll's advancing force. They were encouraged in this belief by the circulation of faked intelligence which suggested that Aberdeen was designated as the venue for the forthcoming encounter. James, painfully aware that Mar was in fact arranging a secret escape for him, was hard pressed to prevent his mask of false optimism from slipping. Indeed, he was sorely tried. The day before the evacuation had been the anniversary of his grandfather's execution, an occasion for sombre reflection which inevitably dwelt upon the inescapable conclusion that the present Stuart heir was more likely to accede to his ancestor's fate than to his throne. With tears in his eyes, James dolefully accosted Mar and delivered the accusation: 'Instead of bringing me to a crown, you have brought me to my Grave'.

On Wednesday February 1, 1716, the Jacobite army arrived in Dundee. After a night's rest, it advanced up the east coast to Montrose, entering the town on February 3. On the same day, the pursuing government force arrived at Dundee. Although the Highlanders were disinclined to employ their strength in running away, nevertheless their effortless achievements on foot put a safe distance between the two armies. In pursuit, Argyll complained that for every three miles the clansmen marched, he could only cover one. At Montrose, the prescient Highlanders began to suspect a plot. The fresh outbreak of suspicion led to more awkward questions. Why had the army's route been directed towards the coast instead of through Angus, as they might have expected? The sighting of two or three French vessels offshore seemed to provide an ominous answer. In an attempt to stifle the rekindled fears of the men, orders were issued for the army to assemble in marching order at 8 o'clock on the night of the 4th to begin its journey to Aberdeen, instead of waiting until the following day. Ostentatious efforts were made to create the impression that James was to be a member of the expedition, while an undercurrent of stealthy intrigue carried forward his secret escape plans.

'At the Hour appointed for their March, the Pretender ordered his Horses to be brought before the Door of the House in which he lodged, and the Guard which usually attended him to mount, as if he designed to go on with the Clans to Aberdeen; but at the same Time he slipped privately out on Foot, accompanied only by one of his Domesticks, went to the Earl of Mar's Lodgings, and from thence, by a By-way to the Water-side, where a Boat waited and carried him and the Earl of Mar on Board a French Ship of about 90 Tuns, called the Maria Teresa of St. Malo. About a quarter of an Hour after, two other Boats carried the Earl of Melford and the Lord Drummond, with Lieutenant General Sheldon, and ten other Gentlemen, on Board the same Ship, and then they hoisted Sail and put to Sea.' (Rae)

Meanwhile the unsuspecting army pushed on up the coast, the foot marching ahead under the command of General Gordon and the horse behind under the Earl Marischal. Both commanders were aware of the true situation. The Earl Marischal had probably rejected an invitation to join the deserters and General Gordon had been entrusted with the unenviable task of breaking the news to the men. It was thus with heavy hearts that they led their duped subordinates towards Aberdeen.

Scarcely one serious interpreter of James's brief part in the rebellion has not concluded in one way or another that he came to Scotland too late and left too soon. His detractors in Hanoverian England eagerly seized upon his dramatic escape and labelled it for propaganda purposes, a 'cowardly flight'. But in fact James did not fit well in the role of absconder and he did not provide his critics with many grounds for calumny. He was far too pious and scrupulous to allow considerations of personal safety to take precedence over his duty, and it was only after every one of his worthy objections to flight had been demolished by Mar that he agreed to leave. Altruism, not cowardice, influenced his decision. He only capitulated when he became convinced that he had become a positive liability to the army and an obstacle to the achievement of favourable surrender terms. He employed his last hours in Scotland in drafting a commission empowering General Gordon as commander-in-chief to negotiate with the enemy for an armistice. He surrendered most of the money in his possession for the future maintenance of the troops. While in Scotland, James had never ceased to promulgate the dogma that he had come with fixed intention of easing the sufferings of his persecuted people. He was, therefore, aware of the fact that he was leaving behind him a damaged, if not grotesquely distorted reputation, if he did nothing to demonstrate his feeling for the victims of the Auchterarder and other burnings. At the eleventh hour, therefore, he made provision in a letter addressed to Argyll for compensation to be paid to the afflicted. Finally, it appears that he left something of a valedictory address to the troops.

Before General Gordon ever reached Aberdeen, the Highlanders' sensitive antennae had picked up muttered rumours of a royal subterfuge. Many of the clansmen, feeling now that there was no dishonour in desertion, took to the Grampians to shift for themselves. Little more than 1,000 men accompanied Gordon into Aberdeen. It was now time for this loyal remnant of a once powerful army to learn that it was destitute. Gordon must have experienced overwhelming distaste when he surveyed his odious lot. At two o'clock on Monday February 6, 1716, a meeting of noblemen, general officers, and chiefs of clans was called in Aberdeen. Before an anxious assembly,

General Gordon read out the contents of the Chevalier's letter.

'General Gordon shewed them a Letter from the Pretender in which he acquainted his Friends, That the Disappointments he had met with, especially from abroad, had obliged him to leave that Country; that he thanked them for their Services, and desired them to advise with General Gordon, and consult their own Security, either by keeping in a Body, or separating, and encouraging them to expect to hear farther from him in a very short Time.' (Rae)

If that had been all, then it would have been a rather terse expression of gratitude for an almost sublime degree of loyalty, but in fact James had expressed himself with more warmth than Rae's précis implies. 'Your safety and welfare was I may say with truth my only view and I resolved not to let your courage and zeal carry you so far as to serve me for your own entire ruin' was the text of his moving message to the men. Although many, in the first heat of their anger, threw down their arms and declared 'They were basely betrayed, they were all undone, they were left without King or General', others, in whom affection for the person of their Prince overrode every other emotion, took comfort from the fact that their hero had fled to safety. However, few could find any complimentary gloss to put on Mar's defection.

There was now no longer any reason to fight, and the government army divided under the command of Argyll and Cadogan was sweeping quickly up-country. The Jacobites left Aberdeen at ten o'clock on Tuesday morning, February 7, and late that same night, Argyll's contingent occupied the town. After following a north-westerly route to Keith and making some desultory enquiries as to the possibility of continuing the campaign, the diminishing Jacobite army turned south and arrived at Ruthven in Badenoch on the 12th, where it made its last halt. On the 14th, General Gordon held a meeting of interested parties at which it was resolved to send a letter to Argyll asking for a general indemnity. The Jacobite army then dismissed itself and broke up into a galaxy of weary individuals seeking the nearest path for home or exile. Later, Adam Cockburn, the Lord Justice Clerk in Edinburgh observed with relief and not a little accuracy: 'Here is this formidable rebellion evanish like smoak'.

The rebellion in Scotland was over. Unlike the insurgents captured at Preston, however, the rebels in the north, who disappeared beyond the Highland Line, vanished also out of the reach of government retribution. Punitive expeditions sent out to scour the Highlands for rebels were largely unsuccessful in winkling them out and it was said that they took fewer than 100 prisóners in all. Nearly all of the prominent noblemen escaped abroad either directly to France, or, after lying low in the Western Isles, they were picked up by rescue ships and taken to the continent. The few Jacobite prisoners secured in Scotland were more of an embarrassment to the government than anything else, and about half were set free without trial and the remainder tried but not sentenced. The Duke of Argyll was accused of deliberately allowing the rebels to slip away from him and he was defamed as a collaborator. Although his nature prompted him to err on the side of leniency, there was not the slightest evidence to substantiate the claim that he had been dilatory in the execution of his duty. Nevertheless, he was disgracefully treated by the government. Stripped of all his high offices, he was allowed to languish in the king's displeasure for some three years after the rebellion officially terminated in 1716. Before long, however, the massive nature of his achievement in Scotland began to reassert itself and Argyll's strong streak of Scottish nationalism was subsequently accepted in London as but a tiny flaw in a giant crystal.

At the time of Argyll's removal and disgrace, however, General Cadogan was left to supervise the mopping up operations in Scotland. He went about his business with gusto and was reputed to have laid waste the area between Stirling and Inverness in his vigorous forays against Jacobite sympathizers. But in fact Cadogan had been given no mandate for revenge and happily there was no human wreckage included in the debris. It quickly became clear, even to his purposeful spirit, that it would be impossible to track down and punish all those implicated in the rising. An amnesty provided that if the Scots were prepared to hand over the weapons in their possession, no questions would be asked. The government had already wreaked vengeance on the Jacobite prisoners taken at Preston and now the climate of opinion was opposed to further unnecessary violence.

Even before James Francis Edward Stuart arrived in Scotland, the Jacobite prisoners taken at Preston had begun to feel the full force of government outrage consequent upon their attempt to bring the rebellion into England. Some of the prisoners were secretly tried in Lancashire and executed. The majority were imprisoned in various jails throughout the county, there to await transportation as slave labour to the American plantations. An élite group of peers, clan chiefs and important second-rankers were taken to London to stand trial. Lords Kenmure, Nithsdale, Nairn, Widdrington, Wintoun, Carwath and Derwentwater were taken to the Tower to await the preparation of articles of impeachment. Forster and Mackintosh were forced into embarassing proximity in Newgate. The trial of the impeached lords was a mere formality and, with the exception of Wintoun, who had received separate treatment because of delays in the preparation of his defence, all pleaded guilty and were condemned to death. In the event, however, Carnwath, Widdrington and Nairn were spared. Lord Wintoun prevaricated long

William Murray, 2nd Baron Nairn, was one of the Jacobite leaders at Preston. He was sentenced to death but the sentence was remitted and he died in 1726.

prisoners found guilty of high treason at this time ran as follows:

'. . you must be drawn to the Place of Execution; when you come there, you must be hanged by the Neck, but not till you are Dead, for you must be cut down alive; then your Bowels must be taken out and burned before your face; then your Head must be severed from your Body and your Body divided into four Quarters, and these must be at the King's disposal.'

It was not the barbarity of this sentence that seemed disgusting to informed eighteenth-century observers interested in the case of the

The Earl of Derwentwater, captured at Preston, delivered a speech, a copy of which is reproduced below, before his execution on February 24, 1716.

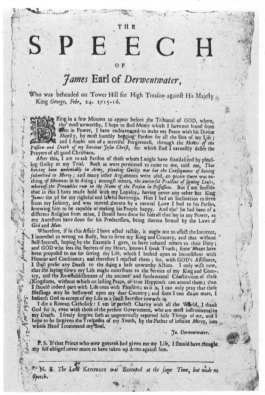

enough to arrange a classic escape by sawing through the bars of his prison window. Nithsdale, too, was rescued by his wife in a daring subterfuge in which the Earl was smuggled out of the Tower in the guise of a lady's maid while his doughty wife mimicked his voice in conversation with her own in the cell. When the lady departed, she acted out a tearful farewell and told the gaolers not to interrupt her husband's prayers. The liberated Earl and his intrepid wife got clean away to France and the success of their joint venture earned them in England the admiration of friends and enemies alike. A similar, and surely more than coincidental, lack of vigilance on the part of gaolers in Newgate also permitted General Forster and Old Borlum of Mackintosh to escape and get clean away. Of those among the peers who were condemned to death, only the Earl of Derwentwater and Viscount Kenmure actually paid the penalty. The sentence passed on two condemned lords, but rather a misplaced and grotesque concern for the observation of the proprieties which prompted them to point out that it was a social solecism for peers to be treated in like manner with common criminals. Thus, after due consideration, Derwentwater and Kenmure had their sentences remitted to the less tasteless exercise of simple beheading. On February 24, 1716, at Tower Hill, after a brief address to the crowd in which he repented of nothing he had done to assist a Stuart restoration, the young Earl of Derwentwater prepared himself for the executioner with impressive, if not invincible composure. Minutes later, he was followed on the scaffold by the sage old Viscount Kenmure, who had so little expected the executions to be actually carried out that he had failed to secure for himself a black suit for the occasion. Once heads had been seen to roll, the Jacobite cause, sanctified by its martyrs could look forward to a return of public sympathy. By the time the rebellion in Scotland petered out, it was widely felt that to persecute a few activists there, would be to arouse a mass of protestors elsewhere. Any fugitive spirit of rebellious fervour still lurking in Scotland was simply left to die away. An Act of Attainder passed against the rebel noblemen and lairds deprived them of their estates, but no strenuous efforts were made to prevent the families of the dispossessed Jacobite exiles from reclaiming an interest in the confiscated property. The loyal tenants of Jacobite landlords stubbornly refused to pay their rents to upstart successors and so the dismemberment of estates was discouraged. Thus, the old order in Scotland was not greatly dislocated by the imposition of savage reprisals. By April 1716, the pacification was virtually complete. Scotland found itself returning to almost the same condition it had been in prior to the 'Fifteen, but it was not left with any of the disfiguring scars that were to commemorate the passage of the 'Forty-five.

The Aftermath

In retrospect, it is not difficult to see the 'Fifteen as a doomed rebellion, a scaled-down, flaccid imitation of the genuine article. As it was originally conceived, it posed a greater threat to Hanoverian security than the 'Forty-five was ever able to be, but as it appeared, in truncated form, it strikes us as a rebellion mined with possibilities that turned out to be damp squibs. Most of the Jacobite army's operations in Scotland were of an undisguisedly paltry nature, while the invasion of England by the southern army resembles nothing so much as an inglorious drift towards the hangman's noose.

The Earl of Mar's culpability for the inconsequential nature of the Jacobites' achievements in the 'Fifteen was, if not total, at least considerable. It was clear from the outset that he did not enjoy the confidence of those prominent figures in the Jacobite movement who were prepared to work and plan in France for a Stuart restoration. Mar was not a confidant of James's, and although he claimed intimate knowledge of the exiled court's affairs, the fact remains that while others such as Bolingbroke and Ormonde, fled to France and tried to organize from there, Mar himself remained in London long enough to offer his services to the new dynasty. It was not until a year after Queen Anne's death that he began to show an active interest in a Stuart restoration, and it was not until his advances had been checked by George I that he contemplated revolt. The sudden eruption of the rebellion in Scotland was the work of a political maverick and any vignette of the Earl of Mar which does not reveal more of the frustrated statesman than the determined general is likely to be distorted.

Mar had neither the authority of his Prince nor the affection of his peers when he began the 'Fifteen rebellion. His reputation among his kinsmen was not of such calibre as to command instant respect. His fulminations against the Union in 1715 did not obscure the fact that he had played a part in its negotiation in 1706. As Secretary of State in the last years of Queen Anne's reign, he had been responsible for the general management of Scottish affairs and he had assumed, in the eyes of his countrymen, the character of an English agent whose motives were suspect. Saddled with a reputation for ambivalence, Mar had thus to contend with a good deal of insolent insubordination from his army and no commander ever had greater difficulty that he in imposing even a modicum of discipline upon his men. This lack of central control, plus the absence of any unifying symbol at the heart of affairs in Scotland, fostered the growth of factions and weakened the fabric of the army. The noblemen and chiefs, who took up the cudgels on James's behalf in 1715, did so for a multiplicity of reasons and a unanimity of purpose did not exist among them. Some were convinced legitimists who believed the right of inheritance of Prince James was more binding than the Protestant Succession. Others were anti-unionists who wanted only to see Scotland restored to independence. A few were sentimentalists who adored the person of the Prince, while some were simple reactionaries opposed to change of any kind and one or two were blustered into the business against their better judgment. The absence of any clear aim might have been offset by the early appearance of James in Scotland, but because he arrived too late to do more than preside over the disintegration of the army, the rebels remained for the most part a mixed-bag of insurgents in search of a goal.

If there was an obvious lack of sparkling leadership from Mar, then the resultant gloom was not enlightened to any startling degree by the personality of Prince James. It is easy to forget that he was only 27 in the year of the rebellion. The morose portrait drawn of him by contemporaries does not fit in easily with the image of a young man. But James, who ought to have been the chief luminary of the Jacobite movement, could point to solid reasons for his melancholic disposition. His life, he maintained had been a series of misfortunes commencing with exile and expropriation in infancy. Even his legitimacy had been questioned. The fiction that he was not his mother's child but smuggled into his mother's bedchamber in a warming pan awoke to taunt him from time to time throughout his life. He was used to bad luck and accepted the collapse of the 'Fifteen as consistent with his lot. James Stuart was never to gain anything like the renown of his dashing son, and with the passage of time and the intensification of his funereal disposition, even the affectionate nicknames by which he was known to his supporters began to indicate the fact that he was not cut out to be a hero. The nickname 'Jamie the Rover' eventually mellowed into the less attractive appellation of 'Old Mr. Melancholy'.

Aside from the personality defects of its leaders, the 'Fifteen as it finally appeared was marred in other, more important ways. When the rebellion began Scotland there was every reason to suppose that a simultaneous rising in England together with 'powerful assistance' from France would render the effort a total success. When both of the support projects collapsed, the mutilated remains of the scheme were patched up in Scotland and Northumberland. Right up until November 1715, the rebels in Scotland were still hoping for a successful conclusion to the Duke of Ormonde's plans to co-ordinate a rebellion in the south-west of England. Once they realized that there was no hope of this and that Scotland was being left to handle the business alone, feelings of disappointment soon hardened into resentment. The rebels in Scotland were always hanging fire, waiting for the arrival of some prospect of support. This gave their army the appearance of irresolution. Nowhere did the antidote of determination combat this debilitating malaise. The secondary issues of the Scottish campaign, such as the bungled attempt on Edinburgh Castle and the mismanaged affair at Dunfermline, displayed in miniature the damaging and occasionally ludicrous results of the Jacobites' dilettante soldiering. A rather more important reflection of this inadequacy was caught in the delays which kept the army inactive in Perth for weeks both before and after Sheriffmuir. Mar's failure to attempt anything more ambitious than a feint towards Stirling at the time of his greatest strength and Argyll's weakest moment represented the worst omission of the campaign, while the splitting up of the army as a result of Mackintosh's expedition was the worst mistake. But at least Mar was not guilty of self-conceit. He was aware of his shortcomings as a soldier and hoped to relinquish his command to the Duke of Berwick. Had be been able to do so, then the outcome of the 'Fifteen might have been entirely different, because James's half-brother was generally held in military circles to be one of the ablest captains of his day. When Berwick failed to appear, however, Mar was left in the position of a man who had bitten off more than he could chew. He had the tools, but was uncertain how to begin the job. The lack of direction offered to the border force was inexcusable, but because Mar was himself mesmerized by the illusion that there were eager thousands waiting to support the cause in Lancashire, it is unlikely that he would have advised against the southward trek. Mar was not a culpable fool. He had shouldered the responsibilities of high office and his ability as a diplomat was never in question. It was just unfortunate for his reputation that the fractured grand design of the project put obstacles in the way of his versatility while shortcomings in the design highlighted his inadequacies. It was not Mar's fault that he was obliged to juggle with uncertainties, but he is remembered as the leader of a rebellion that never really took off. Contrary to all our normal expectations of revolution, the 'Fifteen was ponderous. In-

stead of being dynamic, its mood was apprehensive and its fervour was smothered by indecision and inactivity.

After the collapse of the 'Fifteen, James found on returning to France that he was persona non grata. His presence in that country was no longer tolerable to the Regent Orléans who had reversed the policy of his uncle, the late Louis XIV. The existence of a Jacobite court in France had never been acceptable to the English and, pursuant to the Treaty of Utrecht which ended the Marlborough Wars,

George Keith, 10th Earl Marischal (1694-1778), was a leader of the 1715 Jacobite Rebellion. He also led a Spanish expedition to Scotland in 1719.

James had been forced to move to Bar-le-Duc in Lorraine. Now even this refuge was denied him and he and his swelling retinue of exiled supporters were moved on again, eventually to settle in Rome as guests of the Pope. This close association with Roman Catholicism compounded with James's growing piety to produce a potent mixture for dousing what sympathetic feeling remained in Britain for the expropriated prince.

From this time forward, the Jacobite cause was rated in terms of its disruptive potential by various interested parties in the general mêlée of European politics. In 1716, Charles XII of Sweden showed a brief interest in it when the sale of the formerly Swedish duchies of Bremen and Verden to George I's native Hanover by Denmark moved him to contemplate an invasion of Scotland with 12,000 Swedish troops. Nothing came of the plan. In 1719, it was the turn of Philip V of Spain to raise the Jacobites' hopes to unrealistic levels. For complex reasons surrounding the dynastic struggles over the French throne and in reprisal for the sinking of a Spanish fleet by Admiral Byng off Cape Passaro, Philip V decided to sponsor a Jacobite invasion of Britain. A two-pronged attack was projected in Spain; a large expedition was to be sent to England and a smaller diversionary force to Scotland. In circumstances echoing the failures of the 'Fifteen, the project against England collapsed completely when the main fleet was destroyed at sea. The Earl Marischal, brought out of exile to command the smaller fleet, arrived at his Scottish destination. An army of Spanish mercenaries, Jacobite exiles and Highlanders under the command of the Marquis of Tullibardine met a government force under Major-General Wightman on June 10, 1719, at Glenshiel near Lock Alsh on the west coast. The Jacobites were beaten in the field and the Highlanders who had turned out to support the attempt, once again melted away beyond the Highland Line and beyond the pale of government interference. James,

William Murray, Marquis of Tullibardine, was prominent in the 1715 Rebellion, commanded the Jacobites at Glenshiel in 1719, and accompanied Prince Charles to Scotland in 1745. He died in the Tower in 1746.

who had endured many discomforts to get to Madrid, was ultimately to learn of the expedition's failure and, thus, his personal run of bad luck continued unbroken. This was the last time he stirred himself personally to take an active part in efforts to regain the lost throne of his fathers. On September 1, 1719, he married Clementina Sobieska, descendant of the Sobieski kings of Poland, and the following year she bore him the first of their two sons, Charles Edward Louis John Sylvester Maria Casimir, destined to become known simply as Bonnie Prince Charlie and the guardian of his father's hopes in the field once more in 1745.

3 The 'Forty-Five

From Rome to Britain

The lesson of the 'Fifteen was clear to Jacobites everywhere and especially to the Old Pretender, James Francis Edward Stuart himself — without external assistance, either in the way of foreign aid or national co-operation in Britain, he could not hope to effect a restoration. The aspirations which motivated the rebellion survived the dissolution of the Jacobite army the more easily because the Jacobites remained unbeaten in the field. Their project had not been crushed. It had been merely abandoned until the arrival of a more propitious time. In 1727, George I died in his coach on the way to his native Hanover and his son succeeded him as George II at the age of 44. A long period of peace supervised by Sir Robert Walpole minimized the domestic and foreign grievances upon which the Jacobites relied to promote their cause. In 1739, however, the tide began to change in their favour. England was dragged unwillingly into a war with Spain over the issue of slave shipments to Spanish South America. The Family Compact that existed between the Bourbons of Spain and France meant that war with one country automatically involved hostility towards the other. In 1740, the scene was further complicated by the eruption of the War of the Austrian Succession in which England and Austria ranged themselves on one side of the issue and prepared to face France and Prussia on the other. Somewhat predictably, French interest in the disruptive potential of the exiled Stuarts began to revive.

From 1739 onwards, the interest of emissaries from Scotland and France to Rome, centred on the possibility of launching another rebellion. This time, neither the Scots nor the French were prepared to risk all on chance. The Scots wanted details of any projected invasion and the French wanted the names of those who were prepared to fight. Vague assurances of a spontaneous rising in England were discounted in favour of a systematic collection of the names of likely adherents. A cutting edge was given to the French interest when, in June 1743, a British, Austrian and Hanoverian army inflicted defeat on the French at Dettingen. Towards the end of the same year, an invasion of Britain in the name of the Old Pretender was planned to take place from France. James, now in his mid-fifties, felt that his fighting days were over, but was prepared to delegate his authority to his son, Prince Charles Edward, his 'Carluccio' as he called him, although he was not over-anxious to propel him towards an uncertain destiny. The young Prince, however, had a superabundance of energy, a keen sense of injustice and a conviction that the moment was ripe for action. He welcomed a chance to act. In December 1743, Louis XV invited Charles to France to discuss arrangements for an expedition. With the utmost secrecy, plans were laid for Charles to leave Rome on January 9, with authority as regent of Scotland. The parting between father and son was a sadder affair than either realized, because Charles would never again see his father alive.

It was realized that news of Charles's departure for France would inevitably be interpreted by English commentators as a threat and, therefore, it was imperative that he should gain a head start on his critics by leaving Rome abruptly and travelling without ceremony, in disguise. Not even Charles's brother, Henry, was a party to the plot and the flight was arranged for a day on which the two brothers were engaged to attend a shooting party at Cisterna. Purporting to set off early for the shoot on the morning of the 9th, Charles left the royal residence in Rome, the Palazzo Muti, and so began a journey as fraught with danger and intrigue as that undertaken by his father from France almost 30 years earlier. Travelling through Tuscany to Genoa, then on to Savona, he embarked for Antibes and eventually arrived safely in Paris a month later, on February 10. By this time,

his movements, taken in conjunction with an assemblage of ships at Dunkirk, Calais and Boulogne, were causing considerable unease in London. The French ministry, under the Cardinal de Tencin, was given a strong reminder that the Pretender was a political exile banished from the territories of France.

When he arrived in Paris, Charles looked for the courtesy of a royal welcome, but it seems that he was treated with less respect than the expectations of his birth entitled him to receive. A measure of doubt still exists as to whether in fact he was ever granted an audience with the King of France, but whatever the truth of the matter, he endeavoured to put the best possible interpretation on Jacobite affairs as they stood in France. His principle concern was not for himself but for the success of the expedition, and what he saw was encouraging. Troops to the number of 15,000 were being assembled in Picardy in preparation for a two-pronged attack on Great Britain. One of France's most competent generals, the Comte de Saxe, had been appointed to lead the main invasion on England. He, along with Charles, was to make a landing in Kent with 12,000 men, while the remaining 3,000 were to go to Scotland under the leadership of the Earl Marischal. A swift and deadly attack on the seat of government was seen as a more effective tactic than a slow penetration from the north. It was not in Scotland, but in London that the Stuart fortunes would be decided. A simultaneous rising in Scotland would be a powerful adjunct to the main assault, but George II was not likely to be dislodged by proxy. The 'Fifteen had revealed how the absence of an English rebellion had disabled the struggle.

As activity on the French coast intensified, appropriate defensive measures were being taken in England. Sir John Norris was ordered to take command of the squadron at Spithead, several regiments were marched to the south coast, the Kentish Militia were called out and British troops were withdrawn from Flanders to protect their own shores. The commander of the French fleet was Admiral Roquefeuille and he had already put to sea with the 20 ships that were to act as escort to the transports carrying men to Britain, before Charles actually arrived in Dunkirk. While Roquefeuille patrolled the Channel looking for opposition, the men were embarking and preparing to sail. Quite unexpectedly, the French squadron encountered Norris's fleet and Roquefeuille, fearing the superiority of the opposition, decided to return to France as quickly as possible. He was assisted in this design by an unusually strong wind which, while it rescued him, had a disastrous effect upon the transports lying in the French ports. Gale force winds all but destroyed the entire fleet. Some of the ships went down along with the recently embarked soldiers. Others were damaged beyond repair. Charles and Marshal Saxe, on board one of the vessels which had actually put out from Dunkirk, were lucky to escape with their lives. This trick of the elements had vast repercussions for Jacobite aspirations. The accidental delay occasioned by the storm provided time in which the English could so effectively guard their shores that the enterprise could not be pursued with any hope of success. France and England had so far been enemies only at second hand, as allies of the two main contenders in the Austrian War, but the outright aggression of the proposed French invasion provoked a direct declaration of war from the English. The project had failed so far as the French were concerned and personnel nominated to serve in the expedition were withdrawn for more pressing business elsewhere. From now on material aid would be limited and unofficial.

Meanwhile, Charles found himself in an embarrassing position. He was a leader without a cause. When he should have been descending on England he was in fact kicking his heels in the French coastal town of Gravelines, cursing his bad luck. Later, he moved to Paris, but his proximity to the royal presence did little to revive French interest in the invasion project. In the spring of 1745, the English sustained a defeat at Fontenoy and Charles could see that the moment of England's greatest vulnerability was approaching. The King was out of the country, in Hanover, the army in Flanders was in disarray, and few soldiers were left at home. He decided that the tide of his affairs was running high and he would not be baulked of his mission a second time. The previous year, he had been warned by the Jacobite negotiator, John Murray of Broughton, that unless he came to Scotland with a powerful army and adequate armaments, he could not expect the Highlanders, loyal as they were, to rally to him. He chose to ignore the warning and declared that if he brought only a single footman with him, he was determined to come to Scotland. He was tired of pseudonyms and disguise. He wanted to proclaim his true identity. He had left Rome in a death or glory mood and could not think of returning empty-handed.

The French had largely abandoned Charles to his fate and would neither help nor hinder any project he decided to undertake alone. With the assistance of Antoine Walsh, a Jacobite sympathizer and shipowner, two vessels were procured to furnish a private expedition. Some 1,500 muskets, 1,800 broadswords, 20 field pieces and quantities of powder and ball were accumulated and a sum of 4,000 louis d'or raised. Nantes was chosen as the rendezvous for those who were to take part in the venture. Along with the Prince on board the frigate, the *Du Teillay*, was the Marquis of Tullibardine, veteran of the 'Fifteen and the 1719 attempt, a man now almost 60 and practically disabled by gout. The only English member of the party was Francis Strickland, of whom little is heard hereafter. The four Irishmen included Sir Thomas Sheridan, Charles's old tutor and Colonel John William O'Sullivan, who had been in the French service, and who was to become one of Charles's closest advisers and spiritual mentors in the succeeding campaign. The seventh prominent member of the entourage was Aeneas Macdonald, a Parisian banker and relative of the Macdonalds of Kinlochmoidart, destined to be among the first to parley with the Prince.

The *Du Teillay,* with its passengers on board, waited off Belle-Île for the escort ship, the 68-gunner, *Elizabeth,* which was to carry some of the equipment as well as 700 men, and accompany the smaller vessel to its destination. Before commencing the voyage, Charles dispatched a letter to his father.

Sir,

I believe Your Majesty little expected a courier at this time and much less from me; to tell you a thing that will be a great surprise to you. I have been above six months ago, invited by our friends to go to Scotland, and to carry what money and arms I could conveniently get; this being, they are fully persuaded, the only way of restoring you to the Crown, and them to their liberties. . . . . . Your Majesty cannot disapprove a son's following the example of his father. You yourself did the like in the year '15; but the circumstances now are indeed very different, by being much more encouraging, there being a certainty of succeeding with the least help; the particulars of which would be too long to explain, and even impossible to convince you of by writing, which has been the reason that I have presumed to take upon me the managing of all this, without even letting you suspect there was any such thing a brewing . . . and had I failed to convince you I was then afraid you might have thought what I had a mind to do to be rash; and so have absolutely forbid my proceedings . . . I write this from Navarre, but it won't be sent off till I am on shipboard. . .

Your Majesty's dutiful son,
Charles P.

The letter is deliberately confusing, not to say misleading. Charles was clearly trying to divert his father's gaze from the massive gaps in the plan towards his own vision of its success. In any event, he was careful to advance the project beyond recall before making its existence known to James. Once the escort ship arrived at Belle-Île, there was no further need for delay and the tiny expedition set off with the intention of sailing around Ireland and landing on the west coast of Scotland.

The two vessels had only been at sea for one day when disaster struck again. They were sighted by a British man-of-war, the *H.M.S. Lion.* The *Elizabeth* and the *Lion* engaged in battle, and the French ship described by O'Sullivan as a 'heavy log' was the loser. The vessel was so damaged in the encounter that it was quite unfit to continue on its proposed journey and had to return to Brest. The *Du Teillay,* which had remained beyond the range of the *Lion's* 64 guns, was unharmed, but the expedition had lost more than half its force with the elimination of the *Elizabeth* and her cargo of men and equipment. The enterprise, which had worn the aspect of daring at its outset, now took on the complexion of insanity when the Jacobite Prince absolutely refused to allow the loss of the *Elizabeth* to alter his plans. He still had money, and an inflexible will to appear in Scotland. It was decided that he and his few companions would fly in the face of every adversity to accomplish their mission.

The lone frigate continued on its journey north until it came to Barra in the Outer Hebrides, where a long boat was put out to find a pilot to guide it through the treacherous inland waters. Barra's piper conducted the adventurers safely to a harbour on the tiny island of Eriskay. For two days, the *Du Teillay* had sailed before strong winds and high seas, and on July 23, 1745, when Charles Edward Stuart landed in his father's ancient kingdom, he might have been excused for thinking that he had already weathered the worst of the storms that misfortune could bestow.

Raising the Standard

Charles had been warned that his welcome would be far from hearty should he decide to risk all on a personal venture, and nothing could have appeared to be a more flagrant disregard of the feeling of the Highlanders than the arrival on the shores of Eriskay of the puny eight-man expeditionary force. The morning after his arrival, Charles was to discover that the Highlanders were not so fanatical in their support of the Stuarts as to allow their consideration of men and arms to be swamped by his belief in the abstract virtues of zeal and optimism. Alexander Macdonald of Boisdale came to Charles from the neighbouring island of South Uist and he had a message from Alexander Macdonald of Sleat and the chief of the MacLeods. It was simply this, that if the Prince came without troops he could expect nothing of them, 'not a sou wou'd join with him and their advise was that he shou'd go back and wait for a more favourable occassion'. The news was all the more chastening because MacLeod was one of those pledged to support the cause. On being urged to comply with this advice and return home, Charles replied 'I am come home, sir, and I will entertain no notion at all of returning to that place from whence I came; for that I am persuaded my faithful Highlanders will stand by me'. Of the rest of his party, only Walsh, the captain and owner of the *Du Teillay,* and O'Sullivan supported the Prince's view.

Back on board the *Du Teillay,* the outlook was bleak for Charles. Outside the harbour, a man-of-war was only prevented by contrary winds from drawing near. Inland, there was small hope of support. He would almost certainly be caught if he tried to escape and discouraged if he attempted to proceed. Misfortune had by no means done with him after all. At last, feeling that there was very little left to lose, it was decided to go on. The *Du Teillay* slipped out of harbour at nightfall and passing the islands of Coll, Rhum and Eigg

drew near the Isle of Skye by daybreak. Shortly after mid-day on July 25, she reached Loch-nan-Uamh, in Inverness-shire, between Arisaig and Moidart. Once here, in the Macdonald country of Clanranald, Aeneas Macdonald of the Prince's party was sent off in a boat to Moidart with instructions to return with his eldest brother, Donald Macdonald of Kinlochmoidart, to re-open negotiations once again on the possibility of securing support. When the party of Macdonalds returned, the message delivered to the Prince was the same as that received from Boisdale — to take arms without foreign support could only spell ruin for all concerned. In the *Lockhart Papers,* an account by a 'Highland officer', who wished to remain anonymous, tells of events on board the *Du Teillay.* He recorded that while Charles conversed with the chiefs in an effort to gain their confidence, the rest of the Highlanders who had come on board for one reason or another were entertained in a tent or awning erected on the deck. After the dissolution of the Prince's conference, the chronicler said: 'there entered the tent a pale youth of a most agreeable aspect, in a plain blue coat, with a plain shirt, not very clean and a cambric stock, fixed with a plain silver buckle, a fair round wig out of the buckle, a plain hat with a canvas string, having one end tied to one of his coat buttons, he had black silk stockings, and brass buckles in his shoes'. This youth of 'plain' attire was, of course, Prince Charles himself and 'at his first appearance' the recorder noted that, instinctively, 'I found my heart swell to my very throat'. In fact, Charles now had little left to recommend his cause but the emotional appeal of his presence, and legend has it that it was just this factor which saved the entire project from miscarriage. As he talked with his visitors, Charles is said to have paced the deck of the *Du Teillay.* A young member of the Macdonald family standing guard on the deck and unaware of Charles's real identity soon awoke to the truth when he overheard the heated exchange. His agitation became intense when he realized the extremity of the young Prince's situation. In desperation, Charles at last turned to him, crying 'Will you, at least, assist me?'. 'I will, I will', came the impassioned reply, 'though no other man in the Highlands should draw a sword for you, I am ready to die for you'. According to the conclusion of this apocryphal story, the enthusiasm of the youth infected the other members of his sceptical family, who then relented and offered their service to the Prince in a more sedate manner. It scarcely accords with probability that the family fortunes of the Macdonalds should hang upon the whim of a boy. Nevertheless, a committment of some sort was made by the Macdonalds and they could claim to be the the first to rally to the Prince's call. This slender assurance of support was sufficient to instigate a landing on the mainland, at Moidart, and the Prince's companions thus became known to history as 'the Seven Men of Moidart'. The *Du Teillay* was unloaded and she was told to return to France, leaving the most precious item of her cargo to make his way as best he could.

Among others petitioned for support at this time and who were to become influential in the rebellion, were John Murray of Broughton, James Drummond, titular Duke of Perth, and Donald Cameron of Lochiel. Of these, the last was to become the most important convert for the cause, because the Highland chiefs predisposed to Jacobitism had agreed among themselves that if Lochiel refused to participate in a rebellion, then none of them would co-operate. The account of the rising written by John Home, a 23-year-old volunteer on the government side, gives ample evidence to suggest that Lochiel was as reluctant as the rest to join. In discussion with Charles, Lochiel rehearsed the argument that, because Charles had failed to bring the stipulated aid, no obligation rested with the chiefs to support him. By way of reply, Charles pointed out 'that a more favourable opportunity than the present would never come;

Charles Edward Stuart, known as the Young Pretender, was only 24 when he arrived in Scotland to lead the 1745 Jacobite Rebellion.

that almost all the British troops were abroad, and kept at bay by Marshal Saxe, with a superior army; that in Scotland there were only a few new raised regiments, that had never seen service, and could not stand before the Highlanders; that the very first advantage gained over the troops would encourage his father's friends at home to declare themselves; that his friends abroad would not fail to give their assistance; that he only wanted the Highlanders to begin the war'. Of these considerations, no doubt the one relating to the assistance of friends from France proved the most persuasive. Lochiel relented, and with his capitulation the obedience of other clans was guaranteed. Charles's resolve gained force from the success. 'In a few days', he is reputed to have said, 'with the few friends that I have, I will erect the royal standard, and proclaim to the people of Britain, that Charles Stuart is come over to claim the crown of his ancestors, to win it, or to perish in the attempt'. A rendezvous of Camerons, Macdonalds and Stewarts of Ardshiel was fixed for August 19 at Glenfinnan, at the head of Loch Shiel where the standard would be raised.

Before the official commencement of hostilities, however, an independent action by the Camerons and the Macdonalds of Keppoch against a detachment of royal troops heralded the start of the war. The governor of Fort Augustus had sent for two additional companies of the first Royal Scots regiment of foot, to reinforce the garrison at Fort William. The two garrisons were part of the 'Chain' of three government strongholds (the third being Fort George), strung out along the Great Glen intersecting the Highlands. The Chain was designed to intimidate the Highlanders. The reinforcements were intercepted by the Highlanders and eventually captured with the loss of one or two men on the government side, but no casualties amongst the Jacobites. This small success at the outset of the rebellion had a profound effect upon morale and lent substance to an enterprise which had so far borne all the marks of fantasy. Two days after this skirmish, Charles was joined by Murray of Broughton, who was appointed his secretary. On August 18, Charles left Kinlochmoidart and proceeded towards Glenfinnan, where he arrived shortly after mid-day on the 19th. No one else was at the rendezvous and for two hours the horizon was anxiously scanned for signs of the promised support. Eventually, the Camerons could be seen advancing in two lines, three men deep. Between them were the prisoners of the first skirmish, dragging their feet. There are thought to have been between 700 and 800 insurgents, although many were without arms. Nevertheless, after the strain of his lonely vigil, Charles was only too relieved to welcome anyone. The infirm Marquis of Tullibardine unfurled the standard which was made of white, blue and red silk and, when flown, was almost twice the size of an ordinary pair of colours, according to Home. Supported by a man on each side, he held the staff while the manifesto and commission of regency were read out to the assembled men. After a brief and 'very Pathetick' speech, according to Murray of Broughton, Charles retired to his quarters. About an hour after the first arrivals, Madonald of Keppoch turned up with 300 men and a few renegade Macleods. Since the original expulsion of James II, 56 years had elapsed and the last of the Stuart sovereigns, Queen Anne had been dead for 30 years, but once again the Stuart flag was flying in the ancient kingdom.

At the beginning of the rebellion Charles was acutely conscious of the need to promote his image as that of a Scottish prince, an identity he was only too ready to abandon once he came within sight of England. Nevertheless, for the moment, he took pains to familiarize himself with all things Scottish and took to wearing the Highland costume. He began to pick up a little Gaelic and discovered that his own name in that tongue was 'Tearlach', which sounded to English speakers like Charlie, because the initial consonant was pronounced 'tch'. Thus, he became Charlie, the Bonnie Prince. He was not entirely ignorant of the practices of war, having earned his title 'the Young Chevalier' as a consequence of his attendance at the siege of Gaeta nine years earlier when he was 15. Charles had been allowed to visit this last Austrian stronghold in the Neapolitan war between Austria and Spain. He had apparently shown a keen interest in the proceedings which had earned him the compliments of officers and men alike and the title of Chevalier of which he was proud. News that the Young Chevalier had defied the elements and bad fortune to make an appearance in Scotland soon brought George II back to England. A proclamation was issued putting a price on the Young Pretender's head — 'And to the intent that all due en-

George II succeeded his father in 1727.

had been forgotten in a mood of national outrage. George II had received firm avowals of loyalty from both Houses and all sections of the community. To expect, as Charles did, that all this should be reversed after so short an interval was madness and a misconstruction of the English political mood. In the Highlands, however, there was more reason than ever to look for a way out of the hated union with England. Following the 'Fifteen and the effort in 1719, disarmament acts, although only partially effective, had attempted to reduce the fighting power of the clans. Other measures struck at the system itself and aimed at limiting the autocratic powers of the chiefs and chieftains. Once again, a Stuart was thrown into heavy dependence upon a Highland minority who fought with reactionary zeal to preserve the privilege of an ancient and threatened way of life.

Cope's Near Miss

From an estimated population of 30,000 clansmen, Charles Edward Stuart was never able to draw more than a tiny fraction to his standard and, of these, most were ill-equipped for military confrontation. The disarmament acts which followed the 'Fifteen were only partially effective, relying more on the willing surrender of weapons than enforced confiscation. Not unnaturally, those clans which remained staunchly loyal to the Stuarts found a way around the legislation by surrendering only obsolete equipment and keeping the best of their weapons out of sight until such time as they might be needed again. That time had now arrived, and it was symptomatic of the David and Goliath nature of the confrontation that some of the Highlanders prepared to face the efficiency of a regular army with weapons the condition of which, after 30 years concealment in the earth, was less than pristine.

couragement be given to so important a service we do hereby further, in his Majesty's name, promise a reward of thirty thousand pounds to such person or persons who shall so seize and secure the said son of the said Pretender'. Charles replied by offering a reward of £30,000 to the captor of the usurping Elector of Hanover.

Charles imagined that he had his finger on the political pulse of England. He hoped that the fatal association of his name with the abhorrent French invasion had dimmed in the minds of the English. The Austrian War had been unpopular in the country, the general view being that England was suffering as a result of the Hanoverian connection. But under threat of French invasion, all differences

But, like his father before him, Charles did not really believe that the heavy burden of rebellion would fall upon the Highlanders' shoulders alone. From the tone of his last letter to Louis XV, before quitting France, it is clear that he thought it only required some spirited independent action from himself to elicit the much needed practical help from the French king. 'After having tried in vain all methods of reaching your Majesty in the hope of obtaining from your generosity the help necessary to enable me to play a role worthy of my birth, I have resolved to make myself known by my actions and to undertake alone a project to which even a small amount of help would guarantee success. I am bold enough to flatter myself that your Majesty will not deny it me.' In fact, the Earl Marischal had been left in France to ginger up proceedings. But while French help was still a long way off, there was ample evidence that the British government was planning to nip the rebellion in the bud without delay.

On August 3, 1745, MacLeod of MacLeod wrote to the Lord President of the Court of Session, Duncan Forbes of Culloden:

My Dearest Lord,

To my no small surprise, it is certain that the Pretended Prince of Wales is come on the Coast of South Uist and Barra, and has since been hovering on parts of the Coast of the Main Land that lies betwixt the point of Airdnamurchan and Glenelg . . . . . . His view I need not tell you was to raise all the Highlands to assist him etc. Sir Alex Macdonald and I not only gave no sort of Countenance to these people, but we used all the interest we had with our Neighbours to follow the same prudent method; and I am persuaded we have done it with that success, that not one man of any consequence benorth the Grampians will give any sort of assistance to this mad rebellious attempt . . . . . .

I ever am, most faithfully, Yours
NORMAN MAC LEOD.[1]

Dunvegan
3d Augt. 1745.

The part played by the Lord President in discouraging the Highlanders from joining the Prince turned out to be crucial to the outcome of the rebellion. In the opinion of at least one English Jacobite, the Lord President was nothing less than 'the Oracle of his Country' and an implacable enemy of Jacobitism. He succeeded in diverting some of those sworn to support the Prince's interest away from their original intention. It was also commonly held that, had he been as firm a friend as he was implacable an enemy, the Jacobites should have seen, instead of the 4,000 men who marched into England, 'an army of Eighteen or Twenty thousand men'.[2] By August 8, the news was known in Edinburgh and all military personnel had been put on alert. In London, information concerning the Prince's departure from France had been available since July, but because the post operated only on alternate days from Edinburgh to London, and this was often delayed because of bad weather, detailed intelligence of his subsequent movements was difficult to come by. But in neither capital, at this stage, was there undue panic. The possibility that the Prince's venture might assume the proportions of a serious threat was not seriously contemplated. In Edinburgh, it was held that 'any Commotion these Madmen occasion must be very soon quash'd', and rumour had it that the Prince's army consisted 'mostly of Boys and Old Men' and of these most were deemed the 'Riff-Raff of the Highlands'.[3]

In fact the military situation in Scotland scarcely provided the government with a reason for confidence. On the day that the standard was raised at Glenfinnan, Sir John Cope, Commander-in-Chief of the regular forces in Scotland, was preparing to leave Edinburgh for Stirling, where he was to take command of the army. He had received orders to go in pursuit of the rebels and crush them. According to the *Memoirs* of the Chevalier de Johnstone, who was aide-de-camp to Prince Charles's most prominent General, Lord

1. *Culloden Papers*, London 1815 Pp. 203-4.

2. According to John Daniel. *Origins of The Forty-Five and Other Papers Relating to that Rising*, ed. by Walter Biggar Blaikie. Scottish History Society. Second Series, Vol. II, Edinburgh 1916. From the section, 'A True Account of Mr. John Daniel's

Progress with Prince Charles'. Reprinted from a manuscript preserved at Drummond Castle. Pp. 206-7.

3. *The Rebellion of 1745. An Old Story Re-Told from the "Newcastle Courant"*. Printed for Private Circulation, 1881.

George Murray, and assistant aide to the Prince himself, Cope's army at Stirling consisted of three infantry regiments, Lee's Lascelles' and Murray's, five companies of a Highland regiment, two companies of Guise's regiment and Gardiner's and Hamilton's regiments of dragoons. Apart from Guise's, both horse and foot represented the youngest regiments in the British Army.[4] Meanwhile, the Lord President was zealously distributing commissions for raising several Independent Companies in the North which were to be put under the command of the Right Honourable the Earl of Loudon. Apart from these, and the men under Cope's command, there were in Scotland nine additional companies that had been recently raised there for the national regiments serving abroad. Of these, two had already fallen into rebel hands prior to the official opening of the rebellion, some of the others had already been draughted and most were so weak that they did not exceed 25 men a company. This was the full extent of the Hanoverian force in Scotland in August 1745. The regular troops were for the most part on the continent and these could not be recalled with instant effect. Indeed, everything seemed to point to the accuracy of Charles's instinct for timing. It was, therefore, with some confidence that the Prince dismissed one of the captured English officers with the message: 'You may go to your General; say what you have seen; and add that I am coming to give him battle'.

Cope arrived at Stirling on August 19 and preparations were made to begin the pursuit of the rebels the following day. It was planned that the army should take the Highland road via Crieff and Tay Bridge to Fort Augustus, which Cope hoped to make the centre of his operations. With approximately 1,500 men, he set out on the 20th. One of the regiments of dragoons was left at Leith and the other remained at Stirling, because the countryside to be traversed was unfit for cavalry. Four field pieces (one and a half pounders) were taken, however, and as many *cohorns* (mortars), although it was believed that Cope's army boasted only one trained artilleryman. In addition to this encumbrance, 1,000 stand of arms was taken on the journey to equip the volunteer Highlanders who were reputed to be only awaiting the arrival of arms to bring them out on the government side. Finally, the expedition was hampered with numerous carts and baggage horses carrying the army's provisions. Some 21 days' bread was carried, a necessary providence when venturing into a land that yielded far from plenty.

By the time the government army reached Crieff, Cope realized that any expectation he might have of being joined by Highland volunteers was likely to be disappointed. He had seen no evidence at all of any willingness on the part of the well-disposed clans to arm on the government's behalf and, therefore, he sent most of his surplus arms, some 700 stand, back to Stirling. Indeed, as one of his officers recorded in his journal, this aspect of the affair was very disturbing. 'A march of regular troops, when the country was in its present situation, by themselves, was thought hazardous; but we were told, that we were to be joined at Crieff by a body of the well-affected Highlanders; . . . . But it so happened that not a man of them joined us, neither there nor anywhere else, till we came to Inverness.[5] At Tay Bridge, however, Cope's army was joined by 40 men of Lord Loudon's recently raised regiment.

The opposing armies were now proceeding cautiously towards one another. On the day following Cope's departure from Stirling, the Jacobite army left Glenfinnan and headed in the direction of the mountain of Corryarrak which lay in the path of Cope's progress to Fort Augustus. It was imperative that the Jacobites reach the security of the mountain before the government troops, and therefore, all extraneous equipment had to be abandoned to facilitate their progress. The Prince suffered along with the rest in having to leave

---

4. At the time Johnstone made his observations, Guise's companies were not in Stirling, Hamilton's dragoons were at Leith, Lascelles' regiment consisted of eight companies only, and Lee's was only half a regiment. For a detailed inquiry into the exact state of Cope's army at this time see Rupert C. Jarvis: *Collected Papers on the Jacobite Risings.* (1971)., Vol. 1, Ch. 2, Cope's Forces August 1745.

5. *History of the Transactions in Scotland in the Year 1715-16 and 1745-46* by George Charles, Vol. II Leith, 1819. Pp. 17-18.

12 of the 20 field pieces brought from France in the *Du Teillay* owing to lack of transport. The mountain, towards which both armies were racing, bore the marks of Marshal Wade's influence in the Highlands, being made accessible by a military road. This road extended to the summit in a series of traverses or ramps in a zig-zag manner which caused the Highlanders to refer to the achievement as 'the Devil's Staircase'. If the Highlanders could entrench themselves in the passes on the mountain, they would then clearly be in an excellent position to ambush Cope's small force. They themselves had swollen in numbers since leaving Glenfinnan. Five miles from that place, they had been joined by 300 Macdonalds of Clanranald; later some 250 Camerons joined, 280 Stewarts of Appin and the Macdonalds of Glengarry who, with the Grants of Glenmoriston, were said to make up 400 men in all. The Jacobite army was, therefore, numerically superior to the government force, although largely disorganized. There was never any question of seeking to avoid a confrontation with the enemy. On the contrary, the Highlanders wanted to show their mettle and, prior to reaching their objective, a bond had been drawn up pledging the chiefs 'not to lay down their arms nor to make their peace without the consent of the whole'.

Cope arrived at Dalnacardoch on August 25, and here he received information from the released English officer concerning the state of the Prince's army and the Jacobites' intention to engage the government forces at Corryarrak Pass, on the way to Fort Augustus. From Dalnacardoch, Cope advanced to Dalwhinnie, arriving there the following day, the 26th. Here he received a letter from Duncan Forbes, the Lord President, confirming his intelligence of the previous day and urging him to take great care in view of the rebels' plans. When Cope received this information, he was still some 20 miles away from the south side of the mountain. A Council of War was called to decide the future policy of the army at which it was unanimously agreed that, to pursue the original plan, would be to invite annihilation because the Jacobites were reputed to be 'entrenched to their teeth' along the pass. Cope's force, therefore, decided to go to Inverness. This gave the impression of forward movement without endangering the army, and avoided an obvious retreat to Stirling. When this decision was reached, the Jacobites were already at Abercalder, on the north side of the mountain, preparing for an imminent engagement.

On the night of the 26th, a detachment of Highlanders established themselves in the pass and the following morning Prince Charles was heard to remark as he put on his brogues, 'Before these are unloosed I shall be up with Mr. Cope', but in fact there was no sign that day of Mr. Cope or his army. At last a group of deserters, mostly Highlanders of the London contingent which had recently joined Cope's force, clarified the situation with information concerning the retreat to Inverness. A detachment of government infantry had been sent on towards Fort Augustus to give the impression that the rest of the army was following, but the main body of the army had turned onto the Inverness road and had spent the night at Ruthven, from whence it was to proceed by forced marches to Inverness. There was to be no battle that day.

Cope's plan to march his troops into the Highlands and root out the rebels had misfired badly and he did not escape consequent criticism. The most significant result of the abortive campaign was that Edinburgh and the Lowlands now lay open to the Jacobites if they chose to turn south. In 1715, the Duke of Argyll had persistently blocked the approach to the Low Country, but now the Highlanders had a clear run through to the capital. Instead of pursuing Cope north as contemplated, the Jacobites decided to avail themselves of the opportunity to reach Edinburgh unopposed. The unhappy General

Cope, described by Home as 'one of those ordinary men who are fitter for anything than the chief command in war', was eventually exonerated by a Board of General Officers established later to examine the failure. But the lesson learned from the exercise was that an expeditionary force sent out into the hostile environment of the Highlands would be unlikely to triumph over an indigenous army. Cope's main preoccupation had been not with the enemy but with the geography of the Highlands and the business of surviving in the mountains. According to an officer on the expedition, the army suffered numerous acts of sabotage on this mission. Baggage horses disappeared in the night, grain sacks were ripped open and food was lost. With each loss, the invaders displayed their vulnerability. By the time the army reached Dalwhinnie, on the north side of the Grampians, it had only two days' supply of bread left, and still a long way to go. In the circumstances, Cope had little choice. He had to turn his back on the enemy and present it with a psychological victory. The environment had beaten him.

The Fall of Edinburgh

When Cope reached Inverness on the evening of August 29, 1745, he found that Duncan Forbes of Culloden was already there, attempting to raise the well-disposed clans for the government. Cope himself was not blind to the fact that the Lowlands lay completely unprotected and he immediately arranged for transports to be sent to him at Aberdeen so that he might move his army south by sea, in the hope of reaching Leith before the rebels had a chance to move against Edinburgh. With this in mind, he wasted as little time as possible and marched his men from Inverness to Aberdeen on September 4, where they were embarked on the 16th. The response of the well-disposed clans continued to disappoint even the most modest expectations and a member of the expedition recorded: 'the night before we left Inverness we were joined by 200 of the

Duncan Forbes of Culloden (1685-1747) worked actively to raise support for the government cause in both the 1715 and 1745 rebellions.

Monroes under the command of Captain George Munro of Culcairn, who went along with us to Aberdeen, and were the only Highlanders, not of the regular troops, who joined us in this expedition'.[6]

After abandoning all thoughts of following Cope, Prince Charles and his Highlanders had taken the road across the mountains of Blair Atholl to reach the Low Country. On the way, a valuable accession of strength was secured through the machinations of Macpherson of Cluny, who was thought to have arranged his own kidnap by the Jacobites. In this way, his support of their cause might appear to government agents under the guise of constraint, because Cope had already ordered him to muster his men for the government side. After a pleasant stay in Blair Atholl Castle, the home of the Marquis of Tullibardine, a detachment of Highlanders entered Perth on September 3. The next day at noon, the Declaration, Manifesto and Commission of Regency were read out at the market cross, and in the evening Prince Charles entered the

6. Extract from the account of an officer in Cope's army. *History of the Transactions in Scotland in the Years 1715-16 and 1745-46* by George Charles, Vol. II, Leith, 1817. Pp. 20-21. Even the Monroes disappointed. They marched with the army to Aberdeen, but refused to embark as it was near harvest time and they were required at home.

town mounted on a fine horse, which was certainly not representative of the majority in the Jacobite camp. He wore Highland costume. According to one account, he 'set up a standard with the motto, TANDEM TRIUMPHANS' (At length triumphant).[7] Spies in the pay of the Lord President variously reported Jacobite numbers at this stage as between 1,822 and 1,880. On the day after the entrance into Perth, however, further injections of support came with the appearance of the Duke of Perth, James Drummond, and Lord George Murray with their following. Destined to play a prominent part in subsequent affairs as joint Lieutenant-Generals of the swelling Jacobite army, the two men were of vastly different temperament. Lord George was 45, the brother of the Marquis of Tullibardine and had been present at Sheriffmuir as a boy and he was also active in the abortive campaign of 1719. Assessments of his character were various, but his importance to the campaign is beyond dispute. His aide, the Chevalier de Johnstone, spoke of him in adulatory tones and suggested that he 'possessed a natural genius for military operations' that made him the chief architect of the movement's subsequent success. Personally, he was 'tall and robust, and brave in the highest degree'. According to the same source, 'conducting the Highlanders in the most heroic manner', he was 'always the first to rush sword in hand into the midst of the enemy'. The same author, however, damns the Duke of Perth with faint praise. He was 'possessed of a mild and gentle disposition, was of very limited abilities, and interfered with nothing'. The titular Duke was weak-chested having been crushed by a barrel as a child and, though 'brave even to excess', this weakness imposed restraints upon his bravery. Nevertheless, he was an asset to the cause and apparently did not take umbrage when Lord George displayed a reluctance to share his command, to the extent that he and the Duke of Perth were obliged to direct affairs at one point on alternate days owing to an inability to co-operate. Lord George disliked other things about the arrangement of Jacobite affairs and not the least of these was the influence which the Irishman, O'Sullivan, exercised over the Prince. It will be remembered that he had accompanied Charles from France and was now appointed Quartermaster-General of the army. Although Lord George refused to admit O'Sullivan's military usefulness, the Irishman in fact was credited with considerable skill in the art of what was then referred to as 'irregular warfare'. He had served with distinction in two campaigns abroad and was by no means as ignorant of strategy and tactics as Lord George persistently maintained. The mutual animosity of these two men lasted throughout the campaign. Lord George suspected the motives of the Irish for involving themselves in Scottish affairs and strongly resented any interference by foreigners in his supervision of the Highlanders — 'proud, haughty, blunt and imperious, he wished to have the exclusive ordering of everything; and feeling his superiority he would listen to no advice'. But, in fact, it was Murray's own motives for joining the rebellion that rendered him more vulnerable to criticism than any other member of the high command. His normal Jacobite feelings seem to have suffered a slight relapse in 1745, because two weeks before joining the rebellion, he was the ally and informant of Cope. Although he worked harder than any other individual in the Jacobite army to promote its success, he was never able to drag himself quite clear of the taint of treachery. However, the Jacobites could not afford to reject the services of one who was prepared to undertake the task of drilling the impetuous Highlanders in the proper use of firearms.

The occupation of Perth, coupled with Cope's retreat, combined to produce a mood of jubilation in the Jacobite camp, while on the other side the Hanoverians were forcibly shaken out of their complacency. Before he

7. George Charles. Op. Cit. Vol. II. P. 23.

left Perth, Charles wrote breezily to his father, informing him of his success.

Perth. Sept. 10, 1745.

SIR,

Since my landing, everything has succeeded to my wishes, It has pleased God to prosper me hitherto even beyond my expectations. I have got together thirteen hundred men; and am promised more brave determined men, who are resolved to die or conquer with me. The enemy marched a body of regular troops to attack me, but when they came near they changed their mind, and, by taking a different route and making forced marches, have escaped to the north, to the great disappointment of my Highlanders; but I am not at all sorry for it — I shall have the greater glory in beating them when they are more numerous and supported by their dragoons. I design to march to-morrow, and hope my next shall be from Edinburgh.

I am your Majestys &c. &c.

On his entry into Perth, Charles is reputed to have possessed only one of the louis d'or he brought from France. In the march from Glenfinnan to Perth, he had given generously to the Highland chiefs in order that they might support their followers. At Perth, the public money was levied and personal donations from wealthy sympathizers replenished the exhausted coffers, while parties of Jacobites visited towns in Perth and Fife to raise revenue issued with passes in the name of 'Charles Prince of Wales etc., Regent of Scotland, England, France and Ireland and of the dominions thereunto belonging'. By the time the Jacobites left Perth, their number had increased to about 2,400 with the addition of some MacGregors and Robertsons, as well as those brought by the Duke of Perth and Lord George Murray.

On September 11, they began their march towards the Forth and two days later they crossed the river at the Fords of Frew, some eight miles above Stirling. Meanwhile, in Edinburgh, the authorities viewed the approach of the Young Pretender with horror and dismay. 'Greatly were the friends of the government astonished when they heard the King's army was gone to Inverness and that the rebels were coming to Edinburgh', reported Home. Now, at last, the rebellion had to be taken seriously. Edinburgh was by no means invulnerable. The city walls had never been fortified with cannon and did not represent a formidable obstacle to a determined invader, being in parts, as Home described, 'no better than a garden wall'. The castle, of course had guns as well as a garrison of 600 men, but these were under the direction of the aged General Guest, an 87-year-old invalid. In addition to the trained bands, of which there were some 15 or 16 companies in Edinburgh at this time, the Lord Provost received authority to raise and maintain by voluntary subscription 1,000 foot for the defence of the city. A subscription was accordingly opened on September 9 and, within two hours, money for the maintenance of 600 men was subscribed, and a month's pay advanced. The Edinburgh Magistrates had ordered that each squad of the City Guard be augmented 'to thirty additional men' and a second augmentation was made as the danger increased. The trained bands mounted guard at points of access to the city. Hamilton's dragoons were quartered there, leaving Gardiner's between the Prince and the capital.

As before, the rival armies were racing towards the same objective. Sir John Cope's plan was proceeding as smoothly as might be expected. However, the wind made it impossible to put ashore any nearer the capital than Dunbar. Here, they landed on Sept. 17, the artillery arriving the following day. They were scarcely safe on shore when they heard that the rebels held Edinburgh.

They had come too late. Meanwhile, Charles, who had expected to meet opposition from Gardiner's dragoons at the Fords of

Frew, had encountered none. In crossing the Forth, he was considered to 'have passed the Rubicon' and was now committed to go forward and meet his fate in the Low Country. After a fruitless attempt to pin down the ever-retreating government dragoons, the Jacobite army took possession of Linlithgow on September 15. The following morning, the Highlanders advanced in order towards the dragoons who again retreated in undignified haste to a position only a mile from Edinburgh. By two o'clock on the afternoon of the 16th, Charles had advanced as far as Corstorphine, three miles from the capital. A camp was established at Gray's Mills, two miles to the south-west of the city, and a summons was issued from the camp to the Provost and Magistrates of the city in the following terms:

'Being now in a condition to make our way into this capital of his Majesty's ancient kingdom of Scotland, we hereby summon you to receive us, as you are in duty bound to do. And in order to it we hereby require you upon receipt of this to summon the Town Council and take proper measures in it for securing the peace and quiet of the city, which we are very desirous to protect. But if you suffer any of Usurper's troops to enter the town, or any of the canon, arms or ammunition now in it, whether belonging to the publick or private persons, to be carried off, we shall take it as a breach of your duty and a heinous offence against the King and us, and shall resent it accordingly. We promise to preserve all the rights and liberties of the city, and the particular property of every one of his Majesty's subjects. But if any opposition be made to us we cannot answer for the consequences, being firmly resolved at any rate to enter the city, and in that case, if any of the inhabitants are found in arms against us, they must expect to be treated as prisoners of war.

(signed) Charles, Prince Regent
From our Camp 16th September, 1745.'

The authorities had no choice but to give the summons serious consideration. The plans for the city's defence had already collapsed in a welter of confusion. When positive information was received of the Highlanders' arrival at Linlithgow, it had been agreed that 250 of the recently raised volunteers should march out and support the regular forces and Hamilton's dragoons were ordered to join Gardiner's at Corstorphine. At eleven o'clock on the 15th, the fire-bell was rung in the city as the signal for the volunteers to arm. A little after twelve, the whole city guard, together with a detachment of volunteers, marched out of Edinburgh but returned to the city the same night without having accomplished anything. The same procedure was repeated the following morning and, this time, the volunteers managed to rendezvous with the frightened dragoons at Colt-bridge. With news of the Highlanders' advance, however, the attempt to set up a co-ordinated defence of the city disintegrated and the city soldiers quickly returned to the town while the dragoons rode off by the north side of the city towards Leith. Such was the confusion of the dragoons that they left behind them all their baggage and tents. When Prince Charles's summons appeared in the capital, there was still no news of Sir John Cope and thus the Council was in no position to argue.

Deputies were sent from Edinburgh to the Jacobite camp to discuss terms, but before their return news came in of Cope's landing and the situation was dramatically changed. Instead of considering the rebels' demands, the city Council turned to new proposals, to beat to arms and sound the alarm and reassemble the volunteers. The important thing was to stall the Jacobites until such time as they could be overpowered. Fresh deputies were sent to the camp to prolong the negotiations, but these received a curt dismissal. No decision had been reached by two o'clock on the morning of the 17th. It was time for action. The coach bringing back the dismissed negotiators deposited them in Edinburgh High Street and then drove towards Cannongate. When the Nether Bow port was opened to let the coach out, 800 Highlanders led by Cameron of Lochiel rushed in and took possession of the city. It was five o'clock in the morning. After overpowering the sentries at the other gates and subjugating the town guard, the invaders waited the arrival of daylight. 'When the inhabitants of Edinburgh awaked in the morning, they found that the Highlanders were masters of the city' (Home). While Cope was landing his troops at Dunbar, the herald was proclaiming the sovereignty of King James VIII at Edinburgh.

Confrontation

On September 17, 1745, the entire Jacobite army was within the confines of Scotland's capital city. For Charles Edward, it was a day of immense significance and one that he might, perhaps, have expected to cost his army more in terms of bloodshed. Although the city was taken, the Highlanders failed to secure possession of the castle, which had to be blockaded throughout the occupation to frustrate any counter-measures of the government garrison. The reaction of the authorities towards the coup was predictably hostile, but the common people viewed the affair with unbridled curiosity and an apolitical interest in whatever appeared unusual and exciting. At Corstorphine, before entering the city, the Jacobite army had already encountered numerous casual sightseers from the capital unable to restrain their curiosity. Now, with the prospect of the Prince himself appearing in the city streets, general interest reached a crescendo. The army halted in the hollow between the hills under Arthur's Seat as it approached Edinburgh. After a while, Charles came down to the Duke's Walk accompanied by the Highland chiefs and others of his commanders. The park was crammed with people struggling to catch a glimpse of the celebrity. Home, who was in the crowd, supplied the best description of what might be seen of the pretended Prince on that occasion.

'The figure and presence of Charles Stuart were not ill suited to his lofty pretensions. He was in the prime of youth, tall and handsome, of a fair complexion; he had a light coloured periwig with his own hair combed over the front; he wore the Highland dress, that is, a tartan short coat without the plaid, a blue bonnet on his head, and on his breast the star of the order of St. Andrew'.

After showing himself to the crowd, Charles made his way on horseback to Holyrood House, the palace of the Kings of Scotland.

If Charles cut an impressive figure with the crowd his followers excited only amusement and disgust, with their verminous clothes and miscellany of ancient equipment. 'I observed there armes', recorded one hostile witness, 'they were guns of diferent syses, and some of innormowos (enormous) length, some with butts turned up lick a heren, some tyed with puck threed to the stock, some without locks and some matchlocks, some had swords over ther showlder instead of guns, one or two had pitchforks, and some bits of sythes upon poles with a cleek (ie. a hook), some (had) old Lochaber axes . .'[8] Most of the Highlanders had no proper footwear and one of the first requests made of the Magistracy of the city was for 6,000 pairs of shoes for the army. Nevertheless, it was with such an unimpressive following that, within a month of raising the standard at Glenfinnan, Charles Edward was able to take possession of the capital of his ancestors' ancient kingdom.

At one o'clock in the afternoon of the 17th, the manifesto of James VIII was read out at the market cross, amidst profound silence, followed by the declaration of Prince Charles as Regent. After the commission of regency was heard, the crowd raised a loud huzza, the most ostentatious demonstrations of enthusiasm coming from ladies positioned at the

8. The Woodhouselee MS. A narrative of events in Edinburgh and district during the occupation, Sept. - Nov. 1745. In *The Forty-Five A Narrative of the Last Jacobite Rising By Several Contemporary Hands*. Ed. by Charles Sanford Terry, 1922.

open windows of nearby buildings, who cried themselves hoarse and vigorously waved their white handkerchiefs to represent the Prince of Wales's emblem, the white cockade. Home noted, however, that 'amongst people of condition', these demonstrations of joy were confined to the women, who saw only that the Pretender was handsome. Their male counterparts were more concerned with the practicalities of camouflaging their wealth in such a way that it might not be utilized for the maintenance of the invader's rabble army. For the Young Chevalier, however, the events of that day must have seemed as insubstantial as a dream. The Jacobite army appeared truimphant, but it had in fact done nothing that would usually be associated with the idea of military victory. Had the capital city made any show of resistance, it is difficult to see how the Highlanders could have taken it within a reasonable period of time, bearing in mind Cope's proximity. The Jacobites had yet to prove their worth in terms of solid achievement, and although all was jubilation on this occasion, their success was cheaply bought. A real trial of strength was nearer at hand than any of them knew.

After a couple of days' relaxation in Edinburgh, the Jacobite army set up its camp at Duddingston, about a mile south-east of Edinburgh. Cope's force, after being joined by the exhausted and disgraced dragoons, left Dunbar on September 19, and marched towards Edinburgh with the intention of attacking the Jacobites and relieving the city. The Royal army in transit apparently made a 'great show'. Its cavalry, infantry, cannon and baggage carts extended for several miles along the route, providing a spectacle equal to that of the Jacobite army in provoking the interest of sightseers who turned out once again to view the unusual proceedings. That night, the government forces camped in a field to the west of the town of Haddington. News of Cope's manoeuvres had already sent Charles out to join his army at Duddingston, where,

on the 19th, a Council of War was held in which it was agreed that the Jacobites should march next morning and intercept Cope in his progress towards Edinburgh.

The affection of the Edinburgh crowds had not been so deeply stirred by the arrival of the pretended Prince as to carry more than a handful to the recruiting office. But Jacobite strength was increased at this time by some imported aid in the shape of 500 men of the clan Maclachlan and some Highlanders from Atholl. Among the new adherents were also the Earl of Kellie, Lord Elcho and Lord Balmerino, as well as some other lowland gentlemen. The army was estimated to be about 2,400 strong, but without a contingent that could be accurately described as cavalry. There were perhaps fewer than 50 mounted men, who were mostly gentlemen and their servants, and all were on inferior animals. (In fact the horses were abandoned before the action on this occasion.) The citizens of Edinburgh had taken the precaution of sending most of their serviceable arms to the castle before capitulating to the rebels and thus in this quarter too, there were fewer gains than might reasonably have been expected. Some of the muskets which were to have served the defence volunteers fell into Jacobite hands, however, and went some way towards arming the most impoverished of the Highland soldiers. Nevertheless, there was still sufficient lack of arms for scythes to be visible amongst the Highland ranks that marched from Duddingston to Preston, on Friday, September 20, 1745. The Prince, not unreasonably, was able to brandish a weapon of some distinction, and drawing forth his sword prior to their departure he cried; 'Gentlemen, I have flung away the Scabbard; with God's assistance I don't doubt of making you a free and happy people'.

According to Lord George Murray, it was he himself who led the vanguard and first received the information that Cope's army was heading towards the village of Preston where he was expected to take up a position on the high ground known as Fawside. 'There was no time to deliberate or wait for orders', says Lord George in his *Marches of the Highland Army*. 'I was very well acquainted with the ground, and I was confident that nothing could be done to purpose except the Highlanders got above the enemy, I struck off to the right hand through the fields, without holding any road.'[9] Meanwhile, Cope, in turning towards the plain between the villages of Seaton and Preston, had despatched Lord Loudon to reconnoitre the ground. He soon returned with the news that the rebels were in full march towards them. Sir John quickly decided that the plain was a safe enough place to engage the enemy and set about drawing up his army, facing it to the west, from whence he expected the rebels to appear. 'In a very short time after Sir John Cope had taken his ground, the Highland army came in sight' (Home).

Having gained the high ground with the vanguard, Lord George waited for the rest of the column to join him, after which the whole army proceeded towards the hamlet of Tranent, marching in full sight of the enemy. There, it halted and formed up in line of battle about half a mile from the Royal army. On sighting each other, the soldiers of both armies exchanged deprecating comments. Because the Highlanders had taken a circuitous route from Duddingston, they had not appeared from the direction calculated by Cope and he was forced to alter his dispositions, moving the front of his army from west to south, to face the enemy. There was to be much shuffling between positions for the rest of the afternoon as each side tried to secure the advantage. Although the Jacobites had succeeded in gaining the high ground, it soon became apparent that it was the government army that occupied the superior position, in the plain. On his right, Cope had, at a distance, the village of Preston Pans and nearer, the stone walls of two enclosures, between six and seven feet high. On his left, at a distance, was the village of Seaton and nearer, some marshy ground which terminated in a deep pond. At his rear was the village of Cockenzie and the sea, while in front was Tranent and the Jacobites, who were separated from him by a morass that was virtually impassable, flanked on either side by soft, boggy ground riddled with springs and ditches. Immediately in front of the government position, there was a ditch some ten to twelve feet broad, as well as a thick hedge. The restless Highlanders paced about the ridge looking for an opening which might render Cope's position assailable, but 'the more we examined it, the more we were convinced of the impossibility of attacking it' wrote Johnstone. His impressions were soon confirmed by the testimony of an officer sent to reconnoitre the ground who declared 'it was impossible to get through the morass and attack the enemy in front without receiving several fires'. After nightfall, the Jacobites held a Council of War at which it was decided that they would risk all on a frontal attack at daybreak.

Neither army knew for certain the strength of the opposition it was likely to encounter. Contemporary accounts of events show that there were gross exaggerations on both sides when it came to computing the strength of the rival armies. For example, the Chevalier de Johnstone seemed to think that the Highlanders were faced with an enemy 4,000 strong, while he puts his own faction at a modest 1,800. It emerged later, during Cope's examination by the Board of General Officers, that he imagined the rebels to be some 5,500 in number, although this is inconsistent with his cavalier attitude immediately prior to engagement. In fact the opposing armies were of almost equal size. The Jacobites had 200 or 300 more men than the government total of approximately 2,100.

What the Jacobite leaders badly needed was some inspired plan that would combat the advantages of Cope's position without exposing

9. *Marches of the Highland Army* from the MS. of Lord George Murray, Commander-in-Chief and included in *Jacobite Memoirs of the Rebellion of 1745*. Edited from the MS of Rev. Robert Forbes A.M., by Robert Chambers. Edin. 1834. P. 36.

their own men to unnecessary danger. A straightforward frontal attack clearly lacked these features, and, just when it seemed that courage would have to substitute for inspiration on this occasion, a new element was introduced into their calculations. Present at the Council of War was a local man, named Robert Anderson, who was described by Johnstone as 'proprietor of the marsh' and elsewhere referred to as the son of a local laird. According to Home, he had joined the Jacobites at Edinburgh. Being a native of the country in which the army now found itself, he was familiar with the topography and, although too reticent to express a view during the Council proceedings, he afterwards made public his concern over the decision taken. He thought he knew a way by which the Highlanders might cross the morass without being seen. Anderson went to see Lord George Murray, who, realizing the significance of this disclosure, immediately consulted Charles. It was promptly decided that Anderson should have an opportunity of testing his local knowledge. He was commissioned to guide the Highlanders from the hill on which they were encamped, around the worst part of the morass and into the plain, before sunrise.

The Jacobite army formed up in column of three and, with Anderson leading the way, it decamped in dead silence. The horses were all left behind. As the Highlanders neared the place where Anderson was to lead them across the marshy ground, daylight was beginning to struggle through the frosty mist which had settled over the area. A sharp cry suddenly pierced the chilling air: 'Who's there?'. Some government dragoons on lookout duty had glimpsed the activity going on behind the shrouds of mist. No reply was given. The Highlanders pressed on as quickly and quietly as possible, across the difficult ground. The dragoons galloped off to raise the alarm. The column headed north, led by the Duke of Perth, until it was estimated that the rear would be well clear of the boggy ground. It then halted, faced left and formed into lines.

The Duke of Perth commanded the right wing and Lord George Murray the left. The first line consisted of six regiments, with Clanranald's on the right and Lochiel's on the left. A dispute arose between the Macdonalds and the Camerons as to who was to have the honour of forming the right wing, 'a distinction which was at length yielded, though reluctantly to the Macdonalds'. Next to the Macdonalds on the right stood the regiments of Glengarry and Keppoch; in the centre were the Duke of Perth's men and the MacGregors. The Appin regiment was next to the Camerons of Lochiel on the far left. The second line was commanded by the Prince, because it had been agreed earlier that he owed it to his followers to preserve his person from the worst of the danger.

Meanwhile, Cope had received information from his dragoons that the enemy would be coming from the east. Although the dispositions already made would not need to be altered, the entire line, which was three men deep, had to be wheeled to the left to face the enemy. Five companies of Lee's regiment formed the right wing and nine companies of Murray's made up the left. In the centre were eight companies of Lascelles's and two of Guise's. Flanking the line of foot on the right were two squadrons of Colonel Gardiner's dragoons and on the left flank were two squadrons of Hamilton's, while the third squadron of each regiment remained in the rear. All the artillery was positioned next to Lee's companies on the right wing and was manned by a mongrel company of invalids and sailors, owing to the lack of trained artillerymen. In this new position, the government army had the village of Cockenzie and the sea on its left and its right was protected by the large ditch and morass which had previously lain between the contending armies. The ground which now separated them was 'an extensive cornfield, plain and level, without a bush or tree' (Home).

A grenadier of Barrel's Regiment (4th Foot) and an officer of Bligh's Regiment (20th Foot). The grenadier wears the uniform of the Foot regiments of Cumberland's army, distinguished by mitre caps and shoulder wings. Barrel's Regiment was on the left flank of the Government front line at Culloden. Bligh's Regiment was in the centre of the second line.

These drawings of Highland clansmen show the lack of uniformity among the tartans worn by the Jacobites. One clansman carries the great Lochaber axe, while the other is equipped to fight with the broadsword in the right hand and the dirk in the left. The target is strapped onto the left arm. Both wear the white cockade as a symbol of Jacobite loyalty.

A General Officer and a drummer of Barrel's Regiment (4th Foot). The General wears a cuirass, the last piece of defensive armour to be worn in battle. He is dressed in the style of uniform worn by the Duke of Cumberland in the field. Drummers and fifers of English Foot regiments were dressed in mitre caps and coats sewn with a great deal of decorative lace.

Privates of Ogilvy's and the Royal Ecossais regiments. Three regiments of Scots in the French service were raised by the Duke of Perth. Only detachments of the regiments, numbering about 350, came to Scotland to fight for the Prince. The third regiment (Albany's) wore the same uniform as that of Ogilvy's.

A piper and a corporal of the Royal Highland
Regiment (the Black Watch). These figures show how
Highland soldiers were clothed and equipped. The
piper does not wear the dark green tartan of the
Regiment, but a red sett.

A Highland peasant woman and a Highland lady. In this illustration, the peasant woman wears her shawl as a cowl. The lady's tartan shawl, or screen, is worn in the fashion of ladies of quality. It was often worn to show Jacobite sympathies. This lady wears the added sign of a white hair ribbon.

A trooper of Kingston's Light Horse and a field officer
of Government Highlanders. The trooper's uniform is
typical of Government dragoons in 1745. Regiments
were distinguished by their facing colours. The field
officer is typical of officers of the Black Watch,
Loudon's Highlanders and Highland Militia Battalions.

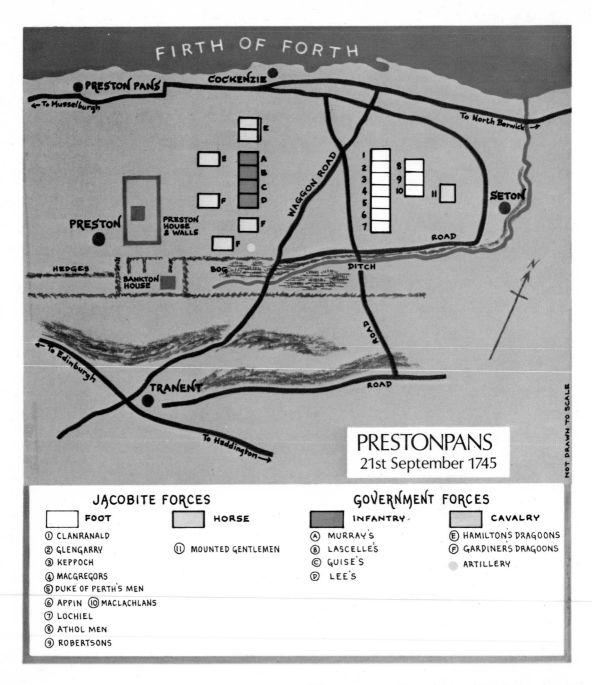

FIRTH OF FORTH

PRESTON PANS
COCKENZIE
← To Musselburgh
To North Berwick →

WAGGON ROAD

E

E A
B
C
F D

F

F

1
2 8
3 9
4 10
5
6 11
7

SETON

ROAD

PRESTON

PRESTON HOUSE & WALLS

HEDGES BOG DITCH

BANKTON HOUSE

ROAD

← To Edinburgh

TRANENT

ROAD

To Haddington →

NOT DRAWN TO SCALE

PRESTONPANS
21st September 1745

JACOBITE FORCES

☐ FOOT   ▨ HORSE

① CLANRANALD
② GLENGARRY
③ KEPPOCH
④ MACGREGORS
⑤ DUKE OF PERTH'S MEN
⑥ APPIN ⑩ MACLACHLANS
⑦ LOCHIEL
⑧ ATHOL MEN
⑨ ROBERTSONS

⑪ MOUNTED GENTLEMEN

GOVERNMENT FORCES

▨ INFANTRY   ▨ CAVALRY

Ⓐ MURRAY'S
Ⓑ LASCELLES
Ⓒ GUISE'S
Ⓓ LEE'S

Ⓔ HAMILTONS DRAGOONS
Ⓕ GARDINERS DRAGOONS
○ ARTILLERY

The map shows the positions of the rival armies at
Culloden (see pages 139-140 and 145-149).

Battle of Prestonpans

As the morning mist melted, the two armies stood revealed. Although the Highlanders had their bravest and best armed men to the fore, the sight of the sun glinting off the equipment of their adversaries must have been a daunting spectacle for them. Referred to by Cope, in his address to the troops, as a 'parcel of rabble, a parcel of brutes', the Highlanders were terrifying in an altogether different way with their reputation for savagery and their wild appearance. With their bonnets pulled down low over their brows, the Highlanders advanced resembling nothing in their approach so much as a 'Moving hedge'. 'Our march up to the enemy till we came near was without pipe or drum, in the most profound silence till the attack was begun, when all our instruments tongues and hands were at work.'[10] The speed of their approach was later described by government officers as unbelievable. In fact, the Jacobite left wing moved before the right and as a consequence the line was uneven. Furthermore, a gap in the line rendered it extremely vulnerable. It was the Camerons who came up directly opposite the government guns. With their quarry in sight, the Highlanders came on with a 'hideous shout' which succeeded in terrifying the makeshift gunners who turned and fled with the powder. A Colonel Whiteford attempted single-handed to fill the gap and succeeded in firing some of the 1½ pounders. In the march from the boggy ground towards the sea, the Jacobite right wing had extended itself so far towards the shore that, being drawn up in a hollow, it had no view of the enemy or its own left wing until the two were engaged. This meant that the Jacobite left and the Camerons received the full attention of the government artillery. This might have proved decisive if the guns had been manned effectively. As it was, despite Colonel Whiteford's effort, a dispatch from the Jacobite headquarters on the day of the battle reported that although 'their Artillery played,

(it) did no other Mischief than carrying off the calf of a Gentleman's leg'.[11] It seems likely, however, that the emergency gunners fired upon their own dragoons, contributing to the utter confusion on the government right and causing the squadron to wheel about, ride over the artillery guard and flee. Colonel Gardiner received orders to repulse the Camerons, and although he himself advanced towards the enemy, he found himself deserted half way by his terrified dragoons. The flight of the gunners and the inefficacy of the dragoons had a depressing effect upon the morale of the nearby government infantry. Without waiting for orders, and seized by panic, they fired once upon the advancing Highlanders, turned and ran. Several of the Jacobites were killed, but the line continued to advance. The Highlanders discharged their muskets and, despite Lord George Murray's training, immediately discarded them, preferring to rush on with sword and dirk to the accompaniment of a furious scream. Within a few minutes, both horse and foot on the right of the government line were routed.

The situation on the government left was little different. Hamilton's dragoons showed themselves no more intrepid than Gardiner's. They similarly fled leaving the flank of foot unsupported with the same result. The regiment next to them gave their fire and then broke up in confusion. The very strength of Cope's position was now turned to the disadvantage of his fleeing men. As the Highlanders hacked their way forward, the redcoats found themselves trapped. Ten or fifteen minutes elapsed between the first shot and the rout and in that time the plain became a charnel house. The vast majority of the government victims sustained their wounds and death blows by the sword, the hideous consequence of which was a battlefield littered with human debris, 'covered with heads, legs and arms and mutilated bodies'. The Highlanders had supplied proof of their celebrated strength in the

10. *From the Journall and Memoirs of P.........C.........Expedition into Scotland 1745-6 by a Highland Officer in his Army*, included in The Lockhart Papers Vol. II, London 1817. Pp. 490-1. (this anonymous journalist is usually taken to be Macdonald of Morar).

11. Dispatch from the Headquarters of the Chevalier, Sept. 21 and included in *The Rebellion of 1745, An Old Story Re-Told from the "Newcastle Courant"*. Printed for Private circulation 1881. P. 22.

most appalling form. Macgregor's company, armed with scythes attached to six foot poles, had hacked its way through horse and rider alike — 'they cut the legs of the horses in two; and the riders through the middle of their bodies' (Johnstone). The Highlanders harboured a superstitious fear of cavalry, which revolved around the mistaken impression that the horses as well as their riders were partisan. They believed that the animals were trained to bite and tear in battle and, therefore, showed no restraint in eliminating them from the contest. They had, in addition, been instructed to aim their blows at the noses of the animals, because the natural movement of a horse wounded in the face is to wheel around. A few animals tormented in this way would be sufficient to throw a whole squadron into disorder. The horses and riders that managed to flee the slaughter formed up again on a nearby hill, but they dispersed towards Dalkeith when the Highlanders advanced towards them. The defeat of the Royal army was complete. None of the government soldiers had attempted to fire a second shot and no bayonets were called for. The Highlanders had not even found it necessary to employ their reserve forces in the second line.

Although the battle itself was brief, Charles remained on the field until mid-day supervising the relief of the wounded on both sides. Contemporary estimates vary as to the numbers killed, wounded and taken prisoner. Lord George Murray stated that 'by the list I caused take that afternoon, by their own sergeants and corporals, we had made betwixt sixteen and seventeen hundred prisoners of which about seventy (were) officers'.[12] Only about 170 of the government infantry managed to escape. Johnstone reported that the victory cost the Highlanders 'forty killed and as many wounded', while Home put the Jacobite losses at 34 killed and 76 wounded. Left in possession of the field, the Highlanders plundered freely. The enemy's standard and other trophies were brought to Charles, as well as

Cope's military chest estimated to contain between £3,000 and £4,000. As was their custom after an engagement, many of the Highlanders, who regarded themselves as volunteers at liberty to come and go as they chose, disappeared towards the hills with as much booty as they could carry.

Contrary to the rumours and ballads that subsequently circulated imputing cowardice to Sir John Cope during the battle, it seems that he attempted unsuccessfully on several occasions to rally his terrified men. The foundation of the Jacobite success had been laid with the successful accomplishment of the dawn operation. Although it was maintained that the government lines were fully formed when the Highlanders attacked, the speed of the Jacobite descent rendered possible by the new line of approach fatally discomposed the regular troops. The *Gentleman's Magazine* for October 1745 published an account of the affair by an officer under Cope. His impression was that 'Neither officers nor general can divest men of dread and panick when it seizes them, he only can do that who makes the heart of man. To their being struck with a most unreasonable panick, and to no one thing else, the disgraceful event was owing'. Once it became clear that the day was utterly lost, Cope had no choice but to assemble the remainder of the dragoons and desert the field. That night, this remnant of the Royal army was at Coldstream. Known to the Jacobites as Gladsmuir and to history as Prestonpans, the battle effectively destroyed the image of the highland army as a bunch of naked, needy miserable wretches. 'The greatest advantage we derived from it', said Johnstone, 'was the reputation that the Prince's army acquired in the onset; which determined many of his partisans who were yet wavering to declare themselves openly in his favour'. Hardly less important was the fact that, apart from the garrisons at Edinburgh, Stirling and the Highland forts, there were now no government troops in Scotland to

12. In *Marches of the Highland Army* from the MS. of Lord George Murray, Commander-in-Chief.

A Race from Prefton Pans to Berwick.

This contemporary engraving depicts the flight of Sir John Cope to Berwick after his army had withdrawn from the field at Prestonpans.

prevent a Jacobite seizure of power. Appropriately enough, when the first Jacobite victors appeared in the Edinburgh streets, it was to the accompaniment of the bagpipes and the old song 'The king shall enjoy his own again'.

From Edinburgh to Carlisle

The victory at Prestonpans encouraged Charles in the delusion that his Highlanders were invincible, and so, without further deliberation, the Young Chevalier was all for pursuing Cope to Berwick. However, practical and political obstacles stood in the way of such a scheme and these were pointed out to Charles by the members of the Council who met regularly at Holyrood to discuss Jacobite strategy and tactics. The first practical difficulty to be acknowledged was the fact

that, after the battle, the army was diminished by desertions on a scale that made it unfit for another immediate confrontation. It was reckoned that if, in its debilitated state, the army was to suffer a defeat, the cause would certainly be ruined and all the previous achievements forfeited. Furthermore, it was argued, an immediate evacuation of Edinburgh would lose for the army the anticipated accumulation of converts, persuaded by the recent success to use the capital as a rallying point. Charles's view was a personal one, founded on impetuosity. The opposition argued along lines of traditional practice and, on this occasion, instinct gave way to reason.

On the political front, the situation was a delicate one for Charles. He knew that, generally, the Scots were still opposed to the Act of Union; among his supporters, in particular, it was deplored. For many Jacobite soldiers, and especially the Highland leaders, the reinstatment of Scotland as an independent kingdom was of more importance than the restoration of the Stuart dynasty in London. There were, no doubt, many who believed, like the Chevalier de Johnstone, that their Prince's 'chief object ought to have been to endeavour by every possible means to secure himself in the government of his ancient kingdom . . . without attempting, for the present, to extend his views to England'. He was strongly advised to dissolve the Union and issue writs for the meeting of a Scottish parliament. However, one consistent element in Charles's approach to the political aspirations of the rebellion was his own eagerness to conciliate English public opinion at all costs. He could not afford to have his father's and his own dynastic ambitions frustrated by Scottish national feeling. He had come to recover all his father's lost kingdoms and nothing less would serve. He must fix his eyes upon London. Dismembering the Union would effectively outlaw him in the English public conscience and this was the last thing he wanted. In order to disarm his father's sternest critics of the prejudice which Charles felt coloured their view of the exiled Stuarts, he issued a proclamation declaring in his father's name the intention to 'reinstate all his subjects in the full employment of their religion, laws and liberties . . . . our present attempt is not undertaken in order to enslave a free people, but to redress and remove the encroachments made upon them'. Calculated to quell the doubts of those who were as yet unable to dissociate the twin evils of Popery and Absolutism from the name of Stuart, the proclamation had little influence with staunch Hanoverians. If Charles hoped to represent himself as the bringer of liberty on the one hand and freedom of conscience on the other, there were those who replied that he proferred gifts already enjoyed.

In opposition to Charles's personal inclination, the Jacobite army remained in Edinburgh for nearly six weeks after the battle of Prestonpans. During this time, Charles solicited the support of recusant Highlanders and the French king, who had as yet shown himself to be an inactive spectator of affairs in Scotland. As the Jacobites worked to attract support, so President Forbes busied himself to the opposite effect with considerable success. Despite his efforts, however, Edinburgh was the centre of much activity. Among the first to join the Prince there was reckoned to be Lord Ogilvy at the head of a company of men from Angus, variously reported as between 300 and 600 in number. He was followed by John Gordon of Glenbucket, a veteran of the 'Fifteen, with 400 men from Aberdeenshire. Next came Lord Pitsligo 'with a great body of gentlemen from the counties of Aberdeen and Banff, attended by their servants, all well armed and mounted'. Some 120 men from Skye came under Mackinnon of Mackinnon. There was still remarkably little response from the citizens of Edinburgh. If Charles needed a reminder that all Scotland was not at his feet, he had evidence in the sporadic fighting which broke out from time to time between the members of the castle garrison and the occupying Highlanders. Unfortunately, in the course of peppering each other, these adversaries inflicted wounds upon several members of the civilian population which did little to recommend the cause to the natives of Edinburgh.

Evidence of some practical help from France came with the arrival, in October, of three ships at Montrose and Stonehaven carrying arms and equipment and a handful of French gunners, as well as an emissary from the French court. It was less than might reasonably have been expected to follow upon the recent demonstration of success, but Charles succeeded in convincing his followers that it was merely the prelude to greater things. Recruits continued to congregate in Edinburgh, but by mid-October it became clear that the Jacobites would require every available man to combat the formidable defence force now being mobilized against them in England. At the end of the month, news came in that Field Marshal Wade had reached Newcastle with the Dutch auxiliaries and some of the troops returned from Flanders. The Duke of Cumberland, George II's third son, was recalled from the Netherlands on October 19, and was followed a week later by Sir John Ligonier's horse, Bland's dragoons, St. Clair's, Harrison's, Huske's and Beauclerks's foot and a troop of hussars. Apart from the force sent to the north-east, there were two other main deployments of regular troops, in the Midlands and on the south-east coast. In addition to these, trained bands and volunteer companies up and down the country prepared for action. The Duke of Cumberland was appointed Captain-General of British land forces and eventually assumed command of the Midland force.

Charles never ceased to press for a decision from his Council on the business of invading England. In truth, the idea was repugnant to some of the Highland chiefs. On October 30, the Council officers met to discuss plans for a projected invasion and Charles declared that he would wait no longer. He suggested that the army march to Newcastle immediately and engage with Wade's forces there before they became too firmly entrenched in their new position. Lord George Murray was still concerned to protect the army until the optimum conditions for its success in any future engagement had been achieved. He argued that if an approach to England was to be made at all, it should be made via Cumberland. At Carlisle, the army would be well placed to attract additional supporters from Northumberland, and even Lancashire, both reckoned to be areas of pro-Jacobite sympathy. Latecomers from Scotland could be picked up in the same place, as well as any new arrivals from France. In principle, it was Lord George's plan that was adopted, although Charles was not entirely prepared to abandon his instinct a second time. A compromise was worked out whereby the army

was to evacuate Edinburgh in two columns. The first, led by the Marquis of Tullibardine and the Duke of Perth, was to follow a route through Peebles and Moffat to Carlisle, while the second, under Charles and Lord George, would take a more easterly path to the same destination at the same time, creating the impression that it was bearing down on Wade. The two armies would rendezvous at Carlisle and, if the plan achieved nothing else, it would surely confound the enemy.

The preparations for this operation were executed with a degree of efficiency entirely absent from the Jacobite manoeuvres of the 'Fifteen. The army was provided with all it needed for a deliberate campaign, and appropriate care was taken to ensure that adequate provisions would be available to the men en route. The entire force now consisted of approximately 5,000 foot and 500 horse. Although the Highlanders were still in a majority the army had lost its strictly Highland identity. According to Home, there were 13 clan regiments, many of which were small, five regiments of Lowlanders, two troops of horse guards and other mounted bodies. The army could now boast a uniformed troop of life guards under the command of Lord Elcho. The artillery train consisted of the field pieces taken at the battle of Prestonpans and six of the pieces brought from France, amounting to 13 guns in all. The men were fresh, rested, better clothed and appointed than they had ever been. Furthermore, most of them were now receiving regular pay. The men in the front rank earned a shilling a day, while the rest of the ranks received half that amount. A captain was paid half-a-crown, a lieutenant two shillings and the ensigns one-and-sixpence a day. The Highlanders chosen to serve in the front rank were allocated their position in accordance with their social status in civilian life. Most were the Highland equivalent of gentlemen, able to provide themselves with the full equipage of musket, broadsword, a pair of pistols, a dirk and a shield, or target. A Highland soldier, wishing to arm himself with particular care, could carry, in addition to the dagger at his belt, a smaller one held in place by the stocking garter on his right leg. But the high standard of accoutrement maintained by the men at the front diminished by degrees the farther back one went, until the undistinguished warriors at the rear bore little or no resemblance to their resplendent kinsmen at the front.

On November 1, 1745, the Jacobite army evacuated Edinburgh. Few among the citizenry were sorry to see it go, and of those most were young ladies who had fallen under the spell of the exotic Royal adventurer. Charles, at this particular time at least, seems to have exhibited a massive indifference to the attentions of women and this tantalizing detachment, compounded with his boyish good looks, made a potent mixture for romantic attraction. To the impressionable young women called to attend the balls given at Holyrood House, he was, if not irresistible, at least challenging. But all alike were doomed to neglect while Charles focused his undivided attention on the problems of the campaign. Had he been aware of the reverberations of his devastating success with the ladies, the young adventurer might have been less amused than grateful, because it was the constant complaint of President Forbes that he could scarcely get a man of sense to act in concert with him '. . . by reason of the necessity under which all laboured of pleasing their mistresses by favouring the Chevalier'. For government soldiers, Edinburgh was subsequently considered a disastrous posting in view of allegations that it was impossible for a loyal soldier to win the smiles of any lady worthy of his attention, 'all of them being in love with the Chevalier and not even scrupling to avow their Jacobitism by wearing white breastknots and ribands'. But Charles was more sensible of the feelings of the men that were to follow him than of the affections of

the women he left behind. The issue might depend largely on maintaining the goodwill of the Highlanders, who, like the men under Old Borlum in the 'Fifteen, grew increasingly restive as the distance between themselves and the border narrowed. By the time they crossed the river Esk into England desertion was commonplace. Charles's secretary recorded that the mood of the men was truculent — 'without any order given at all (the Highlanders) drew their Swords with one Consent upon entering the River, and every man as he landed on t'other side wheeld about to the left and faced Scotland again'.

After halting one day at Kelso, Charles and his men took the road to Jedburgh. On November 9, the column under Charles and Lord George Murray met with Tullibardine outside Carlisle. Tullibardine's column had marched into England via Peebles and Moffat. The appearance of some 50 or 60 mounted Jacobites on 'Stanwix bank, a hill close to Carlisle' excited a gesture of defiance from the Westmorland and Cumberland militia manning the castle garrision under Colonel Durand. The guns were fired and the Jacobites forced to retreat. The following day, a message was sent to the Mayor of Carlisle on Charles's behalf in which it was regretted that the city should have prepared to obstruct the passage of the army, and threatening the town with violence if its gates were not speedily opened. Inside the city walls, all was confusion. Durand and the garrison were pledged to stand firm against the invaders, but the acting Mayor, Thomas Pattenson, believed the rebel army to be in excess of 9,000 men. He despaired of success and was broken by news that the city could not look for imminent relief from Wade's forces as had been originally anticipated. The common people of Carlisle were thrown into the utmost confusion by the prospect of a Jacobite invasion. The women prepared for the event by hiding their children, in the belief that the Highlanders were cannibals.

On November 14, a deputation of townsmen and militia went out to Charles, who had by this time moved to Brampton in anticipation of an advance by Wade. They returned with the message that there would be no terms for the town unless the castle was surrendered simultaneously. The Jacobites were determined to profit by the lesson learned at Edinburgh. When it became clear from the activities of the besieging army that it intended to force an access into Carlisle, the resolve of the militia melted and 'multitudes went off every hour over the walls'. Although Durand himself remained defiant, he had no choice but to admit that, with the few men remaining to him, 'many of them extremely infirm', it was not possible to defend the castle. The town capitulated on the 14th, and on the morning of the 15th it was given up to the Duke of Perth. The next morning, the castle surrendered. In both castle and city, a number of serviceable cannon were discovered, although as a last gesture of defiance Colonel Durand had managed in a single-handed sortie to spike ten of the guns on the ramparts. The Jacobites succeeded to all the militia arms and an additional 1,000 stand secured in the castle. They also found quantities of cannon balls, 'grenadoes, small bombs, pickaxes and other military stores', as well as 100 barrels of gunpowder. In the midst of this welcome legacy, however, the rebels stumbled upon a chastening reminder of the fate of their predecessors in the form of 'many of the broadswords that were taken at Preston in 1715'. On November 17, Charles made his entry into the subdued city.

To Derby and Back Again

The strategy of a twin march into England fulfilled its purpose so far as confounding Marshal Wade and the troops at Newcastle. The city was strongly fortified in anticipation of a rebel advance, and Wade's army encamped upon the Town Moor awaited news of the Jacobites' entry into Northumberland.

Marshal George Wade (1673-1748) opposed Charles in England in 1745. Wade was known in Scotland for the military roads he constructed there in 1726-1733.

A local poet sang in the *Newcastle Courant:* 'Go trusty Wade the War important wage, And execute thy Nation's virtuous rage', but Wade did not go. While the rebels laid a false trail in the east, the real centre of their affairs lay some 60 miles from Newcastle to the west. Carlisle had already fallen before Wade made a move. On November 16, the encampment on the Town Moor was broken up and the government army set off for Hexham, but finding the roads impassable and realizing that Carlisle was beyond relief, the expedition returned to Newcastle. Meanwhile, in Carlisle, the historic decision to march into Lancashire was taken at a Jacobite Council of War held on the 18th. In addition to Wade's presence, an opposition force under Sir John Ligonier was on its way north and, earlier in the month, General Handasyde with Dreus and Ligonier's regiments of foot, the Glasgow, Paisley and Lothian Militia and Hamilton's and Gardiner's dragoons had established a defence at Stirling. The Jacobite army was confronted with an enemy in three directions and so far nothing justified optimism in the popularity of Charles's cause in England.

Leaving behind a garrison of 200 to 300 men, the Jacobite army began to quit Carlisle on November 20. To have stayed longer would have been to invite attack. Furthermore, it was imperative that the government armies in England should be prevented from amalgamating. Each was more than twice the size of Charles's own force. Lord George Murray recorded: 'it was agreed I should march with six regiments and some horse a day before the other six regiments'. He set out on the 20th and the Prince followed the next day. The prospect of invigorating the dormant Jacobites of Lancashire had the same fatal allure for Charles in 1745 as it had for General Forster in 1715. At the Council meeting held in Carlisle, the prevalent view had in fact favoured a retreat to Scotland and it was only the power of Charles's personal faith in the reliability of his many friends in England that swung the issue his way. He assured the faint-hearted that he had received fresh letters from English Jacobites promising him that he should find them all in arms on his arrival in Preston. His own invincible belief in the justice of his cause immunized him against indifference. He believed it was merely a matter of time before the entire English nation awoke to the strength of his claim. It was quite inconceivable to him that vast tracts of the population were happily ignorant of his history and viewed the progress of his crusade as a matter of small interest. The common people of Shap, Penrith, Kendal and Lancaster, who witnessed the passage of the rebel army, felt as little inclined to enlist in such a troupe of banditti as they would welcome hanging. People might turn out to stare amazed at the rugged Highlanders in their bizarre national costume, but if Charles looked for a spontaneous demonstration of affection, then he was sadly disappointed. Even where pockets of Stuart sympathy existed among the aristocracy, individuals required to be certain of the Chevalier's ultimate success before they would commit themselves or their subordinates to such a desperate bid for power.

On November 27, the entire force rested at Preston. The army was received with a feigned expression of pleasure, nothing like the unmitigated joy it had been led to expect. The general Jacobite mood must surely have been one of despondency. The town had depressing associations. A Scottish army had been defeated there in 1648 and the very cause for which the present army was prepared now to fight had been a casualty in the same place in 1715. The weather was bitterly cold and the journey had been exhausting. On the day the Jacobites rested in Preston, the Duke of Cumberland took over Sir John Ligonier's command at Lichfield. The Chevalier de Johnstone recorded that one of his sergeants, named Dickson, tried all day in Preston to attract recruits, but he failed to draw a single one. A more generous response was anticipated from the inhabitants of Manchester. The intrepid Dickson, stealing a march on the main body arrived prematurely in the city and was able to present Johnstone with 180 recruits by the time the army caught up with him on the evening of the 29th. A new regiment consisting entirely of Englishmen was to be raised under the title of the Manchester Regiment and Dickson's recruits were to make up more than half its strength, because it was never to exceed 300 men. Thereby, the clan chiefs were confirmed in their view that the English Jacobites were unreliable at best and treacherous in the main.

After some perfunctory celebrations, the army vacated Manchester on December 1. Lord George reported: 'when we came to Macclesfield (Dec. 1st.) we had certain intelligence that the Duke of Cumberland's army was on its march and were quartered at Litchfield, Coventry, Stafford and Newcastle under Line. We resolved to march for Derby; and to cover our intentions I offered to go with a column of the army to Congleton'.[13] The idea was to trick Cumberland into thinking that the entire Jacobite force was bearing down on him. He would react by

13. *Marches of the Highland Army*. From the MS. of Lord George Murray in *Jacobite Memoirs of the Rebellion of 1745*. Ed. from the MS. of Rev. Robert Forbes A.M. by Robert Chambers. Edin. 1834, P. 53.

collecting his troops and advance to meet the danger, thus leaving the way open for the main Jacobite body to slip around him and reach Derby unmolested. As a result of Lord George's enterprise, it was discovered that Cumberland had at his disposal 2,200 horse and about 8,000 foot. He apparently imagined that the Jacobites were taking a westward course to Wales and had concentrated his men at Stone, seven miles north of Stafford, thus making it a matter of no great difficulty to outflank him to the east. Having completed his part in the subterfuge, Lord George and his detachment slipped away and successfully united with the main column at Derby. In the December edition of the *Gentleman's Magazine,* the following extract from a hostile broadsheet appeared:

'On Wednesday, Dec. 4. about 11 o'clock, two of the rebel van-guard enter'd this town, and at their entrance gave a specimen of what we were to expect from such villains, by seizing a very good horse, belonging to young Mr. Stamford; after which they rode up to the George and there enquiring for the magistrates, demanded billets for 9,000 men, or more. In a short time after the van-guard rode into town, consisting of about 30 men, cloath'd in blue, fac'd with red; most of them had on scarlet waistcoats with gold lace, and being likely men made a good appearance. They were drawn up in the market-place, and sat on horseback 2 or 3 hours; at the same time the bells were rung and several bonfires made, to prevent any resentment from them . . . About 3 in the afternoon Lord Elcho, with the life-guards, and many of their chiefs also arriv'd, on horseback, to the number of about 150, most of them cloathed as above; these made a fine show, being the flower of their army; soon after their main body also march'd into town, in tolerable order, six or eight a-breast, with about 8 standards, most of them white flags and a red cross. They had several bagpipers, who play'd as they march'd along; they appear'd in general to answer the description we have all along had of them, viz. most of their main body a parcel of shabby, lousy, pitiful-look'd fellows, mix'd up with old men and boys; dress'd in dirty plaids, and as dirty shirts, without breeches, and wore their stockings made of plaid, not much above half way up their legs, and some without shoes, or next to none, and numbers of them so fatigu'd with their long march, that they really commanded our pity more than fear.'

The exhausted army had arrived safely, but for how long could it expect to be secure? Wade was coming up on them by forced marches and it would not be long before Cumberland awoke to the true situation. Farther south lay a third army equal in size to the other two. For Charles, the fact was inescapable that he had received a low return on his high investment of faith in the English malcontents and French assistors. Despite scrupulous attention to his public image, he was to those who bothered to read reports of his progress still the 'infatuate son of priestly Rome'. He found himself in hostile country and his army was hemmed in by enemies. It was the middle of winter and London, the soul of his ambition, lay some four days' march away. If, by some freak chance, the Jacobites were to reach the city unscathed, reports showed that they would encounter a vigilante force of massive proportions said to be gathering on Finchley Common to oppose them. By a miracle of ingenuity and determination, the tiny force had penetrated so far unharmed. To venture farther would be to invite annihilation.

The situation was closely debated at a Council of War held in Charles's headquarters in the Earl of Exeter's house. The extremity of their position did not deter Charles from arguing that the Council should pronounce in favour of an advance. 'His Royal Highness had no regard to his own danger, but pressed with all the force of argument to go forward. He did not doubt but the justness of his cause would prevail and he could not think of retreating after coming so far; and he was hopeful there might be a defection in the enemy's army and that severals would declare for him'.[14] It was eloquence bred of despair, because Charles knew that there was little chance of his view prevailing. There had been rumblings of discontent in the leadership of the army for a while. As far back as Manchester, retreat had been the unofficial counsel of many. On this occasion, Charles could carry with him only the Duke of Perth; 'every other officer declared their opinion for a retreat'.[15] John Daniel, one of the English gentlemen to join at Manchester, recorded in his journal an incident of ill-omen:

'Here I cannot pass by an accident that happened somewhat ominous — though I am none of the most credulous — but thence we may date our first misfortune. Great numbers of People and Ladies (who had come from afar to see the Prince) crowding into his room, overturned a table, which in falling overturned and broke the Royal Standard — soon after our return was agreed upon — so I leave the reader to judge and make his reflexions on this.'[16]

News that Lord John Drummond, brother of the Duke of Perth, had landed in Scotland from France with a regiment of his own Royal Scots and Irish picquets (50 men picked from each of six Irish regiments in the French service) appeared to strengthen the argument for retreat. These reinforcements, allied to the additional Scottish recruits being assembled under Lord Strathallan, who had been left in Scotland as commander-in-chief, made up a supplementary force worth falling back for.

Early on the morning of December 6, the retreat began. John Hay, who acted as secretary to Charles during Broughton's illness, recorded that 'very few knew that they were marching back'.[17] The inhabitants of Derby were, in the main, heartily glad to be rid of them. According to one hostile report, they had put up with much in the way of abuse. The Jacobites were accused of stealing tradesmen's good, 'viz. gloves, buckles, powder-flasks, buttons, handkerchiefs etc,; if they lik'd a person's shoes better than their own, demanding them off their feet, without pay . . . they broke open closets, chests, boxes etc. at several gentlemen's houses, took away all the guns, pistols, swords and all other arms they could find, in every house'.[18] A gentleman who had the misfortune to have six officers and 40 privates quartered on him referred to his guests as 'a band of Hottentots, wild monkies in a desert, vagrant gipsies'. Much of the equipment, acquired legitimately or otherwise, was left behind by the retiring army and this was taken as clear evidence of some confusion in their plans. Hay recorded that many of the prominent figures were kept in the dark about the retreat as well as the common men who had no inkling of their true destination when the evacuation began at 7 o'clock, on the morning of the 6th. Charles mounted on a black horse, left his lodging at 9 a.m. and by 11 o'clock, Derby had seen the last of the Jacobites save for a few stragglers. The morning was misty and dark and in the confusion of bodies it was difficult for the men to see exactly where they were going. Most believed that they were advancing towards Cumberland's force. As day dawned, so did enlightenment and the early evacuees, 'the men who had marched in the grey of the morning', wrote Hay, began to note with unease the details of a familiar landscape. '(They) began to know by day-light, from the marks they had taken of the road, that they were going back.' The revelation invoked a 'universal lamentation', and Charles Edward Stuart was not the least among the society of mourners. He had been forced to concede once

14. Lord George Murray. Op. Cit. P. 55.

15. Lord George Murray. Ibid.

16. *A True Account of Mr. John Daniel's Progress with Prince Charles.* Reprinted from a MS. preserved at Drummond Castle, in *Origins of the 'Forty-Five and Other Papers Relating to that Rising,* edited by Walter Biggar Blaikie, Edinburgh 1916. Published by Scottish History Society. Second Series. Vol. II Pp. 177-8.

17. *Account of the Retreat of the Rebels from Derby.* Appendix No. 32, Home.

18. *Gentleman's Magazine,* 1745. P. 707.

more that impetuousity makes a bad master in war, but this time he was utterly crushed by the lesson. He had come within a stone's throw of his objective and his was not the character to sustain with equanimity such a massive blow to his ambition. The retreat from Derby represented for him the dissolution of his hopes. With their death, his vitality, too, was extinguished. All the small acts of personal self-sacrifice, which had excited the admiration of his friends and invited emulation by his followers on the outward journey, now slipped into the realm of legend. Instead of rising at the crack of dawn, animating the men with lively conversation and striding at the head of the army like a Titan, Charles on the return trip rose late, spoke little and rode everywhere. 'He could not walk, and hardly stand' said Hay, 'as was always the case with him when he was cruelly used.' It was a mood of peevish disappointment that communicated itself too effectively to the rest of the army. Now, emulating the degeneration of their Prince, the Highlanders also felt disinclined to foot it back to Scotland empty-handed. Horse stealing became for the first time a commonplace activity. In the interest of the Prince's public image, severe restrictions had been placed on plundering for personal gain on the outward journey, but these rules lost a good deal of their definition with the fading of the Prince's own prospects. On the return journey, discipline was relaxed, although Lord George Murray, who always took a proprietory attitude towards the condition of the Highlanders, intervened frequently to prevent wholesale degeneration. But if the rebels were guilty of a shift in attitude towards the English general public, the defection was by no means unilateral. It only took the appearance of defeat to bring out the worst in the general mass of political equivocators who lined the routes of their return. Army personnel, returning to the billets they had occupied on the outward trip, found themselves

William Augustus, Duke of Cumberland, was the third son of George II. He commanded the Hanoverian forces at the Battle of Culloden.

coldly received. Agents provocateurs sent ahead by the government encouraged local militia and citizens to impede the rebels' progress by denying them essential goods and services and by destroying roads and bridges. The celebrations which had marked the Prince's arrival in Manchester were now definitely shown to be spurious when the mob turned out 'very hearty to have a brush' with the jaded insurgents, and in general the populace displayed a rather unpleasant eagerness to identify with the side of the victors. If Charles needed a reminder that his faith in the Lancastrians had been misplaced, it came in Manchester when an incompetent assassin made an attempt on his life, 'a villain, who mistaking him shot at a Mr. Sullivan, and luckly missed him'. If Charles had not already reached a spiritual nadir, this surely must have grieved him.

4 The Collapse of a Dream

Withdrawal to Scotland

As soon as it was understood that the Jacobite army was in retreat, the Duke of Cumberland made strenuous efforts to overtake and intercept it. Marshal Wade, on the march attempting in vain to halt the advance of the Jacobites, now received orders to cut across country and intercept their retreat. On December 10, the Jacobites were at Wigan and had already slipped past Wade who was at Wakefield on the same day. Wade attempted to make amends by sending his cavalry under General Oglethorpe to join Cumberland at Preston on December 13, while he himself retreated once more to the confines of Newcastle without having accomplished anything beyond his own frustration. The retreating army continued its march through country previously renowned for its strain of Jacobitism, but which now determined to dissociate itself from the cause. Denied bread, the Highlanders scattered barley and oats in straw upon the ground, set fire to it and then picked up the ears and consumed the parched corn. Replying to the hostile reception of their erstwhile friends, abuses committed by the Highlanders intensified. By December 15, the army had reached Kendal, where it was fired upon by the local populace. Here, at least, came the certain information that Wade was left behind and Charles supposed there was little danger now of the retreat to Scotland being cut off. But an army of 4,000 under Cumberland was only two days' march behind. There was at least the consolation that orders given to break down bridges and destroy roads served equally to impede the progress of the pursuing army as it did their own. Nevertheless, the government army enjoyed numerous advantages in pursuit denied the Jacobites in retreat, and eventually the gap between pursuer and pursued began to narrow. On the 18th, the Jacobite rear guard was attacked by government troops.

On December 17, the Jacobite main body arrived in Penrith to the customary hostile reception. The Penrith Beacon was fired to signal alarm and raise the county of Cumberland in protest. The artillery train and baggage under the supervision of Lord George Murray and some 500 Macdonalds, in addition to the normal escort, were trailing behind owing to the bad weather and the frequency of breakdowns among the transport wagons. That the army should have become split up in this was was a dangerous symptom of the growing disunity which infected the personal relationship between Charles and Lord George. As far back in the campaign as the occupation of Carlisle, Lord George had opened up a breach in their affairs by resigning his commission on the ground that the Prince did not sufficiently take him into his confidence. He was persuaded to resume his duties, but the rupture had far-reaching consequences. At Derby, Charles had noted with bitterness, that chief among the opponents of his policy was Lord George himself. Once the retreat began, the petulant Prince found it difficult to control his hostility under a general necessity for co-operation. He appears to have sought vindication against Lord George by frustrating his plans in a petty way. To accommodate the retreat, Lord George requested that two-wheeled ammunition carts be used instead of the normal four-wheeled wagons commonly used on good roads, because he anticipated, quite accurately, that the state of the roads north of Lancashire would be impassable with the heavier vehicles. His request was ignored. As a consequence, the ammunition and baggage train was under constant threat of breakdown and fell farther and farther behind the main body, because the time taken to manhandle the waterlogged wagons put distance between the rear guard and the rest. When the main body reached Penrith, the rear guard was struggling to reach Shap, about ten miles away, and that with 'some difficulty' according to Johnstone who was in the struggling party.

When setting out from Shap on the morning of the 18th to join the rest, the detachment had scarcely begun its march when it discovered a number of light horse continually hovering about, just out of musketshot. According to Home, these were not regular troops but Cumberland people and other volunteers, mounted to harrass the rebels. As the Jacobites prepared to ascend a hill which lay in their path, they were disconcerted to see cavalry patrolling the summit and hear 'a prodigious number of trumpets and kettle-drums' (Johnstone). It was quite impossible to calculate the numbers that might be grouping beyond the hilltop, but nevertheless, the Jacobites bounded up the slope and were agreeably surprised to discover, on reaching the summit, not a panorama of potential aggressors but only 300 light horse and chasseurs who immediately fled in disorder.

The march was resumed, but in less than an hour after the disturbing incident, they were forced to halt again because of a broken wagon. Because Lord George had received strict instructions from Charles to leave nothing behind that could be utilized by the pursuing army, 'not so much as a cannon ball' — it was necessary to send to a nearby farm for a replacement, and await its arrival. In the interval, the Duke's men came within striking distance of their quarry. The Jacobites had resumed their march and covered two miles when the government army fell on the Macdonalds in the rear of the column. Because the road was narrow and flanked by hedges and ditches, the government cavalry could not be deployed to any great advantage. The technique adopted by the Highlanders in such conditions was to stand firm against attack and, after repulsing their aggressors, to turn and rejoin the tail of their own retreating column. They continued in this way for a mile, 'the cavalry continually renewing the charge, and the Highlanders always repulsing them, repeating the same manoeuvre, and behaving like lions' (Johnstone). When Clifton Hall was reached, a few miles south of Penrith, Macpherson of Clunie and some reinforcements came to the aid of the embattled Macdonalds. An anonymous journalist described what happened then in the following narrative:

'After the Baggage was sent to Penrith, a Battalion of Foot and some Horse, went thro' Lord Lonsdale's Parks of Lowther, thinking to find some of the Light-Horse about his House, as he was Lord Lieutenant of the County; Accordingly some of them were seen at a Distance but rode off upon Sight of the Highlanders: Some Shots were fired after them. At the same Time, some Parties scouring the Parks, took a Running Footman of the Duke of Cumberland's, and another Person clothed in Green, who appeared to be an Officer; who informed that the Duke of Cumberland was within a Mile, with about 4000 Horse and Dragoons, besides Light-Horse and Militia; upon which Lord George Murray, who always commanded the Rear Guard, took Possesssion of a Village called Clifton, being a Mile from Lord Lonsdale's House, upon the Highway to, and two Miles short of Penrith.'[1]

With the main body of the Jacobite army not far distant, and nightfall coming on, Lord George decided to send for reinforcements to Penrith, in case the brush with Cumberland's detachment should develop into an engagement. Shortly after sunset, his fears began to take shape and almost simultaneously came the reply from Penrith that the main body of the army was going to leave immediately for Carlisle. Lord George was ordered by Charles to abandon all thought of an action and march in pursuit at once. Lord George, however, was confident that he could 'dislodge' Cumberland's men by a 'brisk attack', because in his view the enemy

numbered less than 500. In any event, the affair was now too far advanced for abandonment. The same anonymous Jacobite narrator takes up the story:

'. . the Enemy form'd upon an open Muir, facing Clifton, and within half Cannon-Shot; where they continued for a considerable Time: At last, about an Hour after Sun-set, they dismounted several of their Dragoons, who came to the Bottom of the Muir, and lin'd the Hedges and Ditches that were next to it. There was a pretty smart Fire on both sides, for about half an Hour; but at last the Dragoons firing very fast, a Battallion of Highlanders was ordered down Sword in Hand upon them, with Orders to drive them from their Posts, but not to advance upon the Muir. Accordingly they went on with the greatest Alacrity and Swiftness, and after passing two Hedges, drove them from the third, which was the last of all, and then returned, as they were ordered, to their former Posts. But twelve of the Highlanders, having past the bottom Ditch, and run up the Muir are still a-missing, which is the whole Loss on their Side. How many of the Dragoons were killed and wounded is uncertain; but several Circumstances, such as Broad-Swords taken from the Dragoons, and the Report of the Wounded dressed at Penrith next Day, cannot be less than a hundred.'

Despite the fact that the action had taken place in opposition to his command, Charles was well pleased with the outcome.

After the small but decisive affair at Clifton, the Jacobites marched all night for the relative safety of Carlisle where the whole army congregated on the 19th, the rear guard arriving ragged and footsore in the grey light of dawn. The day was spent in resting, while plans were worked out for the next move. Although Lord Drummond's reinforcements and the fresh recruits collected under Lord

---

1. *Journal of the Marches of His Royal Highness the Prince Regent's Army, from the Time they entered England the 8th of November till their Return to Scotland, the 20th December 1745.* Reprinted in *Historical Papers relating to the Jacobite Period.* Edited by Colonel James Allardyce, Vol. I. Printed for the New Spalding Club, Aberdeen MDCCCXCV, Pp. 283-6.

Lord John Drummond, brother of the titular Duke of Perth, raised the Royal Scots Regiment in France and served at Falkirk and Culloden.

Strathallan at Perth had been ordered to march south, it became clear that they were not coming and would have to be sought in Scotland. Charles, highly reluctant to abandon his last foothold in England, decided to march the main body back across the border, while leaving a garrison of between 300 and 400 men at Carlisle. All but Charles himself seemed to appreciate that Carlisle was in no condition to withstand a siege. Johnstone wrote: 'it was not in a condition to resist a cannonade of four hours being utterly untenable, and a thousand times worse than an

intrenched camp in an open country'. Charles placed great reliance in the fact that Cumberland's force was without heavy artillery, but this was an omission easily supplied, as later events were to demonstrate. The project developed a grim aspect when it was interpreted as a deliberate sacrifice of unwilling victims to the army's convenience. The garrison, it was rumoured, would act as a bait to amuse Cumberland's men while the rest of the army escaped clean away. But, according to John Daniel's account of the business, the Colonel of what was left of the Manchester regiment, on discovering that some of his men were opposed to the idea of entering Scotland, petitioned to be left behind, and O'Sullivan, who had a strong claim on the Prince's confidence said in his narrative: 'It was agreed upon in the Counsel that there should be a garrison left, those of the officers that stayed there, desired it themselves'.[2] Furthermore, it seems that in selecting the men who were to constitute this forlorn hope, Charles was at pains to choose a number of officers who held French commissions and would therefore be entitled, in case of capture, to be treated as prisoners of war rather than rebels. Once again, there was friction between Charles and Lord George. Recent experience had exposed the danger of hauling artillery across rough country in bad weather, and Murray wanted to leave all the guns behind at Carlisle. Charles protested, having a kind of blind faith in the efficacy of these engines of destruction which was quite independent of experience. The guns had so far proved nothing but an encumbrance and had been lugged about to no beneficial effect. Nevertheless, Charles insisted that at least three of them should accompany the army to Scotland. This was eventually agreed.[3]

The main body left Carlisle on December 20, the Prince's birthday, according to the English calendar.[4] He was 25 years old. At about two o'clock in the afternoon, they reached the River Esk, swollen by heavy rains

2. John William O'Sullivan's narrative reproduced from Stuart Papers at Windsor in *1745 and After* by A. & H. Tayler. P. 110 The published list of officers and men taken at Carlisle shows the names of only eight Frenchmen, while the number of English taken exceeded 100, and over twice that number of Scots were sacrificed.

3. 'I think that Charles, who had set his heart on leaving not a cannon ball behind placed the garrison to guard his guns, all

but three of which he could not carry across the Esk'. Andrew Lang in *Prince Charles Edward*, 1900. P. 150.

4. The new or Continental Reckoning was eleven days in advance of the old or English style. Old Style was used in Great Britain until 1752 and the birthday of Prince Charles Edward is sometimes given as December 20, Old Style, or December 31, New Style.

and almost impassable. Using a technique whereby a section of the river was marked off by placing cavalry above and below the chosen point of crossing, the soldiers linked arms and forded the flood, ten or twelve abreast, often with little more than their heads visible above the water. This particular crossing took almost two hours and was accomplished without loss among the men, but sadly, one or two of the stalwart female camp followers were swept to a watery grave. Once safely established on the other side, the bedraggled men thawed their limbs and warmed their spirits by breaking into reels. 'The pipes began to play so soon as we passed and the men all danced reels, which in a moment dried them', said Lord George. The army had left Scotland on November 8, and now returned in circumstances vastly different from those envisaged by its leader. For the men, however, it was sufficient to have survived the ordeal and be back once again in their native country:

'It is certain, that by all Accidents, such as Deaths, by Sickness (of which 'tis believed there were more in one Day in General Wade's Army, than was in six Weeks in his Royal Highness's Army) and the People that went astray in Plundering (which notwithstanding all the Officers were able to do, could not be entirely prevented) and were not heard of again, that his Royal Highness's Army did not lose forty Men in the Expedition, including the Twelve at Penrith. Upon the Whole, never was a March performed with more Chearfulness, and executed with greater Vigour and Resolution; . .'[5]

The return was inauspicious, but at least the retreat had preserved the characteristics of a planned withdrawal where it might easily have degenerated into headlong flight.

The army now divided with the object, again, of confounding any pursuers. One body

quartered that night at Annan in Dumfriesshire and the other at Ecclefechan. The van of the army reached Glasgow on Christmas Day, and Charles arrived with the main body the next evening. The Jacobites had completed a round trip on foot of nearly 600 miles in 56 days, an impressive achievement when bad roads, freezing weather, and the hardships of the return journey are considered.

Meanwhile, at Carlisle, the garrison was forced to surrender to Cumberland on December 30, after he had procured some 18-pounders from Whitehaven with which to bombard the castle. The composition of the Duke's army at this time, according to Johnstone, was as follows: of infantry regiments, he had those of Ligonier, Richmond, Sinclair, Albemarle, Howard, Skelton, Bland, Semphill, Bligh, Douglas, Leslie, Bernard, Roper, Sowle, Johnson, Gower, Montague, Halifax, Granby and Cholmondeley; of cavalry, he had the regiments of Montague and Kingston, plus the horse detached from Wade's army earlier and a force of Dutch auxiliaries. Each infantry regiment was reckoned to be over 800 strong and the cavalry regiments about 300. The city was surrounded the day after the Jacobite army left and the castle garrison managed to maintain the semblance of a defence only until the arrival of the big guns on the 28th. On the 30th, Mr. Hamilton, the governor hung out the white flag. The garrison surrendered under terms that saved the defenders from being put to the sword but reserved them for 'his Majesty's pleasure', which was just a euphemism for death deferred. After taking Carlisle, the Duke of Cumberland returned to London. A detachment of government troops under the command of General Hawley was ordered to pursue the rebels into Scotland.

There can be little doubt but that Charles was badly shaken by the loss of Carlisle. He had been guilty of a strategic error and the loss of the garrison at Carlisle represented the worst blow in a campaign so far remarkable for its lack of military action.

5. *Journal of the Marches of His Royal Highness the Prince Regent's Army.* Supra.

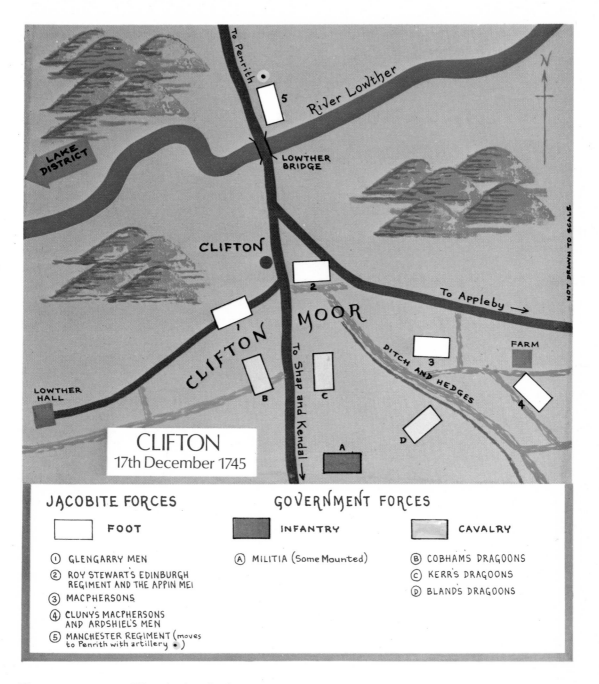

CLIFTON
17th December 1745

JACOBITE FORCES

☐ FOOT

① GLENGARRY MEN
② ROY STEWART'S EDINBURGH REGIMENT AND THE APPIN MEI
③ MACPHERSONS
④ CLUNY'S MACPHERSONS AND ARDSHIEL'S MEN
⑤ MANCHESTER REGIMENT (moves to Penrith with artillery ●)

GOVERNMENT FORCES

■ INFANTRY   ☐ CAVALRY

Ⓐ MILITIA (Some Mounted)
Ⓑ COBHAMS DRAGOONS
Ⓒ KERR'S DRAGOONS
Ⓓ BLAND'S DRAGOONS

Map labels: To Penrith · River Lowther · LOWTHER BRIDGE · LAKE DISTRICT · CLIFTON · CLIFTON MOOR · To Appleby → · NOT DRAWN TO SCALE · To Shap and Kendal → · DITCH AND HEDGES · FARM · LOWTHER HALL

The engagement at Clifton is described on pages 117-118.

A private of the Lally Regiment and a gentleman of the Prince's Life Guard. Picquets of
three Irish regiments (Dillon, Lally and Roth)
were present at Culloden. These regiments
(The Wild Geese) were all in the French service
and, because of this, were among the few to
be well treated as prisoners-of-war after the
battle. The Prince's Life Guard were among the
few Jacobite 'cavalry' to retain their horses after Culloden.

A gunner and an officer of the Royal Artillery. Unlike
the 1715 uprising, the Crown had a standing body of
artillery with trained men at the time of the second
rebellion. Although the pieces were handled by
soldiers, the drivers and waggoners were still
civilians, often hired locally to move the guns. The
transport of artillery was a problem in the Highlands,
but the cannon were used to good effect by Cumberland's gunners at Culloden.

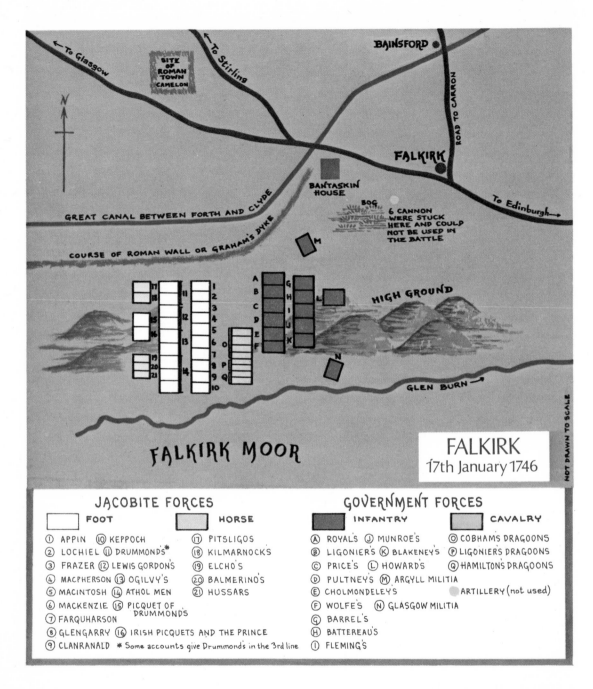

The map shows the positions of the rival armies at Falkirk (see pages 127-131).

The Battle of Falkirk

During the period of Charles's absence in England, Jacobite affairs in Scotland did not come to a standstill. On the contrary, the interval produced a significant improvement in Charles Edward's prospects of raising a healthy, powerful army. Under the impression that the Jacobites were blazing a victorious trail through England, the clan Fraser eventually decided to come out on the side of the victors and, under their chief's son, they staged a somewhat ineffectual blockade of Fort Augustus. More successful was Lord Lewis Gordon, who established a Jacobite headquarters at Aberdeen. He succeeded in raising men and money from neighbouring counties to strengthen the cause, and scored a military victory over a party of MacLeods mobilized on behalf of the government. Lord Loudon and President Forbes of Culloden continued, as before, to organize well-disposed clans in the King's interest and the far north was effectively under their control, with Inverness as the headquaters for those taking up arms on behalf of the government. Perth resumed the purpose it had served 30 years earlier, during the 'Fifteen, as the rallying point for further Jacobite recruits. On a high estimate, it was thought to contain some 4,000 fresh supporters by the time the jaded army returned from England. Of French reinforcements to leave their native shore, only a small proportion actually arrived in Scotland owing to the efficiency of English cruisers in the Channel. The most notable casualty of English vigilance was Fitzjames's regiments of horse. Out of the full complement embarked, never more than a few troops were ever employed on active service in Scotland. In addition to these and Lord John Drummond's Royal Scots raised in France, and the Irish picquets, the remainder of the new recruits fell into two categories — those that were tardy members of the clans already gone into England, and those newly converted to the cause. It was a heterogeneous

force and disputes had not been uncommon among its leaders. This was the principal reason for its having remained immobile, in opposition to injunctions to move south.

It was anticipated that the Jacobites would go to Edinburgh when news of the return crossing was received in Scotland, and immediately the government troops at Stirling marched back to the capital to protect it from the ravages of a second occupation. Glasgow, as a destination, had little appeal for Charles, because its citizens were distinguished by their unswerving devotion to the Hanoverian dynasty and the Protestant Succession. During the week of his sojourn there, Charles was heard to remark that 'nowhere had he found so few friends', and while the city had raised at its own expense some 1,200 men for the suppression of the rebellion, the Jacobites made fewer than 60 recruits in a week. In the same time, the army lost more than that number of deserters. After placing an order for 12,000 shirts, 6,000 cloth coats, 6,000 pairs of stockings and 6,000 waistcoats with the refractory tradesmen of Glasgow, a partially refitted army was reviewed on Glasgow Green. John Daniel, still with the Jacobites and a long way from his Lancashire home, said: 'we marched out with drums beating, colours flying, bagpipes playing and all the marks of a triumphant army to the appointed ground, attended by multitudes of people, who had come from all parts to see us'. His narrative began to falter, however, when he described the person of the Prince on this occasion, an old Cavalier's devotion obviously clouding his perception and colouring his judgment.

'I am somewhat at a loss to give a description of the Prince as he appeared at the review. No object could be more charming, no personage more captivating, no deportment more agreeable than his at that time was; for, being well mounted and princely attired, having all the best endowments of both body and mind, he appeared to bear a sway, above any comparison, with the heroes of the last age; and the majesty and grandeur he displayed were truly noble and divine.'

A less flattering observer, who managed to get 'so near him . . that I could have touched him with my hand', remembered most vividly after an interval of years only the dejected air and melancholy aspect of the Prince, and took this for a sign that 'he evidently wanted confidence in his cause'.

On January 3, 1746, the same day that the Duke of Cumberland left Carlisle for London, the Jacobite army left Glasgow and made its way towards Stirling, with the object of capturing the city and castle. Once again the army divided. Charles took one column via Kilsyth to Bannockburn where he established his headquarters, and Lord George Murray with six battalions of the clans proceeded via Cumbernauld to Falkirk. According to O'Sullivan, the Prince had sent 'expresses upon expresses to Lord John Drummond to joyn him Armes & Bagage with all the diligence possible near Stirling', but Lord John had discovered an impediment in the transportation of the heavy guns he had brought with him from France. When, finally, a junction was made and new and old recruits combined alike in one body, the Jacobite muster-master, Patullo, put their total number at 9,000, certainly the greatest mass of men Charles was ever able to attract to his standard at one time, during the Rebellion.

On January 8, Stirling town surrendered to the invaders after only slight hesitation, but the castle remained independent, under the protection of 74-year-old Major-general Blakeney, who retired with men and provisions into the impregnable fortress built upon a precipitous rock and refused to surrender. It was a familiar situation. The Jacobites mounted a siege operation which eventually became more remarkable for its doggedness than for any success it enjoyed.

Men were picked off by the garrison, batteries erected to elevate the Jacobite guns collapsed, trenches were laboriously hacked out of the stony ground, and none of this made the slightest impression on the fortress or its occupants. Meanwhile, on January 6, General Hawley, appointed to the command of government forces in Scotland, had reached Edinburgh. He had under his command not only that part of Cumberland's army ordered to pursue the rebels into Scotland, but also all the British infantry regiments in the army commanded by Wade, which had been ordered to march from Newcastle to Edinburgh. From New Year's Day onward, government troops were arriving in Edinburgh, the whole concentration eventually amounting to three regiments of dragoons, and 14 battalions of foot, plus volunteers.

For Lieutenant-General Henry Hawley, the prospect of striking a decisive blow against Jacobitism represented not only his official duty, but it was also a private indulgence, because he had been present as a Major of Evans's Dragoons at Sheriffmuir in 1715 and he now welcomed the chance to superimpose upon his memory of the indecisive engagement a fresh impression of total success. He was a man reputedly 'brave and able, with no small bias to the brutal', and his opinion of the rebel army was contemptuous — 'I do and allwayes shall despise these Rascalls', he wrote to the Duke of Newcastle. In his view, the Jacobites were incapable of standing against well drilled cavalry. With the experience of Dettingen and Fontenoy behind him, he had no doubt of his ultimate success, but nevertheless took the precaution of warning his men about the fighting tactics of the Highlanders to abate their fears. If they remembered their training and retained their composure they would find the Highlanders 'the most despicable Enemy that are', he averred. On January 13, Hawley sent an advance guard under General Huske from Edinburgh in search of his quarry. On the 15th, the main force followed, with Hawley himself bringing up the rear escorted by Cobham's dragoons. The object of the expedition was to relieve Stirling of its oppressors, but the army was never to get beyond Falkirk.

A reconnaissance party under Lord George Murray encountered the van of the regular army at Linlithgow on the 13th. Once it was established that an engagement with Hawley was imminent, the Jacobite soldiers were withdrawn from their various encampments in and around Stirling and were concentrated around Bannockburn, with the exception of some 1,200 men who were left to continue the siege of the castle. Beginning on the 15th, the army drew up in line of battle for three successive days in anticipation of an attack from Hawley. On the 17th, when the expected attack once again failed to materialize, the decision was made to take the offensive. In Council, Lord George's topographical knowledge led him to suggest that the army make for a piece of rising ground known as the 'hill of Falkirk', a ridge of barren moorland lying less than a mile above the government camp. This was agreed to and accorded well with the Highlanders' predilection for establishing themselves in an elevated position prior to battle. All things being in accord, between twelve and one o'clock on the 17th, the Jacobite army headed for Falkirk, but not before a diversionary tactic had been set up, whereby Lord John Drummond was sent off earlier to pursue a different course to that proposed for the main force in order that his activities might distract the attention of any government spies away from the principal manoeuvre. As one of the features of the landscape separating the rival armies was a large wood, it was not difficult to have Lord John appear on the north side of it, while the army proceeded quietly to the south.

The tactic was a complete success if the memoirs of government partisans in the ensuing battle are to be believed. One, William Corse, serving with the Glasgow regiment in Hawley's force, said 'about eleven o'clock we got the alarm, & in a very short space were all under Arms . . . Then we found out it was a false alarm'.[6] The first alarm was given when Drummond's activities were spotted. A little before two o'clock, a second alarm was sounded and there could be no doubting its seriousness this time. The surprise was complete. General Hawley was not even present in the camp when the main force of Jacobites was identified just a mile and a half away and heading for Falkirk Muir. In his absence, company commanders began drawing up their men in front of the camp. When Hawley arrived, flushed from his entertainment at Callender House, an order was given for the three dragoon regiments to march up the hill which as yet still separated the armies and establish themselves upon it before the Highlanders could do so. Home, who was present as a volunteer on the government side remarked that 'the cavalry was a good way before the infantry and for some time it seemed a sort of race between the Highlanders and the dragoons, which of them should get first to the top of the hill'. But the Royal army was not only disadvantaged by being surprised: 'at the very instant the regiments of foot began to march the day was overcast, and by and by a storm of wind and rain beat directly in the face of the soldiers'. The Jacobites had this foul weather at their backs and were able to form up and protect their weapons from the rain. Under a lowering sky, the government infantry struggling up the hill in the teeth of the gale could scarcely see where they were going and were completely unable to prevent the driving rain from soaking their firearms. As a consequence, not one in five of their firelocks was serviceable. Most of the infantry failed to reach the plateau at the top of the moor and the King's regiments of foot were positioned on the downward slope of the hill during the action. The government side had not the slightest possibility of getting its cannon up the slope, pitted as it was with folds

6. *Culloden Papers*. Published from the originals in the Possession of Duncan George Forbes of Culloden, Esq., London 1815. P. 270.

and ridges and intersected at one point by a deep ravine. Most of the guns stuck fast in the mud at the bottom of the hill, 'so that we were upon an equal footing with them in that respect, we bringing none with us' remarked John Daniel on the Jacobite side. It had certainly not been Charles's intention to jettison his precious guns, but in the final race for the hill the Jacobites had been obliged to leave the artillery behind. It was the only point of parity between the rival armies. In all other respects, the Jacobites had the advantage. Theirs was the numerically superior force, it had the advantage of surprise and descent and even the wind was blowing their way. Perhaps more important was the fact that the initiative gave them licence to meet Hawley's men on ground unsuitable for regular troops.

When the Jacobite front line was drawn up, it consisted entirely of Highlanders. The three Macdonald regiments of Keppoch, Clanranald and Glengarry had the right of the line. Next to them stood a small battalion of Farquharsons. To the left of these were the Mackenzies, Macintoshes, Macphersons and then on the left came the Frasers, Camerons and Stewarts of Appin. The second line consisted of Lord George Murray's Atholl brigade, Lord Ogilvy's and Lord Lewis Gordon's regiments, some Maclachlans and Lord John Drummond's regiment, the last having rejoined the main body after the feint. It rankled with Lord George that O'Sullivan, who was made Adjutant-General, should not have nominated in advance the commanders who were to serve the various parts of the line. He said in an aggrieved tone, 'I had asked twice that morning who was to command in the different stations, and his Royal Highness went and talked of it to some others, but I got no answer'. In the event, Murray himself took command on the right and Lord John Drummond was reputed to have served the left, although Murray in his querulously critical account of the battle said that he was not in position

when the action commenced. Charles Edward, himself, was in the rear of the second line with the French regulars and Irish picquets and some horse as a body of reserve. O'Sullivan commented wryly that most of the Jacobite horse 'was not fit to be set in Line of Battle'. The battleground itself was reminiscent of Sheriffmuir, with patches of marshy ground and undulations so great that it was frequently impossible for the men on either side to see the full extent of their own or their enemy's lines.

The Royal army was also drawn up in two lines with a body of reserve. The front line consisted of a battalion of the Royals, of the regiments of Wolfe, Cholmondeley, Pultney, Price and Ligonier. The Royals[7] had the right and Wolfe's the left. The second line contained Barrel's regiment, Blakeney's, Munro's, Battereau's and Fleming's. Barrel's had the right and Blakeney's the left. Howard's regiment formed a body of reserve. The opposing lines, it appears, were not drawn up directly opposite each other. The right of the government front line stood opposite the ravine mentioned earlier. It was separated by the ravine from the Camerons and Stuarts on the left of the Jacobite line and it outflanked them by at least two regiments, whereas the left of the government front line was itself considerably outflanked by the Jacobite right. The dragoons, which had been sent off first, were so spaced out that they covered the greater part of the whole Jacobite front line and gave rise to O'Sullivan's impression that 'the most part of the enemy's first ligne was all horse'. On the morning of the battle, Hawley's army had received a fresh injection of support in the shape of three companies of Lord Loudon's regiment and some of the Black Watch. The 12 battalions of foot each contained about 400 men; the dragoon regiments 200 each and the Glasgow regiment, which being newly raised was not allowed a place in either of the lines but stood apart, was about 700 strong. Hawley had at his disposal slightly

7. St. Clair's, the oldest foot regiment in the British Army, were referred to as the Royal Scots, or the Royals. Lord John Drummond on the Jacobite side gave the same nomenclature to his regiment which was composed of Scottish exiles. Drummond's regiment are often referred to as the Scots Royals to prevent confusion with St. Clair's, the Royal Scots.

less than 7,000 men. The Jacobites numbered about 1,000 more.

The action commenced when, from the right and left of the government horse, two columns were detached and began to advance at a fast trot. Half of the government infantry had yet to line up when Hawley gave the order for the dragoons to advance and Colonel Francis Ligonier commanding them is reputed to have said that it was the 'most extraordinary order that ever was given'. Hawley perhaps wanted to test his theory that the Highlanders could not stand against a cavalry charge. The dragoons themselves were horrified by the idea of attacking unsupported by foot, but they came on 'as boldly as any troops in the world'. Lord George Murray, advancing on foot at the head of the Macdonalds on the right with his sword drawn and target ready, encouraged the Highlanders forward 'foot by foot', continually trimming their line, exhorting them to keep their ranks and commanding them to hold their fire. The dragoons pounded towards them through the sleet. When they were within ten or twelve paces of the Highlanders, Lord George gave the order to fire. When the first shot rang out, an observer noted the time to be ten minutes to four. The Macdonalds of Keppoch began the discharge and the fire ran down the line from them to Lord Lovat's regiment of Frasers. In 'the third part of a minute', the torrent which had threatened to sweep all before it was stemmed. Immediately Hamilton's and Ligonier's (previously Gardiner's) dragoons wheeled about and, in a manoeuvre not entirely unknown to them, fled the field, leaving about 80 of their number dead on the spot. Cobham's dragoons turned to the right and galloped off at full speed between the lines, 'as if they run'd the gauntellet, exposed to the fire of almost all the ligne', said O'Sullivan. If Johnstone is to be believed, however, some of the dragoons penetrated the Highland line and set about 'trampling the Highlanders under the feet of their horses', while the Highlanders replied by stretching on the ground and thrusting their dirks into the bellies of the animals. For William Corse, on the government side, who was only two-thirds of the way up the hill with the Glasgow regiment, the battle must have appeared lost before it had properly begun. The fleeing dragoons fell in with the militia '& carry'd off about a Company of our people, among whom I was', said Corse. 'Some of us they rode over, and some of us ran and rode so well that we got quit of them in about 5 or 600 yards, with the utmost difficulty'. The civilian drivers of all but three of the government gun teams still struggling up the hill immediately ran off with the horses. It was a disastrous start for the King's army.

Five minutes after the first fire, the Jacobite left wing consisting of Camerons, Stewarts, Frasers and Macphersons was charged by the enemy's foot and 'also a body of horse' reported Lord George Murray. Some of the Highlanders on the left, being unable to resist the temptation to fire off pot shots at Cobham's dragoons fleeing through no man's land, now found themselves with empty guns. The weather being what it was, the Highlanders had abandoned the idea of trying to reload their muskets (they did not use cartridges) and a good many were without answering fire when attacked. Those whose weapons were primed aimed at the oncoming horses and then all fell to with drawn swords upon the men. It was the type of attack the regular troops most abhorred and in no time impetuosity triumphed over orthodoxy. The regular soldiers were driven down the hill amid terrifying scenes of slaughter. Meanwhile, on the opposite wing, despite Lord George's restraining influence, order had given way to chaos. With a rousing huzza, the Highlanders followed up their first successful blow by breaking ranks and descending in their characteristic wild stampede upon the fleeing dragoons. They fell in full cry on the first line of government foot. It was what Lord

George had feared most; he had lost control of them. But the Highlanders' greatest strength was their recklessness and the government troops, with their temperamental guns, were in no mood to withstand shock tactics. After giving their erratic fire, they did not pause to draw their bayonets or short swords but fled in droves from the torrent which threatened to engulf them. The second line did not even pause to fire. With the exception of Barrel's regiment, the entire line disappeared. Only parts of Ligonier's and Price's regiments of foot remained of the first line. It was now left to this tripartite remnant of a once disciplined army to salvage what it could of the day. Acting in concert and following orders to fire on the flank of the pursuing Highlanders, these stalwarts began to gain a little ground on the hill but were spared a greater effort by the prevailing air of incredulity on the other side. It was difficult for the Jacobite leaders to grasp the fact that so few remained of their formidable adversaries. Drummond refused to believe that men who had fought at Fontenoy could be so easily broken. 'Surely this is a feint', he was heard to cry and, believing that the few resistors were luring the Jacobites into an ambush, the rebel pursuit was called off.

Neither of the triumphant Jacobite wings could perceive the success of the other because the two were separated by ground too uneven to permit a clear view. Lord George Murray could only see that on his side the enemy was in full flight and that unless he could rally the Highlanders nothing could be done to cut off the retreat. He tried desperately to regroup his men, but it was hopeless. For the Highlanders, victory came when the enemy showed a clean pair of heels. Any deeper tactical consideration had little appeal for them. With the expenditure of all their energy in the opening gambit, they responded but limply to the suggestion of reassembly. Moreover, they were highly superstitious, and Lord George said, 'one vast loss was that not a pair of pipes coud be got'. Without them, the Highlanders refused to rally and although it appears a trivial oversight, Lord George evidently regarded the omission as important. The pipers, who normally charged with the rest of the line, threw their instruments to their boys who could not be found at the crucial moment.

On Drummond's side, the situation was less clear cut. When the pursuit was called off, some of the Jacobites, imagining that they had sustained a defeat, began to wander about in a state of confusion. Some left the field altogether and numbers of them turned up later that evening in Bannockburn to report on how they had lost the day. The space between the two wings was virtually empty save for stragglers and Charles came forward with the Irish picquets to fill the void and encourage the bewildered men to recover their muskets and re-form their companies. A principal factor in the general chaos was the disobedience of the Jacobite second line. Instead of holding its position, all, save the Athollmen on Lord George's wing had fallen in with the first line, over-anxious to have a share in the action. Lord George's fears might well have attracted their logical conclusion if the government army had been in the slightest degree capable of exploiting the ill-discipline of its adversaries, but it was not.

It began to grow dark and the rain continued to fall. 'At this moment', said Home, 'the field of battle presented a spectacle seldom seen in war. Part of the King's Army, much the greater part, was flying to the eastward and part of the rebel army was flying to the westward'. Neither side was inclined to prolong the action. The Royal army was soundly, even disgracefully beaten. The fact that a fragment of Hawley's army remained in possession of part of the field when the Jacobites withdrew was interpreted by government partisans as evidence of a drawn match, but Hawley writing that night to the Duke of Cumberland confessed 'My heart is broke'. It had taken his contemptible foe just 20 minutes to shatter his illusions.

The Jacobite losses in the Battle of Falkirk, as the action came to be known, amounted to about 50 killed and between 60 and 80 wounded. Hawley was unwilling to publish the true facts about government losses. The official return showed 12 officers killed and 55 privates as well as 280 wounded and missing, but Home thought that at least 16 officers were lost and between 300 and 400 privates. O'Sullivan intimated that it was fairly clear that a number of regular officers had been killed because 'goold watcheses were at a cheap rate'. The action was barely over before the Highlanders fell to stripping the bodies of the fallen. The Chevalier de Johnstone, forced out onto the battlefield on the night of the 18th to mount guard over some captured cannon, lost his way in the dark and eventually found himself wandering about in a ghoulish landscape of plundered dead, 'among heaps of dead bodies, which their whiteness rendered visible, notwithstanding the obscurity of a very dark night . . I even remarked a trembling and strong agitation in my horse which constantly shook when it was forced to put its feet on the heaps of dead bodies and climb over them'. It was a grisly enough memorial to the previous day's work. The next day, a pit was dug on the battlefield by local people, into which the bodies were unceremoniously piled. 'The rustics who stood around easily distinguished the English soldiers from the Highlanders, by their comparative nudity, and by the deep gashes which scarred their shoulders and breasts - the dreadful work of the broadsword. It was also remarked that all the Highlanders had bannocks or other articles of provision concealed under their left armpits.'[8]

Up and down the country, the news of Hawley's unexpected defeat was received with incredulity. Government partisans, who had not contemplated a reverse, distorted the facts to suit their own bias. The *London Gazette* carried the following misleading account of the action by a writer who chose to take a part of the action and represent it as the whole:

'The rebels by all accounts lost many more men than the King's forces, and could not improve the advantages they had at the beginning of the action, but were driven back by, and fled before, a handful of our army, and we remain'd masters of the field.'

Less prominence was given to the news that a court martial was ordered for some officers and men 'who behaved ill' in action, or indeed to the fact that some were cashiered, others hanged and still more whipped for desertion or cowardice, once Hawley recovered his broken spirit.

Three days before the Battle of Falkirk, King George had opened a new session of Parliament with the statement that he did not think it proper to lay anything before the Lords and Commons for their consideration but what immediately related to 'the present unnatural Rebellion'. He reminded both Houses, 'I have not only sent a considerable body of our National Forces into Scotland, and ordered the Hessian Troops in my pay, to be landed there, but have also made such a Disposition of the rest of my Forces by Land as well as by Sea, that I hope, by the Blessing of God, this Rebellion will, in a short Time, be extinguished'. At court, therefore, Hawley's failure was not unnaturally regarded as a disaster of the first order. It seemed to indicate that the Jacobite victory at Prestonpans was by no means the adventitious thing it was held to be in Whig circles. Hawley's seasoned campaigners had gone the way of Cope's raw recruits. Of the 12 government battalions at Falkirk, all but two were old regiments and nine of them had been recalled from Flanders. The King's army had been humiliated and every forward movement of the Jacobites increased the danger of a support invasion from France. The Duke of Cumberland, who had been recalled from Carlisle to command an

8. Robert Chambers, *History of the Rebellion in Scotland in 1745, 1746*. Vol. 2., P. 24. Traditions at Falkirk. Lord George Murray was instrumental in having the Highlanders issued with small bags in which to keep food and one can only assume that the bannocks etc. were found in these containers.

anti-invasion force on the south-east coast now received a new assignment, of the utmost urgency. He was to assume control of his father's forces in Scotland and preside over an all-out effort to crush the rebellion.

Strategic Retreat

If the Jacobite victory caused consternation in Whig circles, there was little evidence of jubilation in Bonnie Prince Charlie's camp. Jacobite leaders were far from intoxicated by a victory which many felt was marred by being incomplete. Lord George Murray, in particular, was mortified by the safe retreat Hawley had effected. The Jacobites' failure to follow up their initial success by an active pursuit which might have driven the dispirited Royal army out of Scotland, if not annihilated it altogether, was he felt an omission which had consequences far beyond the immediate present. Recriminations flew between Murray and O'Sullivan in which the one was criticized and the other calumniated. The already strained relationship between Charles and Lord George deteriorated even further and, among the common soldiers, there was the usual lack of compunction about wandering off home after an action with all the booty they could carry. Another battle had been won without any benefit to the Stuart cause.

Hawley, on his side, looked for a convenient peg on which to hang his defeat and found one in the complacent attitude of those Hanoverian Scots who had informed the world that the Jacobite army was nothing but a parcel of rabble. He seemed to have all but forgotten that he himself had subscribed only too readily to that view, and in a complete volte-face, he now declared, 'I never saw any troops fire in platoons more regularly, make their motions and evolutions quicker, or attack with more bravery and better order, than those Highlanders did at the battle of Falkirk last week'.[9] Hawley's change of view is not important in itself and was no doubt not without its selfish aspect, because he sought to minimize the shame of his defeat by magnifying the strength of his enemy. More significant was the change of attitude which followed upon the realization that the rebel army was not likely to be snuffed out by a regular army hidebound by the recommendations of its fighting manual. Some new method of combating the Highland menace had to be found and, with every engagement, the clansmen lost a little of their psychological advantage as the regular troops began to familiarize themselves with the Highlanders' idiosyncratic tactics and observers on the government side looked for a breakthrough.

The day after the Battle of Falkirk, Charles returned to Bannockburn and the attack upon Stirling Castle was intensified. The Duke of Perth had been left to command the 1,200 men detached from the main force to prosecute the fruitless siege. The whole operation cost the Jacobites dear in expenditure of time and lives. An extract from a contemporary journal of the transactions at Stirling written by a Whig townsman under the title *Stirling Neuse,* gave the following devastating information: 'they lost during the siege above six hunder of their best men, being almost all French. There was only one man killed in the Castle'. Understandably the siege became unpopular, and on January 29, 1746, the following address to Charles was written by eight of the clan leaders.

'We think it our duty, in this critical juncture to lay our opinions in the most respectful manner before your Royal Highness.

We are certain that a vast number of the soldiers of your Royal Highness's army are gone home since the battle of Falkirk, and notwithstanding all the endeavours of the commanders of the different corps, they find that this evil is increasing hourly, and not in their power to prevent; and as we are afraid Stirling Castle cannot be taken so soon as was expected, if the enemy should march before it fall into your Royal

9. Robert Chambers. *History of the Rebellion in Scotland in 1745, 1746.* Vol. 2., 1827. Notes to Chap. 1. No. 14.

Highness's hands, we can foresee nothing but utter destruction to the few that will remain, considering the inequality of our numbers to that of the enemy. For these reasons, we are humbly of opinion that there is no way to extricate your Royal Highness and those who remain with you, out of the most imminent danger, but by retiring immediately to the Highlands, where we can be usefully employed the remainder of the winter, by taking and mastering the forts of the North . . .

SIGNED by LORD GEORGE MURRAY
             LOCHIEL
             KEPPOCH
             CLANRANALD
             ARDSHIEL
             LOCHGARY
             SCOTHOUSE
             SIMON FRASER,
                   master of Lovat.'

According to John Hay, acting Secretary, when Charles read the address, 'he struck his head against the wall till he staggered, and exclaimed, "Good God! have I lived to see this".' However he soon discovered that hysteria was an inadequate response to the demands of a critical situation. Although consistently unconvinced by the strategic benefits of retreat, Charles was now growing used to the idea that he was not omniscient. In quieter mood and with a good deal of magnanimity, he replied to the chiefs expressing his personal disapproval of their scheme but adding, 'I am too sensible of what you have already ventured and done for me, not to yield to your unanimous resolution if you persist in it'. But he could not find it in his heart to forgive Lord George Murray, the pivotal figure of the confederecy, in Charles's view.

The retreat north began on February 1, 1746 and was not remarkable for its efficient organization. Plans for the army to rendezvous at St. Ninian's and disperse in an orderly manner were altered, which put Lord George once more into an irritable mood. 'It seems after I left Bannockburn they changed the concert that was taken when I was present and orders were sent to Stirling to evacuate it by break of day. I never got so much as a message, nor knew nothing of any change.' Next day at Crieff, he 'complained much of the retreat'. Here, at a Council of War, it was decided that the army should proceed north in two divisions. The clans under Charles were to follow the military road over the Grampians, while the Low Country regiments and horse went with Lord George via the coast road through Angus and Aberdeen. Inverness was to be the rendezvous.

The chiefs' concern about the strength of the Royal army vis-a-vis their own, was not without some solid foundation. After retiring piecemeal to Edinburgh, it was known that the defeated force had been augmented by the arrival of two fresh battalions of infantry and an additional regiment of cavalry, Lord Mark Ker's. On January 30, William Augustus, Duke of Cumberland arrived in the capital to take up his command and was greeted enthusiastically by citizens and soldiers alike. He was just 24 years old, but looked a good deal older because of his excessive bulk. He was narrow-shouldered, fat and undeniably bovine in feature, but none of this detracted from his popularity with the men who had served under him at Fontenoy, by whom he was called affectionately 'bluff Bill'. He was generally considered a competent soldier and was not on this occasion disposed to linger in Edinburgh while his enemies were at liberty. After staying less than 36 hours, he set off on the morning of the 31st with the army, with every intention of forcing the Jacobites to an immediate engagement. He was given a rousing send-off. One delirious observer, apparently at a loss to flatter the Royal Soldier, blessed him and told him he was 'far bonnier than the Pretender'. The podgy Duke, equally deluded, addressed the crowds and told them he would return soon with news of victory.

Next day, while the government army marched towards Falkirk, news came to the confident Duke that his quarry had taken itself off to the Highlands.

As Charles had feared, news of the Jacobite retreat was widely interpreted as defeat. It was thought that the history of the rebellion of 1715-16 was being repeated, that the rebels were retiring northward in order to disperse and that Charles, in imitation of his father, would very soon be seeking a passage to France. On February 4, Cumberland began his pursuit, but before he caught up with them the rebels were to demonstrate quite plainly that they were still a force to be reckoned with.

On Sunday, February 16, Charles reached Moy Castle, seat of the Laird of Mackintosh and about ten miles from the rendezvous at Inverness. It will be remembered that Inverness had been established as the headquarters of members of the clans who had taken up arms on behalf of the government. Lord Loudon was now supervising a force of considerable size there, consisting of his own regiment and 18 independent companies, as well as some 100 Macdonalds and MacLeods brought from Skye under Sir Alexander Macdonald and chief MacLeod. Under the direction of Lord Loudon, a plan emerged to seize the Prince.

The custodian of Charles's safety at Moy was Lord George Murray's 20-year-old cousin, the Lady Mackintosh. She was informed of the plot and, without more assistance than that afforded by her domestic staff and a local blacksmith, one Donald Fraser, and a few companions, managed to prevent a party of Campbells from gaining access to the castle where her guest was alone except for his personal bodyguard. Under cover of darkness, Fraser audaciously impersonated a whole army by rushing about calling out regimental names and thus duped the night raiders into thinking they had stumbled on the main Highland force in the dark. The ruse was a complete success and the plotters fell over

themselves in their anxiety to get away. Lady Mackintosh appears to have been a spirited lady, because she followed up this success by raising some 500 of her husband's men and, as soon as he went off to command a company of militia on the government side, she promptly took to the field for Charles and became known as Colonel Anne, 'la belle rebelle'.

The Earl of Loudon subsequently retired across the Moray Firth into Ross with his army and left the way clear for Charles to enter Inverness. In the usual way, a few regular troops, militia and volunteers barricaded themselves in the nearest armed citadel and put up a token resistance against the invaders. In this instance, the fortress was Fort George, built upon the site of the ancient castle of Inverness and recognized by the Highlanders only as a modern symbol of Hanoverian oppression. To the delight of the clansmen, once the garrison surrendered, the hated monument was blown up. This event took place on February 20, by which time Lord George Murray and his column had arrived, after a gruelling journey. John Daniel gave a graphic account of the privations of the men, after they left Aberdeen: '. . it blew, snowed, hailed and froze to such a degree, that few Pictures ever represented Winter, with all its icicles about it, better than many of us did that day; for here men were covered with icicles hanging at their eyebrows and beards'. The snow and hail drove into the faces of the travellers and it became 'impossible to see ten yards before us', he said. Lord George recorded that he had 'above three hundred carriages' with him and the trials of such a journey can only be guessed at. When he arrived in Inverness, he reported to Charles that the fatigue and trouble he had undergone was 'inconceivable' and no doubt his temper was the worse for it.

When the Duke of Cumberland commenced his pursuit of the retreating army, he was little more than a single day's march behind it, but with a rate of progress at little more than half the rebels' capability, he soon found himself outpaced. When he arrived at Perth, the weather was so bad he decided to halt there and await a more propitious time for venturing into the Highlands. While the Royal army rested at Perth, the Prince of Hesse arrived in the Firth of Forth with the auxiliaries referred to by the King in his address to Parliament. There were 5,000 in all, most of whom were to remain in Perth after the English army moved on to Aberdeen. In the meantime, the Jacobites made continual forays from Inverness. On March 5, Fort Augustus was captured; Lord Loudon's force was dispersed by the Duke of Perth later the same month; on March 21, some of Cumberland's Argyllshire militia occupying Keith were surrounded and captured; Lord George Murray and Cluny Macpherson made a daring march into Perthshire and laid siege to Blair Castle. At last, on April 12, intelligence was brought to the Jacobite headquarters that the Duke of Cumberland was advancing with his whole army. 'They had been for a fortnight before that, lying all the way from Aberdeen to Strathbogie' said Lord George. There could be no doubt that a concerted attack was imminent. The events of the next few days would settle the destiny of the Stuarts. Messages were sent everywhere to bring in all the men.

Night Raid on Nairn

The 'Forty-five was about to enter its final phase. On·this, the eve of its greatest trial, the Jacobite army found itself less capable of resisting attack than ever before. After the privations of a hard winter, the army was run down, inadequately provisioned and desperately short of money. Because the Highlanders had endured much and achieved a great deal, Charles had slipped into the error of believing they could endure all and achieve still more. But Lord George Murray, whose vision of hell was an inefficient commissariat, realized that an army was only as strong as its weakest link and he railed against

the lack of foresight which had led to the army being holed up in Inverness devoid of essential supplies with its enemies closing in around it The men had received no pay for weeks and even the meal which was doled out as a substitute was in short supply. The chiefs had exhausted their personal financial resources and Charles himself had barely enough money left to distribute among his officers. Cut off from potential sources of revenue in the Lowlands by the advance of the English army and prevented from receiving succour from France by the navy, the Jacobites found themselves facing the barren Highlands, hedged in by frustrations which began to be expressed in their gradual decline. It seemed at last that the shades of the 'Fifteen were beginning to haunt the 'Forty-five. For the first time, Charles was negligent of his duties, investing all his hopes in a desperate, irresponsible optimism. In the absence of any real inducement to remain in the camp, common clansmen in their hundreds abandoned their conditioned clan loyalty in favour of an instinctive drive towards self-preservation. They left the camp for the spring-time planting at home.

The army was in a seriously weakened state when the intelligence was received in Inverness of the Duke of Cumberland's advance. In addition to individual deserters, several detachments were absent pursuing local objectives. Lochiel and Keppoch's Highlanders were laying siege to Fort William; Cluny and the Macphersons were in Badenoch; Simon Fraser, Master of Lovat was away recruiting another battalion for his regiment of Frasers; an army of about 700 Mackenzies, Macgregors and Macdonalds was in Sutherland pursuing Loudon's disintegrating force. Many participants in affairs believed that at least a third, and probably half the army was absent. Recruitment had been nothing like as brisk as anticipated. Lady Mackintosh had come in with her 500 and, when Lochiel and Keppoch returned in the nick of time before the battle of Culloden, their following was greater than when they left. A squadron of Fitzjames's horse managed to get through from France and land at Peterhead, but most of these for want of horses, were destined to serve on foot in the forthcoming battle. At the time of its departure from Aberdeen, the government army was officially recorded at 7,179 strong and it was to receive further reinforcements before it reached Culloden. With the odds so heavily stacked against them, the Jacobite leaders reacted to the news of Cumberland's progress with predictable gloom. Many were in favour of retiring farther into the hills to recoup, and when news came in that they were not to expect any further military support from France, oblivion must have appeared attractive if only for a while.

In direct contrast to the straitened circumstances of the Jacobites, the government force exulted in its condition as the spearhead of establishmentarian endeavour, with all the machinery of the state at its disposal. A convoy of ships accompanied the government expedition as it followed its coastal route and carried all the impedimenta of an intensive campaign. It became apparent, however, that well-maintained armies are as likely as destitute ones to indulge in looting and that the offenders in such cases are not found only among the lower ranks. After a six weeks' halt in Aberdeen, the Duke of Cumberland and Hawley in particular left behind them disgraceful reputations with the unsuspecting civilians who had the misfortune to surrender up their homes as billets. Hawley was especially ruthless and the home of one, Mrs. Gordon, was apparently divested of all its moveable assests as a consequence of his short tenancy. 'I was deprived of everything I had but the clothes on my back', reported the outraged owner. '(Hawley) packed up every bit of china I had, all my bedding and table linen, every book, my repeating clock . . . . my worked screen, every rag of Mr. Gordon's clothes, the very hat, breeches, night-gown, shoes and what shirts there was of the child's,

twelve tea-spoons, strainer, and tongs, the japanned board on which the chocolate and coffee-cups stood, and put them on board a ship in the night time, directed to himself at Holyrood House at Edinburgh'.[10] A similar confiscatory exercise was practised by the Duke of Cumberland elsewhere, as a rehearsal in miniature of what the Scots might expect from a conquering army.

When Cumberland left Aberdeen, he took his army north on the road by Old Meldrum and Banff. When this was learned at Inverness, a Jacobite detachment under the command of Lord John Drummond was sent to Elgin and ordered to throw up entrenchments along the banks of the Spey separating the two armies, with the object of disputing the passage of the river. This was an improvisatory tactic designed to buy time in which the fragmented Jacobite army might reunite. The stratagem was a complete failure and, with its collapse, the Jacobites were precipitated into a full-scale emergency. William Anne, Second Earl of Albemarle, who was to command the government front line in the forthcoming engagement, wrote to the Duke of Richmond on April 15, the day before the battle, giving him an account of the army's progress.

'My Dear Duke,
    My letter must be short, for my time is very precious, besides my usual Idleness. I shall therefore give you but a short narration of ourselves. I joined ye army Last friday at Cullen from Strathbogie, where I commanded ye advanced post 19 Days, 30 milles from Aberdeen, consequently Lying ye whole time in Hott water, hardly ever pulling off my coat and breeches. Saturday wee ford'd ye Spey, and encamped on this side, meeting with little or no opposition; Sunday we marched to Alves, half-way between Elgin and Forres; yesterday we ford'd ye Findhorn and Nairn (ye first very deep); near ye last wee took our camp; wee mett with no difficultys at any of these

10. *Extraordinary Conduct of the Duke of Cumberland and General Hawley at Aberdeen.* Jacobite Memoirs, P. 214 ff.

Rivers. The Rebels might with ease and no danger to themselves have disputed ye passage of every one; . . . '[11]

On the Jacobite side, Johnstone recorded that 'the astonishment which prevailed at Inverness when the information came upon us like a clap o'thunder, that the Duke of Cumberland had forded the river Spey, without experiencing the least opposition, may be easily conceived'. In the face of superior numbers, Lord John's force was hopelessly inadequate for the task to which it had been assigned. On April 14, 1746, the King's army came to rest at Nairn, some 17 miles from Inverness. It had been augmented and was now reputed to be in the region of 9,000 strong. It remained at Nairn on the 15th, which was the Duke of Cumberland's twenty-fifth birthday.

Now, against a background of urgency, the conflicting personalities of the main protagonists on the Jacobite side were thrown into bold relief. Charles was predictably in favour of challenging the government army without waiting for absentees from his own force to return. Audacity had served him well in the past and his ability to discriminate between the bold and the rash had never been acute. There were as many shades of opinion on the sanity of such a strategy as there were individuals in the camp. Lord George later stated quite categorically that there was no Council of War.[12] He deplored this breakdown in official procedure not only because it contravened his bias towards the correct, but also because it facilitated an increasing tendency in Charles towards scheming with his favourites, including the Irishmen, O'Sullivan and Thomas Sheridan, whom Murray detested. Meticulous, as usual, Lord George set himself the task of deciding what was best for the army. On the day that Cumberland arrived in Nairn, Charles led his army out of Inverness towards Culloden House, the currently vacant property of the Lord President, Duncan Forbes, who had worked so sedulously to quash the rebellion. With his

men quartered in and around Culloden Park, Charles took up his quarters in the vacant house. Some 12 miles now separated the rival armies and, with a battle imminent, Lord George Murray began to cast about for the most suitable site for the Highlanders' stand. 'My Opinion, and that of the Chiefs . . was to retire to a strong ground on the other side of the Water of Nairn; where if the Duke of Cumberland should attack us, we were persuaded we could have given a good account of him.'[13] Two officers were sent to examine the ground and they returned with a favourable report. It was hilly and boggy, ideally suited to the Highlanders' way of fighting and prohibitive to cavalry and cannon. O'Sullivan, however, 'haveing examined this famiouse field of Battle, found it was the worst that cou'd be chosen for the highlanders & the most advantagiouse for the enemy'. His choice alighted on an area of 'plain moor' about a mile and a half to the south-east of Culloden House. Early on Tuesday morning, April 15, the army was drawn up in line of battle on Drummossie Moor and, even as the dispositions were being made, Lord George was protesting: 'I did not like the ground: it was certainly not proper for Highlanders'.[14] O'Sullivan was not entirely unaware of the importance of selecting a favourable position and he carried on with his arrangements, assuring Lord George that the moor was sufficiently pitted with hazards to prevent the enemy's horse and cannon from operating decisively. At this time, O'Sullivan was ill and utterly exhausted and he was debilitated owing to the purgings he had undergone to alleviate his condition. He was also thoroughly weary of Lord George's hectoring manner and had already been put to the inconvenience of making 'two or three Orders of Battle to Satisfy Ld. George', because 'one time he'd have it one way, another time another way'. A strong current of desperation began to flow through the final arrangements.

The army had spent the night of the 14th

11. *The Albermarle Papers*, being the correspondence of William Anne, Second Earl of Albemarle, Commander-in-Chief in Scotland 1746-47. Ed. by Charles Sanford Terry, MCMII, Pp. 3-4. The Earl took over from the Duke of Cumberland in July 1746.

12. In a letter dated 5th of August 1749 to William Hamilton Esq. (under the pseudonym De Vallignie).

13. In the letter cited.

14. *Marches of the Highland Army.*

sleeping under the stars, 'among the furze and trees of Culloden wood'. In the morning, the men were stiff, cold and hungry, but O'Sullivan said they 'had but very little or nothing to eat'. Macdonald of Morar said 'the poor creatures grumbled exceedingly . . . To appease them we had oblidged ourselves to give them payment of all their arrears . . . which we not being able to perform, made the fellows refractory and more negligent of their duty'. Charles tried to satisfy the pressing demands of the moment by giving them all a shilling a man 'which he promis'd to continu 'em every week as far as what little he had cou'd reach'. The mood of the men on the moor was understandably truculent. The army waited for Cumberland's appearance and when he failed to arrive it was concluded that there would be no battle that day. 'We lay under our arms upon the hill all day expecting the enemy, without any other provision but a sea bisket to each man', said one participant. Elsewhere, it is recorded that the army was dispersed at about 2 p.m.

Reversing the policy of recent weeks, Charles properly assembled his principal officers in a Council of War to discuss strategy. This meeting evolved a plan sufficiently inspired to produce a recrudescence of the Prince's old ebullience. It was agreed that a dawn raid upon the Duke of Cumberland's camp at Nairn should be attempted. If rumours of the celebratory exercises taking place in the government camp to mark the Duke's birthday were to be believed, the troops would be less than alert first thing the following morning. Lord George Murray, who was not usually given to mad-cap schemes, was so utterly averse to facing the government army on the ground chosen by O'Sullivan that he was prepared to stake everything on a bold stroke. He later made his position quite clear in a letter written in 1749: 'I was for the night attack, as well as all the principal officers', but he added the important proviso that the thing must be executed

'before two in the morning, so as to surprise the enemy'. Any failure to achieve their objective before dawn would fatally impair the element of surprise, and therefore it was a matter of some importance to mobilize the army with the utmost expedition. The plan misfired from the start. Efforts to assemble the disintegrating army began to disclose the bitter consequences of an inefficient commissariat. The starving men had scattered in all directions, but principally towards Inverness, in an effort to find food. Even those who were overtaken by their officers and threatened with death for desertion refused to acknowledge their duty before they had satisfied their hunger. At least 2,000 men were lost in this way. It was clear to all concerned, save Charles himself, that the scheme had aborted. Everyone was opposed to persevering with it 'but his Royal Highness continued bent on the thing'. In solemn mood and in complete silence, the night march to Nairn began just after eight o'clock. The army advanced in two columns, one behind the other with Lord George leading the first and Charles himself at the head of the second.

Consistent with the breakdown in discipline which marked the commencement of the project, it was not long before dislocations in organization appeared to jeopardize the progress of the night march. The Highlanders, with Murray in the van, were nocturnal predators of some experience, the dawn raid being a characteristic tactic of clan warfare. The Irish picquets and others with Charles in the rear were quite unused to covering ground quickly at night. Lord George recorded that he was stopped at least 50 times in six miles with alarming reports of a widening gap between the two columns. The cross country route contained unexpected pitfalls and hazards difficult to overcome on a black night. Many took advantage of the darkness to steal quietly away. Lord George disobeyed frequent injunctions to halt and allow the rear column to catch up. The gap widened and, by two o'clock in the morning when the van was forced to halt, it was still three or four miles from Nairn, with the second column trailing miserably half a mile behind. It was already light and quite clearly, if the army was to continue on its way, it would be forced to march the last mile to Nairn within full view of its enemy and, therefore lose the advantage of surprise, which it so desperately needed in its depleted state. Without waiting for Charles's command, Lord George decided to retreat. John Hay, whose responsibility it was to distribute the rations and who by this time must have been feeling the weight of his own culpability for the fiasco, recorded that 'Charles who was on horseback set out immediately, and riding pretty fast met the Highlanders marching back. He was extremely incensed and said, Lord George Murray had betrayed him'.[15] Betrayed he had been, but not by Lord George. It later emerged that the Duke of Cumberland had information of the night march and that spies, speaking Gaelic and wearing the Highland costume, mingled with the marchers.

At five o'clock in the morning, the army returned to Culloden, exhausted and demoralized. For those who had gone all day without food and all night without sleep, the limit of endurance had been reached. Many simply collapsed in fields and hedgerows. Others went off to look for beds in Inverness and some were not to wake before the enemy was upon them. Charles, too fretful to rest, declared publicly that no one in future would command his army but himself.

Culloden Moor

Among the exhausted night-raiders to return to Culloden were John Daniel and Chevalier Johnstone, both of whom committed to paper their surprise at succeeding events. 'We had no sooner reached our camp again', wrote Daniel, 'than news came of the enemy's being in full march towards us, and of their intention to attack us'. Johnstone, who had made off in the direction of Inverness to recruit his strength with a little sleep, explained, 'I tore off my clothes, half asleep all the while; but when I had already one leg in the bed and was on the point of stretching myself between the sheets, what was my surprise to hear the drum beat to arms, and the trumpets of the picquet of Fitzjames sounding the call to boot and saddle, which struck me like a clap of thunder'. Those who were yet awake to hear the call were no doubt similarly struck. Too many were already sunk into oblivion exhausted by hunger and fatigue, and Cumberland was not disposed to allow them to recuperate from the night's activity.

If Cumberland was not a brilliant commander, he was at least thorough and he was not the man to relinquish an advantage. Each brush with the Highlanders had seen a little of their fabulous reputation swept away. In the erosion of the enigma which had cloaked their existence in mystery and vague terror, Cumberland saw an opening to vindicate the sullied reputation which the musket and bayonet had so far received at the hand of the sword and target. His men were instructed in a new technique for resisting the Highlanders in close combat. Instead of each soldier confining his attack to his immediate opposite, he was advised to thrust his bayonet at the adversary of his right-hand neighbour. In this way, the point of his weapon, instead of being caught on the target which the Jacobite carried on his left arm, would find an unprotected way to the sword-arm and right breast of the foeman, who would be caught unaware by such an oblique assault. The soldiers were also impressed with the importance of reserving their fire until the advancing Highlanders were almost upon them. It was certain if they failed to do this and fired too soon, as they had done in the past, they would have no time to reload before the broadsword could intervene. The entry in Cumberland's Orderly Book dealing with the matter laid down, 'at three deep, to fire by

15. Appendix No. 43 Home.

ranks diagonally to the centre, where they come, the rear rank first, and even that not to fire till they are within ten or twelve paces'. Thus equipped with new principles, and confident and determined to retrieve the laurels lost at Falkirk and Prestonpans, the Royal army appeared in the vicinity of Culloden.

Colonel Ker, on the Jacobite side, was sent out to reconnoitre the position when rumour rather than sound intelligence heralded Cumberland's approach. He returned and reported that the foot were marching in three columns with their cavalry on the left, so that they could form their line of battle in an instant. There was no time now for the Jacobites to march to the ground they had occupied the day before. Charles, had himself scarcely rested since his return to the camp, because he had been preoccupied with the necessity of getting supplies of meat and meal distributed among his starving men. He had claimed the command of the army for himself. He must decide what was to be done. The emissary from the French court, Marquis d'Eguilles, later wrote to King Louis:

'I requested a quarter of an hour's private audience. There I threw myself at his feet. In vain I represented to him that he was still without half his army; that the great part of those who had returned had no longer their targets — a kind of defensive armour without which they were unable to fight to advantage[16]; that they were all worn out with fatigue by a long march made on the previous night and for two days many of them had not eaten at all for want of bread.'

Although d'Eguilles's concern was less for the army in general than for the French contingent in particular, his objections were common currency. Lochiel and Keppoch, both lately returned, were also opposed to fighting that day, April 16, 1746. As usual Lord George Murray was uneasy about any operation undertaken in haste. Reacting against advice on all sides to retire to Inverness and there await the remainder of his scattered forces while allowing his recently exhausted followers 24 hours respite, Charles decided 'on giving battle, let the consequences be what they might' (Johnstone). Supported by his belief in the supernatural strength of his Highlanders, Charles could see no reason why he should back away from a fight. '. . he was rather too hazardous and was for fighting the enemy on all occasions', said Lord George, in his *Marches of the Highland Army*. D'Eguilles, seeing that his entreaties fell on deaf ears, wrote, 'proud and haughty as he was . . . (he) could not bring himself to decline battle even for a single day'. When the alarm was raised, there were no more than 1,000 men in the immediate vicinity ready to take to the field.

O'Sullivan was again Adjutant-General and he recorded that 'the Prince order'd the Pipes to play immediately', although it was clear to all that there was small chance of rallying the men scattered about in neighbouring fields and villages, or snoring in Inverness. Much less was there a possibility that those detachments yet to come in would reach Culloden in time to participate in the fight. 'Cluny was not arrived', said O'Sullivan, 'we had above two thousand five hundred men absent'. His estimate was a conservative one. According to Patullo, the Jacobite muster-master, the Prince could command on paper 8,000 men, but in fact he knew he would be lucky to scrape 5,000 together. In the event, he was probably even less fortunate. Lord George Murray later asserted that the Jacobite army at Culloden consisted of 'not above 3,000 in the field, and those not in the best order', but this was certainly a low estimate. The total number of Jacobites at Culloden was probably between 4,000 and 5,000, approximately half the strength of the opposing army, and not all of these were actively engaged.

16. Many of the exhausted night-raiders had thrown away their targets on the return journey.

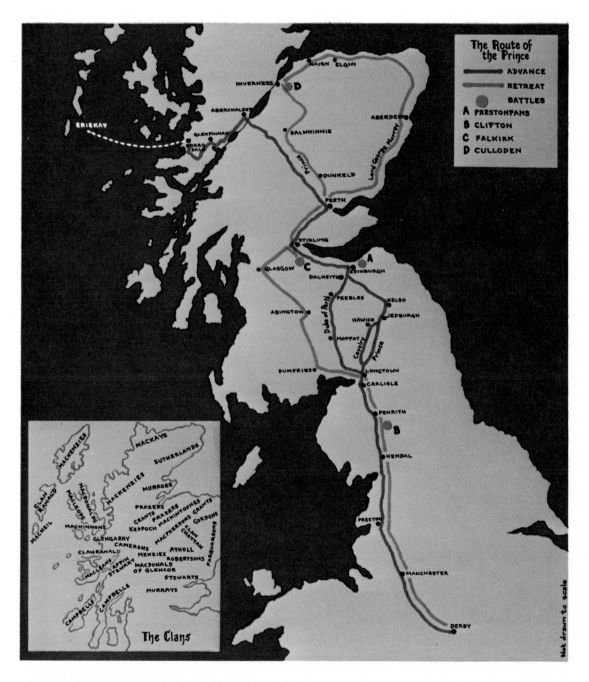

The map shows the route of the Prince through
Scotland and England.

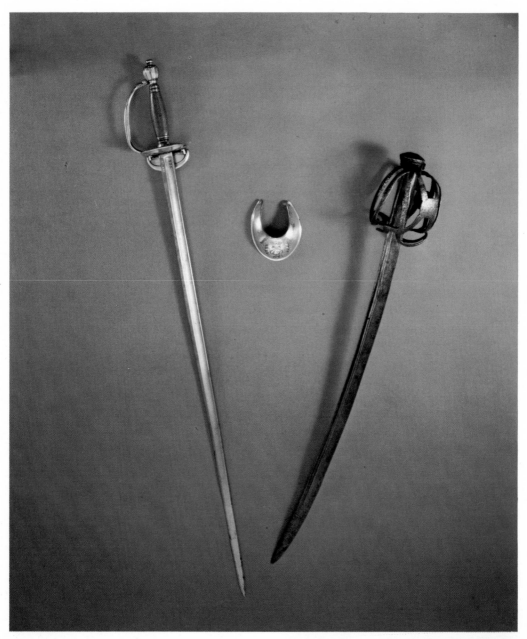

Short all-steel swords were, with bayonets and muskets, standard weapons of British infantrymen. The longer weapon is an infantry officer's sword. The crescent-shaped gilt gorget was worn by infantry officers.

Lord Ogilvy

Lord Elcho

Cameron of Lochiel

Lord George Murray

FOUR PROMINENT JACOBITES OF 1745

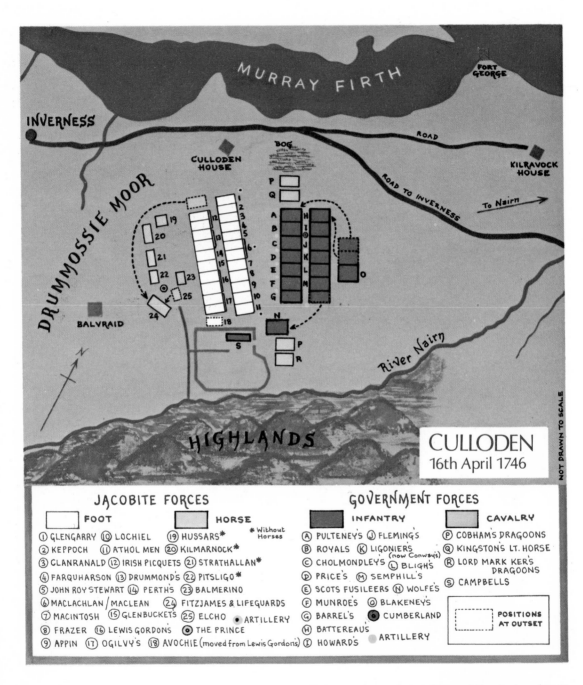

CULLODEN
16th April 1746

NOT DRAWN TO SCALE

MURRAY FIRTH

FORT GEORGE

INVERNESS

ROAD

KILRAVOCK HOUSE

CULLODEN HOUSE

BOG

ROAD TO INVERNESS

To Nairn

DRUMMOSSIE MOOR

River Nairn

BALVRAID

HIGHLANDS

JACOBITE FORCES			GOVERNMENT FORCES		
☐ FOOT		☐ HORSE	■ INFANTRY		☐ CAVALRY

* Without Horses

① GLENGARRY   ⑩ LOCHIEL   ⑲ HUSSARS*
② KEPPOCH   ⑪ ATHOL MEN   ⑳ KILMARNOCK*
③ CLANRANALD   ⑫ IRISH PICQUETS   ㉑ STRATHALLAN*
④ FARQUHARSON   ⑬ DRUMMOND'S   ㉒ PITSLIGO*
⑤ JOHN ROY STEWART   ⑭ PERTH'S   ㉓ BALMERINO
⑥ MACLACHLAN/MACLEAN   ㉔ FITZJAMES & LIFEGUARDS
⑦ MACINTOSH   ⑮ GLENBUCKET'S   ㉕ ELCHO   ◉ ARTILLERY
⑧ FRAZER   ⑯ LEWIS GORDONS   ◉ THE PRINCE
⑨ APPIN   ⑰ OGILVY'S   ⑱ AVOCHIE (moved from Lewis Gordons)

Ⓐ PULTENEY'S   Ⓙ FLEMING'S   Ⓟ COBHAM'S DRAGOONS
Ⓑ ROYALS   Ⓚ LIGONIERS (now Conways)   Ⓠ KINGSTON'S LT. HORSE
Ⓒ CHOLMONDLEY'S   Ⓛ BLIGH'S   Ⓡ LORD MARK KER'S DRAGOONS
Ⓓ PRICE'S   Ⓜ SEMPHILL'S
Ⓔ SCOTS FUSILEERS   Ⓝ WOLFE'S   Ⓢ CAMPBELL'S
Ⓕ MUNROE'S   Ⓞ BLAKENEY'S
Ⓖ BARREL'S   ◉ CUMBERLAND
Ⓗ BATTEREAU'S   ● ARTILLERY   ☐ POSITIONS AT OUTSET
Ⓘ HOWARD'S

The map shows the positions of the rival armies at Culloden (see pages 139-140 and 145-149).

The Battle of Culloden

Having gone so far, there was nothing for it but for Charles to go on and he apparently found his talent for dissembling useful at this critical juncture. 'The Prince got a horse-back, & went up upon the Moor with Lochiels Regmt.', said O'Sullivan, 'not the least concern appear'd on his face, he has that tallent superiorly, in the greatest concern or denger, its then he appears most chearful & hearty'. But what Charles saw must surely have made him wince, if just a little. Cumberland's approaching host of about 9,000 contained nearly 800 well-mounted men in opposition to Charles's own miserably depleted mounted arm. The Jacobites had fewer than 150 horse between the mounted regiments, which meant that most of the cavalry were obliged to appear on foot in the action. To answer the erratic fire of the Jacobite amateur gunners came a team of artillerymen under Brevet-Colonel William Belford, who had entered the Royal Artillery on its formation in 1726 and had served with distinction in Flanders. Finally, as a compelling reminder that the struggle was not one between the English and Scottish nations, three Scottish regiments of foot could be seen among Cumberland's 15 regular battalions, as well as the kilts of the Campbells in the Argyll Militia.

Cumberland formed his lines at a distance and marched in order to the field. It must have been a withering sight for the bedraggled Jacobites recently pulled from their beds in the fields. According to Home, the first government line consisted of six regiments of foot; the Royal had the right; on their left stood Cholmondeley's, Price's, the Scots Fusiliers, Monro's, and Barrel's. The second line consisted of the same number of regiments; Howards had the right; on their left stood Fleming's, Ligonier's, Bligh's, Semphill's and Wolfe's. The reserve line was made up of Pultney's, Battereau's and Blakeney's. (Before the hand to hand fighting began, Pultney's regiment was moved to the right of the

Royals in the front line and Battereau's to the right of Howard's in the second line). The Duke of Kingston's light horse and one squadron of Cobham's Dragoons were placed on the right of the first line; Lord Mark Ker's Dragoons and two squadrons of Cobham's were on the left. Cumberland's unmistakable 18-stone bulk could be seen on a powerful grey near the right of his second line.

The field which necessity forced upon the Jacobites was about a mile farther to the west of the ground chosen the previous day, and a mile and half to the south of Culloden House. It had not been reconnoitred. The Jacobites drew up in two lines which they had 'much difficulty in forming' owing to lack of numbers, reported Johnstone. Their right extended towards a stone enclosure which was to prove crucial to the outcome of the battle. Their left extended towards Culloden House and Parklands. Their front line was longer but a good deal thinner than its opposite number, nor was it straight but stretched obliquely for 1,000 yards across the moor roughly southeast to north-west, putting the Jacobites on the right of the front line about 500 yards away from the enemy and those on the left some 800 yards distant. Lord George commanded on the right, where his Athollmen stood next to the fatal enclosure. If he was upset by the disposition, the Macdonalds who pressed for their traditional place in the line were even more disgruntled. 'We of the Clan McDonalds thought ominous we had not this day the right hand in battle as formerly .. as at Gladsmuir (Prestonpans) and Falkirk, and which our clan maintains we had enjoyed in all our battles and struggles on behalf of our Royal family since the battle of Bannockburn', said Alexander Macdonald of Morar in the *Lockhart Papers*. The Duke of Perth, who was to command on the left, attempted to sweeten the Macdonalds with blandishments, suggesting they would make a right of the left if they fought with their customary zeal. According to Home, between the Athollmen on the right and the three Macdonald regiments on the left of the front line, there stood Lochiel's regiment of Camerons, the Appin Stewarts, the Frasers, the Mackintosh regiment, a united regiment of Maclachlans and Macleans, Colonel John Roy Stewart's Edinburgh regiment, and the Farquharson regiment. The second line, which was commanded by General Stapleton, consisted of Lord Ogilvy's regiment of two battalions on the right, Lord Lewis Gordon's regiment, also of two battalions, Glenbucket's regiment, the Duke of Perth's, Lord John Drummond's and the Irish picquets. On the eve of Culloden, the French envoy calculated the total number of French troops in Charles's service at 780.[17] For want of numbers, the second line was not continuous but disposed in three bodies to protect the two wings and the centre. Three four-gun batteries of mixed calibres were sited in the centre and on the wings of the front line. Charles patrolled the line of Highlanders, commanded to wear their kilts this day, and tried to fire their minds with the enthusiasm that affected his. 'Here, they are comeing, my lades, we'l soon be with them. They dont forget Glads-mur nor Falkirk, & yu have the same Armes & Swords.' From the hungry wretches on the moor came a hesitant huzza. Stooping to examine a sword, Charles confidently asserted, 'I'l answer this will cut of some heads & arms today. Go on my Lads, the day will be ours & we'll want for nothing after' (O'Sullivan). For the most part, the men stood disconsolately on the moor, only anxious to be parted from an affair which destiny long since had branded as fatal. Orders had been issued the previous day that no one was to throw away his gun, everyone was to remain in his appointed place until ordered to move, and there was to be no plundering until the battle was over. This was clearly an attempt to correct the abuses of Falkirk, but the wind had already been sown on that occasion and, as Lord George had prophesied, they were about to reap the whirlwind. As the

Jacobites waited, a little snow and hail began to fall and this time it blew against them.

The opposing armies faced each other across the moor for two hours. In the five intersections between the battalions of the government front line, Belford had placed two three-pounders. At five minutes past one, in answer to the Jacobites' opening shot, the ten guns exploded into action and poured their first decimating fire of round-shot into the Jacobite lines. This cannonade once begun was to last for almost 30 minutes. John Daniel, with Charles in the rear with his Life Guards and the few hussars which made up the pitifully scant Jacobite 'reserve', observed that 'the whole firing of the enemy's Artillery seemed to be directed against us in the rear, as if they had noticed where the Prince was'. He was not entirely wrong. Horrifying gaps were appearing elsewhere in the lines, but Belford had in fact observed the body of horse with Charles and had ordered two pieces of cannon to be directed at them. With the first round, they succeeded in decapitating a servant not 30 yards behind the Prince. Removed to a position of greater safety, Charles was unable to see precisely what was happening at the front, where the Highlanders were growing increasingly restive at being exposed to these terrifyingly accurate engines of destruction without being allowed to reply, their own guns being but a very feeble match for those of the enemy. They waited until they could endure no longer, and finally the Mackintosh regiment in the right centre broke. Hitching up their kilts, casting off their plaids and 'scrugging' their bonnets low down over their brows, they charged followed shortly afterwards by their neighbours. In fact there had been a breakdown in communications. Charles had already issued the order to charge, but the messenger taking the instruction to Lord George Murray had been killed before the order was delivered. By the time the enraged Frasers, Stewarts, Camerons, Athollmen, Maclachlans and Macleans

17 *Origins of The 'Forty-Five and Other Papers Relating to that Rising'.* Ed. Walter Biggar Blaikie. Scottish History Society, Second Series, Vol. II, Edinburgh 1916. Footnote P. 178.

This engraving, depicting the Battle of Culloden, was made in the year following the battle.

followed the Mackintosh regiment, they were impelled by the grief and certainty that their army had already received a mortal wound.

When the galled Highlanders descended on the government line, they had already disobeyed one injunction and were in no mood to adhere to any counsels of restraint. Many of them threw away their muskets without even firing first, so eager were they to be unencumbered in the fray. When the charge began, Brevet-Colonel Belford switched his ammunition from round-shot to grape-shot and the Highlanders were raked with an explosive mixture of leaden balls, nails and old iron as well as the running fire of the facing battalions. The Highland centre regiments, in order to avoid the worst of the

discharge, veered off to their right, crowding in and squeezing out some of their compatriots on that wing. It was thus for Barrel's and Munro's on the left of the government front line to bear the brunt of the descent, although the Highland ranks were dramatically thinned before there was any hand-to-hand fighting. The importance of the enclosure which had seemed to protect the right flank of the Jacobite line now became apparent. Its east wall had been breached and a party of Argyll militia and dragoons occupied a position from which they could pour their fire onto the advancing Jacobite right wing. 'Their fire, from the circumstance of their being quite close to our right was so terrible, that it literally swept away, at once, whole ranks', said Johnstone. Facing both front and flank fire, the Atholl brigade lost 32

147

of its officers in the charge and was so shattered it stopped short. Lord George himself was carried by his careering horse beyond the government cannon where he was badly thrown, his hat and wig blown off and his sword broken in the heat of the action. Despite the enormous number of casualties, the knot of mixed clans which had been the original centre and right of the Jacobite line, pressed on, ploughing through the marshy ground and stumbling over their own dead until they fell upon their executioners. '. . and tho' they were received by them with their Spontoons and Bayonets, the two Regiments of Foot that were upon the Enemy's left, would have been entirely cut to Pieces, had they not been immediately supported by two other Regiments from their Second Line. As it was, these two Regiments (being Barrel's and Munro's) had above Two Hundred Men killed and wounded.'[18] In the second line, immediately behind Barrel's, stood Semphill's regiment, which during the attack had advanced 50 or 60 paces, 'and their front rank kneeling and presenting, waited till Barrel's men got out of their way' before releasing their fire on the Highlanders, bringing most of them down and forcing the rest to turn back. A captain in Munro's was later to write 'Our lads fought more like Devils than Men'. Barrel's were no less tenacious 'not a Bayonet in the Regiment but was either bloody or bent' in the imbroglio. Lord George Murray ran back to bring forward the second line, but it was already too late to save the right.

The Macdonalds, in their unaccustomed position on the left of the line, had still not closed with the enemy when the action was thickest on the right. They had a greater distance to cover in the charge and were showing an unprecedented reluctance to move. Eventually, when they were prevailed upon to advance, they did so hesitantly, stopping to fire their pistols and brandish their swords at a distance from the enemy. The ground between the armies in this area was swamp and marshland and many of the Macdonalds, knee-deep in water, no doubt realized that a Highland charge robbed of speed was also bereft of its impact. They were still facing heavy fire from the battery opposite them, while Cumberland's disengaged troops on the right of his front line waited only for them to get close enough before firing. Lord John Drummond urged them on and Keppoch advanced alone sword in hand, with messianic fervour, crying 'O, my God, has it come to this, that the children of my tribe have forsaken me'. They might have been prevailed upon to make a supreme effort had it not been that the whiff of defeat had already begun to stink in their nostrils. Johnstone, who advanced with his friend Macdonald of Scothouse, on the Jacobite left was later to claim that 'if our right could only have maintained its ground three minutes longer, the English army, which was very much shaken, would have been still more so by the shock of our left wing, which was yet at the distance of from fifteen to twenty paces from the enemy, when the disorder began on the right'. The sight of their fleeing countrymen was scarcely one to inspire heroism in the Macdonalds, nor is it likely that had they closed they would have incurred anything but the same fate as their companions on the right.

At this point, O'Sullivan ran to O'Shea, commanding Fitzjames's squadron. 'You see all is going to pot', he called, 'You can be of no great succour so before a general deroute which will soon be, Seize upon the Prince & take him off'. O'Sullivan had spotted a body of horse moving towards the Jacobite left as if to cut off their retreat and he was anxious that Charles should not lose a second in making his escape. The Prince, distracted by a sight he never thought to witness, refused to admit the evidence of his eyes and thought there was yet a chance to rally the men. O'Sullivan pointed out that the army was disappearing on all sides. 'Then, they won't take me alive', replied Charles, too proud to admit defeat by quitting

18. *A Particular Account of the Battle of Culloden April 16, 1746.* From the Blaikie Collection of Jacobite Pamphlets, Broadsides and Proclamations formed by Walter Biggar Blaikie (1847-1928) and presented to the National Library of Scotland.

the field. His aged tutor, Sir Thomas Sheridan, pleaded with him to look to his own safety. A nearby standard bearer, who later alleged that he was a witness to this vital exchange wrote that the entreaties of Sheridan and Charles's other friends would have been in vain, if 'General Sullivan had not laid hold of the bridle of Charles's horse and turned him about'.[19] Charles left the field to the vindictive cry of 'Run, you cowardly Italian' from Lord Elcho. In turning his back Charles knew that he had seen the last of the English crown.

Scotland's Agony

The Battle of Culloden lasted approximately 40 minutes and was distinctly a Highland affair on the Jacobite side. None of the Lowland regiments of the second line did more than cover the retreat of the repulsed men. That the Highlanders should have been defeated is scarcely surprising considering the extremity of their situation and the circumstance of the coup manqué of the night before. That they were able to wring from their drooping spirits sufficient passion to participate in such an unequal contest is the astonishing thing. It did not require Cumberland's full force to crush them, and only a small proportion of the government army was actively engaged. (Some of the Royal troops were not even called upon to discharge their muskets). For the losers, there was consolation in the many acts of individual and group heroism that might be set alongside the disappointment of a general defeat. Lochiel, shot in both ankles had continued to harangue his men into the attack. Macdonald of Keppoch died with his sword and pistol raised in lonely defiance against a foe that had brought him down twice with musket fire. Some of the Highlanders died trapped between the government lines after penetrating the front centre rank which closed with sickening ease behind them. In a harrowing display of courageous dementia, many clansmen, having cast away their guns and lost their swords, had torn stones

from the ground with their bare hands and hurled them crazily at the neat rows of white-stockinged exterminators ranged against them. There was scarcely a man in the front rank of each of the regiments that attacked who escaped death, and many more besides. For the government, the victory was cheaply bought. The official account put the number of Hanoverian killed, wounded and missing at 310, a mere fraction of the Jacobite losses.

When the field was cleared of combatants, it was not the defeated force that departed with a crumpled reputation. On the contrary, the victors interpreted their leader's tacit approval of no quarter in such a zealous fashion that the reputation of the government army at Culloden has remained sullied ever since. Some of the worst offenders in the regular army were Lowland Scots. Ample evidence exists to demonstrate that the notorious barbarities committed by Cumberland's men were not just a fiction put about by a defeated force eager for sympathy and revenge. Chambers, the editor of *Jacobite Memoirs*, has informed us that the authentic details of violence and cruelty to be found in that work 'will greatly exceed the previous conceptions even of those who have been accustomed to hear the least favourable version of the story'. It seems that after the government's infantry regiments swept the field, the cavalry closed in upon the fleeing Jacobites and there followed, in the words of one Hanoverian observer, 'a general carnage'. He went on to say, 'the moor was covered with blood; and our men what with killing the enemy, dabbling their feet in the blood; and splashing it about one another, looked like so many butchers'.[20] But it was less the random killing of the moment that earned the victors their ruthless reputation, than the systematic extermination which followed. As rebels, the Jacobites knew they could look for none of the courtesies customarily exchanged between regular armies in the eighteenth century. For that reason, they took off as many of their woun-

19. Home. Footnote P. 240.

20. Charles. *History of the Transactions in Scotland in the Years 1715-16 and 1745-46*. Leith 1817. Vol. II. Pp. 328-9.

ded as they were able to bear. They realized that the practice of treating enemy wounded in common with the victor's own was not likely to be adhered to in their case, even though the Jacobite record in relation to prisoners taken at Falkirk and Prestonpans was virtually unblemished by gratuitous violence. Lord George was proud of the Jacobite reputation for clemency and said, 'in nothing was I more careful than about prisoners, even the common soldiers', and recorded with pride, 'I had many letters full of acknowledgement from the officers'. The case was rather different for the Jacobite wounded on the field of Culloden. Those that survived the onslaught, but were too severely wounded to drag themselves clear of the battlefield, endured subsequent storms and the depredations of looters. After two days, any of them still showing signs of life were done to death in various ways. There was a notorious incident in which a barn providing shelter for some Jacobite fugitives was fired and its occupants killed. Accounts of indiscriminate killings among the inhabitants of nearby hamlets and villages were legion. Even Duncan Forbes, who had worked sedulously in the government's interest in Scotland to frustrate the rebellion, objected to the manner in which Cumberland chose quite arbitrarily to treat the Scots as a conquered nation. The purges continued in Invernesshire for weeks after the battle, until at last in Smollett's words, 'all was ruin, silence and desolation', for 50 miles around. 'Bluff Bill' had successfully justified the exchange of his affectionate soubriquet for the chillier appellation 'Butcher Cumberland'.

The defeat at Culloden was interpreted in various ways by the Jacobites, and not all of them regarded it as the end. A hard core of enthusiasts saw it merely as a temporary setback. John Daniel recorded that when he arrived at Ruthven in Badenoch, there were assembled the Duke of Perth, the Marquis of Tullibardine, Lord George Murray, Lord John Drummond and about 1500 to 1800 men, all of whom were optimistic about the prospect of rallying. 'I am thoroughly convinced', said Johnstone, 'that in the course of eight days, we should have had a more powerful army than ever capable of re-establishing without delay, the state of our affairs'. There later appeared a table of Resolutions drawn up by 'the Rebel Chiefs' in which the subscribers, heads of clans, commanders and leaders unanimously agreed and promised 'fortwith with the utmost expedition to raise in arms, for the interest of His Royal Highness, Charles Prince of Wales, and in defence of our country all the able-bodied men that all and every one of us can command or raise, within our respective interests or properties'.[21] Although no official account of Culloden was published under the authority of Charles, a version appeared in London in 1749 in the form of a letter, supposed to have been written by Lord George Murray:

'. . . before I conclude, I must acquaint you with a proposal that was made six weeks before the battle of Culloden: Some officers proposed sending up meal to several places in the Highlands, and in particular towards Badenoch, that in the event of the Duke of Cumberland's marching to Inverness before the army was gathered, they might retreat for a few days, till they could assemble: or, if a misfortune should happen by a defeat, there might be some provisions in those parts; but this was reckoned timorous advice, and was rejected as such: though I have reason to think it was the opinion of almost all the Highland officers, who were not for precipitating any thing. There is no doubt to be made, but that the Highlanders could have avoided fighting, till they had found their advantage by so doing: they could have made a summer's campaign, without running the risque of any misfortune; they could have marched through the hills to places in Banffshire, Aberdeenshire,

21. Resolutions reprinted 'in full in Appendix No. 47. Home.

the Mearns, Perthshire, Lochaber and Argyllshire, by ways that regular troops could not have followed; and if they ventured among the mountains it must have been attended with great danger and difficulty; their convoys might have been cut off, and opportunities might have offered to attack them with almost a certainty of success; and though the Highlanders had neither money nor magazines, they would not have starved in that season of the year, so long as there were sheep and cattle; they could also have separated themselves in two or three different bodies, got meal for some days provisions, met again at a place appointed, and might have fallen upon the enemy where they least expected; they could have marched in three days what would have taken regular troops five; . . . in short, they might have been so harassed and fatigued, that they must have been in the greatest distress and difficulties and at length probably been destroyed . . .'

(dated Lochaber 16th May 1746)

But Charles had little interest in prolonging the agony in Scotland. He continued, as before, reluctant to commit himself to Scotland alone. The only throne he had been interested in was that of Great Britain and the farther he withdrew from London the greater his isolation became. To realize his aim, he knew that nothing less than a coup de main could be effective. That blow had already been delivered, and with daring, but it had stopped short of its mark at Derby. Although Charles Edward Stuart was undoubtedly possessed of a mercurial personality that bloomed in the air of success and shrivelled at the first touch of adversity, he had reasons beyond mere temperament to feel aggrieved at his misfortune. His hopes were almost certainly better founded than might at first appear. The English Tories, although by no means all Jacobites, had definite leanings towards the Stuart family and Tories at that

time formed the bulk of the nation. It is certain that a considerable part of the English aristocracy expressed itself in favour of the attempt while Charles remained at a distance and then deserted him when he appeared in their midst. A brief glance at the history of the 'Fifteen might have afforded Charles a vision of his own future. Once again, France had given nothing but the most insignificant assistance and thereby contributed massively to the ruin of the rebellion. If the Jacobite Prince, alternately buoyed up by hope and dashed by disappointment, began now to exhibit signs of the paranoia that was to afflict him in later life, his neurosis might be said to have had its roots in bitter experience. '. . . he had taken it into his head he had been betray'd', said Lord Elcho.[22] Charles's suspicion alighted as usual on Lord George Murray, as the chief machinator, and here he was wildly mistaken. 'I could shew, in a thousand instances, that nothing was wanting on my part to forward the cause', said the accused man, forced into a defensive posture and recommending his virtues with all the urgency of a man who knew himself to be disliked. 'I will venture to say, that never an officer was more beloved of the whole, without exception that I was.' But Lord George was not alone in being misjudged by Charles. The Prince's jaundiced view extended to cover the Scottish Jacobites in general, whom he thought might be planning to make their peace with the government by handing him over. He was coldly polite to the Scots officers after the disaster, and 'seemed very diffident of Every body Except the Irish Officers', said Lord Elcho. A message was sent to the insurgents at Badenoch telling them curtly to disperse and advising each man to shift for himself. The rebellion petered out in a welter of mistrust and it was only the magnificent tribute of loyalty paid by the Highlanders to the Prince that repudiated his accusation of intrigue and cleared the end of the rebellion of its odious taint.

22. In, *A short Account of the Affairs of Scotland in the years 1744, 1745, 1746* by David, Lord Elcho etc. Reprinted in *The Forty-Five, A Narrative of the Last Jacobite Rising by Several Contemporary Hands.* Ed. By Charles Sanford Terry, 1922, P. 143.

While the Duke of Cumberland received an extra £25,000 a year from a grateful nation and became the 'blooming hero' of sickening panegyrics published in magazines up and down the country, Bonnie Prince Charlie was skulking about the Western Highlands and Islands with a price of £30,000 upon his head, and dependent upon the fidelity of his Highlanders for his life. There were many in addition to the redoubtable Flora Macdonald who refused to violate his shaky trust in exchange for a fortune. 'I must do justice to the several clans', said James Maxwell of Kirkconnell, who was a Major in Elcho's Life Guards, 'by letting the world know that each of them had some share of the merit. The Prince was at Different times in the hands of McDonalds, Camerons, McKenzies, Chisholms, Grants, Frazers, Macphersons, Stuarts, MacLeods and even Campbells tho' that clan was in arms against him . . . Necessity frequently drove him to employ people he knew nothing about, but all gave him convincing proofs of the most zealous attachment . . .'[23] In an age in which strength in adversity was regarded as one of the highest ornaments of virtue, the Highlanders had little to be ashamed of here.

On September 19, 1746, Charles boarded the inappropriately named vessel, *L'Heureux,* and left Scotland for ever, to return to France. Among others to reach the Continent in safety were Lord John Drummond, O'Sullivan and Sir Thomas Sheridan. The sickly Duke of Perth died on the voyage to France and Lord George Murray, disdaining the exiled clique of Jacobites surrounding the Prince, made his chief residence in Germany but died in Holland in 1760. A number of tribunals were established in different parts of the country for the summary trial of prisoners and Jacobites went to the gallows in batches of 20 or 30 a day in London, Carlisle, York, Edinburgh and various other places in England and Scotland. A still greater number of prisoners were transported to the plantations

Flora Macdonald (1722-1790) was the daughter of a farmer at Milton, South Uist. She was imprisoned for aiding the Prince but she was released in 1747.

and many died in transit or while awaiting trial in prison. The Marquis of Tullibardine, veteran of previous Jacobite risings, eventually gave way to his infirmities and escaped the ignominy of a public execution by dying in the Tower, but Lords Balmerino and Lovat were sent to the block. Some of the prominent Highland chiefs, among whom were Macdonald of Clanranald and the convalescent Cameron of Lochiel, escaped abroad, while others like Macpherson of Cluny in his famous cave, Cluny's Cage, were forced to go underground, literally, for years. But in fact, the whole of Highland society felt the full force of government outrage. For it, Culloden came to mean much more than the end of a rebellion. It spelled the end of the Highland way of life.

23. *Narrative of Charles Prince of Wales's Expedition to Scotland in the Year 1745.* Maitland Club 1841. Reprinted C. S. Terry Op. Cit. P. 188.

Charles Edward Stuart, in later life, was a very different person from the bright-eyed and adventurous youth who sailed for Scotland in 1745.

'No man, or boy, within that part of Great Britain called Scotland other than such as shall be employed as Officers and Soldiers in His Majesty's forces shall, on any Pretence whatsoever, wear, or put on Clothes commonly called Highland Clothes; that is to say the Plaid, Philabeg, or little kilt, Trowse, Shoulder-belts, or any part whatsoever of what peculiarly belongs to the Highland Garb.'

The Highlanders were to be yoked by violence to the rest of the community.

Charles Edward Stuart had been in Britain for little more than a year and he was to survive the disappointment of his hopes for a further 42 years. He never returned to Rome while his father lived and stayed away for some 20 years, returning immediately after James's death on January 1, 1766. With the passage of time, the cherubic, bright-eyed youth of early portraiture degenerated into the lugubrious old man of later descriptions. Happily for Charles, the legend of the chaste adventurer survived the years of alcoholic indiscretions, and the persona of the Bonnie Prince became the quintessential element of his renown. In old age, however, when questioned about the 'Forty-five, he was liable to turn apoplectic, a condition much aggravated by drink, heightened by bitterness, and complicated no doubt by a guilty conscience concerning his faithful Highlanders.

Twice in a generation, the warlike Highlanders had shown themselves capable of defending with arms the claims of their royal clan and there was to be no possibility of their ever again being able to provide a Stuart claimant with a cradle for rebellion. In a process known euphemistically as 'the pacification of the Highlands', their distinction as a nation was systematically destroyed. When the dust had settled on the desolate landscape created by Cumberland, acts were passed in London for disarming the clans, abolishing the system of heritable jurisdiction, whereby the Scottish lairds had been used to administer the law on their own estates. A law was even introduced for outlawing the national costume of the Highlanders:

Conclusion

History has compensated the Jacobites for their failure by granting them a reputation for selfless endeavour which looked beyond the principle of personal gain. Loyalty to the House of Stuart became the badge, and renunciation the hallmark of the true Jacobite. But in fact, the principal figures who took to the field in 1715 and 1745 knew very well that they were playing for very high stakes indeed, and anticipated proportionately great rewards should their efforts be crowned with success. Most of their virtues stem from having failed. For those who were dragged into the rebellion at the instigation of their clan chief or landlord, however, the case was somewhat different. They could expect little material reward for their efforts and any service rendered willingly by them could reasonably be considered disinterested. Despite coercion in recruitment, the Jacobite armies were considered volunteer forces and, as such, they were expected to perform more zealously than those who fought merely for pay. There is every indication that the Highland and Lowland peasants did not always wear the aspect of men who fought with halters round their necks. In the 'Forty-five especially, it was a matter of some astonishment to the fiercely independent English rustic to see the thousand personal miseries these creatures endured without complaint, wrapped in an imperfect notion of the justice of their cause and warmed by a sentimental attachment to the person of their Prince.

The army Charles Edward Stuart led into England in the late autumn of 1745 was only half the size of the docile force superintended by the Earl of Mar in 1715 and a mere fraction of the total clan strength then available of about 30,000. It is easy to forget that this tiny army had as its objective the conquest of three kingdoms and lacked every necessity for the accomplishemt of the task beyond the abstract virtues of ingenuity and courage. The incompetence of the government's counter-invasion measures left the issue in doubt just long enough to translate the drama of a lucky escape into the tragedy of a near miss. Luck was certainly something the Stuarts never enjoyed in large measure. In fact, it is difficult to escape the conclusion that Providence damaged the prospects of the Stuarts more effectively than the connivance of their enemies. Prior to the 'Fifteen, in 1708 when feeling against the new Union was running high in Scotland, James Francis Edward Stuart, the Old Pretender, put himself at the head of an expedition guaranteed to find massive support in Scotland. At the critical moment of departure from France, he fell ill with measles and when the fleet eventually sailed it was battered by gales and unable to make a landing in Scotland. Six years later, in 1714, when Queen Anne died, consultations which might have settled the throne on her half-brother and effected a peaceful restoration were left incomplete. About a year after, the prospects of the 'Fifteen were wrecked when the death of Louis XIV left the rebellion bereft of essential foreign aid. In 1744 the ships assembled at Gravelines in preparation for a French invasion were destroyed by freak gales and the project subsequently abandoned, leaving the Young Pretender to embark upon the enterprise alone. The Stuarts appeared to be at the centre of a destructive vortex, and inevitably the rebellions of 1715 and 1745 came to be identified with the characteristics of their Royal figureheads. The 'Fifteen, dull and uninspired, reflects the melancholia and irresolution of James. Even in parts ludicrous, the rebellion, like the man, however, has a tragic element which renders our amusement less than complete. The 'Forty-five on the other hand appears brilliant and bold with its mixture of brief triumph and slow decline, reflecting the career of the Prince himself.

Time was always the greatest of Jacobite foes. In 1715 when the right of primogeniture, which Jacobites held dear, were sacrificed to the imperatives of the Protestant Succession and the dead Queen's half-brother was passed over in favour of the German Elector, then Stuart sympathizers could point to a fresh invitation for revolt. But the constitutional guarantees secured by the accession of the Hanoverians diverted loyalty into a new channel and reduced Jacobitism in England to the status of a sentiment, as Bonnie Prince Charlie discovered to his cost. Had no apprehension existed that a restoration of the Stuarts would be accompanied by a revival of the old issue of arbitrary power, then there would probably have been few who would not have preferred the ancient to the new dynasty. But by 1745, those who nursed a fondness for the old line had also grown to love the guaranteed liberties offered by the new. It is rather to be wondered at, therefore, that some 30 years after the accession of George I and 57 years after the expulsion of James II, so many men should have been discovered who were willing to swim against the tide of history in support of the Stuart claimant. Essential to an understanding of this aspect of the rebellions is the view of the Highlands opened up by the eruption of violence and the glimpse the rebellions afforded into the unique life-style of the most numerous and zealous of active supporters, the Highlanders.

Although the Highlands and Islands constituted approximately one-fifth of the area of England, Scotland and Wales, little was known of the region or its inhabitants south of the Highland Line. The barren mountains, rugged sea coast and remote islands resisted exploration by all but the most intrepid of eighteenth-century travellers. The Highlanders, themselves subsisting in small enclaves marked off from the rest of society by distinctions of language, dress and tribal customs, lived a life withdrawn from their neighbours and virtually untouched by the moderating influences of church and government. In so far as they were considered at all by the rest of society, the Highlanders were regarded as the abhorrent remnant of a barbaric era whose warlike temperament and legendary feuds were the disgrace of a civilized age. After the 'Fifteen, inroads were made, quite literally, into the Highland way of life when the area was opened up by Marshal Wade's 250 miles of military road. Slowly, an ancient way of life began to feel the influence of new ideas, but a gradual adjustment to change was not to form part of the history of the Highlands. Instead, in the holocaust that followed the 'Forty-five, the Highlanders' distinction as a nation was

destroyed in the interest of conformity and effective governance. In 1773 Dr Johnson made his tour of the west coast and had this to say of what he found:

'There was perhaps never any change of national manners so quick, so great, and so general as that which has operated in the Highlands by the last conquest and the subsequent laws. We came hither too late to see what we expected — a people of peculiar appearance and a system of antiquated life. The clans retain little now of their original character: their ferocity of temper is softened, their military ardour is extinguished, their dignity of independence is depressed, their contempt of government subdued, and their reverence for their chiefs abated. Of what they had before the late conquest of their country there remains only their language and their poverty.'

Such was the legacy left by the Stuarts to the Highlands. Nevertheless, it would be wrong to see the Highland clansmen of the Jacobite Rebellions of 1715 and 1745 as a race of noble savages whose primitive virtues were trampled underfoot by the Stuarts in their headlong flight towards the English throne. Many of the chiefs looked resolutely into the past and refused to relinquish their hold on a tribal system that exalted them. They turned to the Stuarts as to a means of prolonging their privilege and protecting their way of life. If they were used by the Stuarts, then the Stuarts were used by them. For both, it was a desperate alliance against progress.

'A wind that awoke on the moorland came sighing,
Like the voice of the heroes who perished in vain:
"Not for Tearlach alone the red claymore was plying,
But to win back the old world that comes not again.'

SOURCES

The 'Fifteen: Primary Sources

1. *The History of the Late Rebellion with Original Papers, and Characters Of the Principal Noblemen and Gentlemen Concern'd in it,* by the Reverend Mr. Robert Patten. London, 1717. The author was curate of Allendale in 1715 and joined Forster at Wooler to become his chaplain. He was captured at Preston and earned the hatred of loyal Jacobites by turning King's evidence.

2. *The Earl of Mar's Journal,* printed at Paris. Reproduced as an Appendix to Patten's *History.* London, 1717 ed. P. 241 et seq.

3. *The History of the Rebellion Rais'd against His Majesty King George I By the Friends of the Popish Pretender,* by the Reverend Mr. Peter Rae. Second Edition to which is now added, *A Collection of Original Letters and Authentic Papers relating to that Rebellion.* London, M.DCC.XLVI. The first edition of Rae's history appeared in 1718. Rae was minister of Kirkconnel and died two years after the publication of the second edition, in 1748. The title of his book indicates his personal bias.

4. *Letters from a Gentleman in the North of Scotland to his Friend in London,* by Captain Edward Burt. London, 1815. (2 Vols..) Burt was one of the few English gentlemen to penetrate beyond the Highland Line in the eighteenth century. His observations on the Highland way of life reveal its severity, but Burt's description of the Highlanders helped to dispel the illusion that they were barbarous savages.

5. *The Lockhart Papers: Containing Memoirs and Commentaries upon the Affairs of Scotland from 1702 to 1715* by George Lockhart, Esq., of Carnwath. London, 1817, 2 Vols. Containing also, *Journals and Memoirs of the Young Pretender's Expedition in 1745,* by a Highland Officer in his Army. Lockhart was arrested as a Jacobite in 1715. His *Memoirs concerning the Affairs of Scotland, from Queen Anne's Accession to the Throne, to the Commencement of the Union of the Two Kingdoms,* London 1714, is a valuable document on the progress to the eighteenth-century rebellions.

6. *The History of the Union between England and Scotland with a collection of Original Papers Relating Thereto* by Daniel Defoe. London, 1786.

7. Historical Manuscripts Commission. 1904. MSS. of the Earl of Mar and Kellie.

The 'Fifteen: Secondary Sources

1. *Scottish History from Contemporary Writers. The Chevalier de St. George and the Jacobite Movements of 1701-1720.* Ed. by Charles Sanford Terry. London, 1901. Including inter alia, extracts from: *Memoirs of the Insurrection in Scotland in 1715* by John, Master of Sinclair. Abbotsford Club. Edinburgh, 1858. Sinclair was not an enthusiastic rebel. He belonged to what Mar referred to as the 'Grumblers' Club', and was consistently critical of all Mar's actions. Sinclair was attainted but was pardoned in 1726. *The Life of the most illustrious Prince, John Duke of Argyle and Greenwich* by Robert Campbell. London, 1745. *A True Account of the Proceedings at Perth; the Debates in the Secret Council there; with the Reasons and Causes of the suddain breaking up of the Rebellion.* Written by a Rebel. London, 1716. At one time this booklet was attributed erroneously to Sinclair. It is currently thought to be the work of Defoe. *Accounts of the Burning of the Villages of Auchterarder, Muthill, Crieff, Blackford, Dalreoch and Dunning.* Printed in the Maitland Club's Miscellany Edin., 1843 Vol. iii. *A Journall of Severall Occurrences from 2nd November 1715, in the Insurrection (began in Scotland) and concluded at Preston in Lancashire on November 14, MDCCXV,* kept by Peter Clarke. The narrative appears both in Ware's *State of Parties in Lancashire before the Rebellion of 1715,* Manchester, 1845, and in the Scottish History Society's *Miscellany,* Edinburgh, 1893. Clarke was an attorney's clerk at Penrith. He may have been employed by Derwentwater to deal with his personal correspondence. Although his diary covers the events of only two weeks, they were at least the most active weeks of the campaign.

2. *The Peerage of Scotland* by Sir Robert Douglas of Glenbarvie, Bart. 2nd Edition. Ed. by John Philip Wood. 2 vols. Edinburgh, 1813.

3. *The Jacobite Relics of Scotland; Being The Songs, Airs and Legends of the Adherents to the House of Stuart.* Collected and illustrated by James Hogg. Second Series. Edinburgh, MDCCCXXI; 2 vols. Both volumes contain some interesting Notes.

4. *Sketches of the Character, Manners and Present State of the Highlanders of Scotland* by Colonel David Stewart. Edinburgh, 1822 2 vols.

5. *History of the Rebellions in Scotland under The Viscount of Dundee and the Earl of Mar in 1689 and 1715,* by Robert Chambers. Edin., 1829.

6. *Memoirs of The Pretenders and Their Adherents* by J. H. Jesse. London, MDCCCLVIII.

7. *A History of the Highlands and of the Highland Clans* by J. Browne. 1849.

8. *Tales of a Grandfather* by Sir. Walter Scott. London, 1898.

9. *James Francis Edward The Old Chevalier* by Martin Haile 1907.

10. *The Social Life of Scotland in the 18th Century,* by H. G. Graham. 1909.

11. *The Jacobites and The Union. Being a Narrative of the Movements of 1708, 1715, 1719* by Several Contemporary Hands. Edited by Charles Sanford Terry. C.U.P., 1922.

12. *The Life of the Right Honourable James Radcliffe Third Earl of Derwentwater with an account of his Martyrdom for the Catholic Faith and Loyalty to His Rightful King etc*, by Major Francis John Angus Skeet. London, 1929.

13. *The Old Chevalier, James Francis Stuart*, by A. & H. Tayler. 1934.

14. *1715: The Story of the Rising*, by A. & H. Tayler. 1936.

15. *The Jacobite Risings of 1715 and 1745*, by Rupert C. Jarvis. Cumberland County Council, 1954.

16. *The Stuarts* by J. P. Kenyon. 1958.

17. *Northern Lights: the Story of Lord Derwentwater*, by Ralph Arnold. 1959.

18. *The Jacobite Movement* by Sir Charles Petrie. 3rd Ed., 1959.

19. *A History of Scotland* by J. D. Mackie. Penguin, 1964.

20. *The Jacobite Rising of 1715*, by R. E. Hutchison. A pamphlet written by the Keeper of the Scottish National Portrait Gallery. Edinburgh, 1965.

21. *The Glorious Revolution of 1688* by Maurice Ashley. 1966.

22. *A History of the Scottish People 1560-1830*, by T. C. Smout. 1969.

23. *The Jacobite Rising of 1715* by John Baynes. 1970.

24. *Scotland in the Age of Improvement*. A collection of essays edited by N. T. Phillipson and Rosalind Mitchison. Edinburgh U.P., 1970.

25. *Inglorious Rebellion. The Jacobite Risings of 1708, 1715 and 1719* by Christopher Sinclair-Stevenson. 1971.

26. *Beyond the Highland Line. Three Journals of Travel in Eighteenth Century Scotland*. Edited by A. J. Youngson. 1974.

27. *The Northumberland County History*. Various vols.

The 'Forty-Five: Primary Sources

1. *The Blaikie Collection of Jacobite Pamphlets, Broadsides and Proclamations*. The Collection was formed by Walter Biggar Blaikie (1847-1928) and on his death was presented to the National Library of Scotland. Inter alia: *A Particular Account of the Battle of Culloden April 16, 1746 In a Letter from an Officer in the Highland Army to his Friend at London*. London 1749. *A Compleat and Authentick History of the Rise, Progress, and Extinction of the Late Rebellion And of the Proceedings Against the Principal Persons Concerned Therein etc*. London MDCCXLVII. *Acts for Restraining Highland Dress*.

2. *Historical Papers relating to the Jacobite Period 1699-1750*. Edited by Colonel James Allardyce, LL.D. Vol. I. Printed for the New Spalding Club MDCCCXCV. Containing inter alia: *Wade's Report on the Highlands, 1724*; *Cope's Battle* (By an Eye-witness); *Journal of the Marches of His Royal Highness Prince Regent's Army, from the time they entered England the 8th of Novemebr, till their Return to Scotland the 20th December 1745; A Plain, General and Authentic Account of the Conduct and Proceedings of the Rebels during their stay at Derby 4th to 6th December, 1745*; and Two accounts of the Battle of Falkirk.

3. *Memoirs of the Rebellion in 1745 and 1746 by The Chevalier de Johnstone, containing a Narrative of The Progress of the Rebellion from its Commencement to the Battle of Culloden etc*. Third Edition. London 1822. Translated from a French MS originally deposited in the Scots College at Paris. Johnstone was aide-de-camp to Lord George Murray and, later assistant aide to Charles himself. From the confidential positon he occupied, he was able to get to know the principal characters in the Rebellion. His comments on the character of the Prince are often acid while he champions Lord George as a military genius.

4. *The History of The Rebellion in the Year 1745* by John Home. London 1802. Home served as a volunteer on the government side and his account of the rebellion was submitted in manuscript to the reigning family prior to publication six years before his death. It can therefore be taken as the authorized version of the event from the government point of view. Important appendices include Hay's account of the retreat from Stirling and his version of the abortive night raid on Nairn, as well as a reprint of Lord George's letter of 5th Aug. 1749 under the pseudonym, De Vallignie, relating also to the night raid.

5. *Jacobite Memoirs of the Rebellion of 1745*. Edited from the MS of Rev. Robert Forbes A. M. by Robert Chambers. Edinburgh 1834. The 1834 volume contains inter alia. *Lord George's Marches of the Highland Army*, a narrative of the rising with particular reference to his own part in it, a section entitled 'Extraordinary Conduct of the Duke of Cumberland and General Hawley at Aberdeen and Colonel Ker of Gradyne's account of The Battle of Culloden'.

6. *The Lockhart Papers*. (See under Sources for the 'Fifteen) The section entitled 'Journall and Memoirs of P......C..... Expedition into Scotland 1745-46 by a Highland Officer in his army', in Vol. 2 is useful. The anonymous author is thought to have been Macdonald of Morar. Col. Ker of Gradyne's account appears in this volume under the title of *Account of Events at Inverness and Culloden*.

7. *O'Sullivan's Narrative. In 1745 and After* by A. & H. Tayler 1938. John William O'Sullivan was born in County Kerry about 1700. He was educated in France and accompanied Charles as one of the original Seven Men of Moidart. His account is confused, difficult to follow and often unreliable. He and Lord George Murray seem to have fought for the affections of the Prince and O'Sullivan emerges as the victor.

8. *Culloden Papers.* (See under Sources for the 'Fifteen) Contains William Corse's account of Falkirk.

9. *Origins of the 'Forty-Five and other Papers Relating to that Rising.* Edited by Walter Biggar Blaikie. Edinburgh 1916. Scottish History Society. Second Series Vol. II. Contains inter alia: *A True Account of Mr. John Daniel's Progress with Prince Charles.* Reprinted from a MS preserved at Drummond Castle. Daniel served in Balmerino's and was one of the few English Jacobites to remain with the army till the end. After suffering severe privations after Culloden, Daniel got a passage to France. His account is remarkable for the unswerving loyalty he exhibits towards the Stuarts.

10. *The Stuart Papers at Windsor.* Ed. by A. & H. Tayler. London 1939. A collection of correspondence from the archives at Windsor Castle.

11. *The Albemarle Papers.* Being the Correspondence of William Anne, Second Earl of Albemarle, Commander-in-Chief in Scotland 1746-47.

The 'Forty-Five: Secondary Sources

1. *Gentleman's Magazine:* 1745, '46.

2. *The Forty-Five.* A Narrative of the Last Jacobite Rising By Several Contemporary Hands. Ed. By Charles Sanford Terry. 1922. Contains inter alia, extracts from; *A short Account of the Affairs of Scotland in the years 1744, 1745, 1746,* by David, Lord Elcho; *Memorials of John Murray of Broughton,* sometime Secretary to Prince Charles Edward 1740-7; *Narrative of Charles Prince of Wales' Expedition to Scotland in the year 1745.* By James Maxwell of Kirkconnell; *A complete history of England, to the Treaty of Aix-la-Chapelle,* by Tobias George Smollett; *Carlisle in 1745: authentic account of the occupation of Carlisle in 1745,* by George G. Mounsey; *The Scots Magazine.*

3. *History of the Transactions in Scotland in the Years 1715-16 and 1745-46,* by George Charles Vol. II. Leith 1817.

4. *The Jacobite Relics of Scotland,* collected and illustrated by James Hogg. 2 vols. Edinburgh 1819-21.

5. *History of the Rebellion in Scotland in 1745, 1746,* by Robert Chambers. 2 vols. Edinburgh 1827.

6. *Memoirs of Prince Charles Stuart (County of Albany) commonly called the Young Pretender; with Notices of the Rebellion in 1745,* by Charles Louis Klose. Second Ed. in 2 Vols. London 1846.

7. *The Rebellion of 1745. An Old Story Re-Told from the Newcastle Courant.* Printed for Private Circulation 1881. A collection of details with interconnecting comments. From the files of the Newcastle Courant.

8. *Prince Charles Edward,* by Andrew Laing. 1900. Limited Ed. of 1500 No 1253.

9. *The Young Pretender,* by Charles Sanford Terry. 1903.

10. *Culloden Moor and the Story of the Battle,* by Peter Anderson Stirling 1920.

11. *Battles of the '45,* by K. Thomasson and F. Buist. Batsford, London 1962.

12. *Culloden,* by John Prebble. Penguin 1967.

13. *Collected Papers on the Jacobite Risings,* by Rupert C. Jarvis. Vol. I. Manchester University Press. 1971.

14. *Bonnie Prince Charlie,* by Moray McLaren. Rupert Hart-Davis. 1972.

15. *Charles Edward Stuart. The Life and Times of Bonnie Prince Charlie,* by David Daiches. Thames and Hudson. London 1973.

16. *The Rash Adventurer. The Rise and Fall of Charles Edward Stuart,* by Margaret Forster. Secker & Warburg. London 1973.

17. *Over the Sea to Skye,* by John Selby. Hamish Hamilton 1973.

18. *Beyond the Highland Line.* Three Journals of Travel in Eighteenth Century Scotland, Burt, Pennant, Thornton. Edited by A. J. Youngson. Collins 1974.

Index

Note: Numbers in bold type indicate an illustration.

Act for Encouraging Loyalty in Scotland 16, 31
Act of Attainder 74
Act of Settlement 6
Act of Union (1707) 6-7, 12, 107-108
Ainsley, Sgt William 22
Albemarle, Earl of 136
Albemarle's Regiment 120
Anderson, Robert 96
Anne, Queen 6, 9, 12
Appin, Stewarts of 88, 128, 146
Appin Regiment 45, 96, 146
Ardshiel, Stewarts of 84, 133
Argyll, Duke of **21** (portrait)
    Vulnerable position (1715) 15, 20-21
    Forced march to Edinburgh 25
    Stalemate at Leith 26
    Reinforcements 40-41, 43
    Sherriffmuir 44-49
    Gaining ascendancy 65-66
    Loss of reputation 68, 72
    Advance to Perth 69
    Occupation of Aberdeen 71
Argyll Militia 145
Artillerymen **36, 123**
Atholl, Duke of 13, 15, 16
Atholl Brigade 128, 130, 145, 146, 147-148
Auchterhouse 13
Augustus, William *see* Cumberland, Duke of
Auldbair 13
Austrian Succession, War of 78, 80, 85
Balfour, Colonel 44
Balmerino, Lord 94, 152
Barrel's Regiment **97** (grenadier), **99** (general), **99** (drummer), 128, 130, 145, 147, 148
Battereau's Regiment 128, 145
Beauclerk's Foot 109
Belford, Brevet Colonel William 145-147
Bellingham, Madam 51
Bernard's Regiment 120
Berwick, Duke of 17, 40, 76
Bill of Rights 10
Black Watch *see* Royal Highland Regiment
Blakeney, Major-general 126
Blakeney's Regiment 128, 145
Bland's Dragoons 109, 120
Bligh's Regiment **97** (officer), 120, 145
'Bobbing John' 12
Boisdale, Alexander Macdonald of *see* Macdonald, Alexander (of Boisdale)
Bolingbroke, Viscount 11, 13, 74
Bonnie Prince Charlie
    Origin of name 84
    See Stuart, Charles Edward
Breadalbane, Earl of 16, 31
Broadswords 19, **58, 59**
Burntisland raid 23-24
Burt, Captain 19-20
Byng, Admiral 77
Cadogan, General William 68, 71, 72
Cameron of Lochiel, Donald 83, 93, 96, 133, 135, 140, **143** (portrait), 149, 152
Camerons 45, 84, 88, 96, 105, 128, 129, 146, 152
Campbell, John *see* Argyll, Duke of

Campbells 16, 134, 145, 152
Carnwath, Earl of 13, 31-32, 43, 72
Carpenter, General George 30, 32, 42, 50, 51, 54
Carpenter's Dragoons 46
Cathcart, Colonel 27, 48
Chambers, Robert 48, 68, 149
Charles XII of Sweden 77
Chevalier de St George 13
    See Stuart, James Francis Edward
Cholmondely's Regiment 120, 128, 145
Churchill, Arabella 17
Churchill's Dragoons 30, 54
Clan 7, 14
Clan Act 11
Clanranald, Macdonald of *see* Macdonald of Clanranald
Clanranald's Regiment 47, 96, 128
Clifton, Battle 118, **121** (map)
Cobham's Dragoons 30, 54, 127, 129, 145
Cockburn, Adam 31, 72
Cope, Sir John 86-96, 105-107, **107** (flight to Berwick)
Corse, William 127, 129
Cotton, Colonel 55
Culloden, Battle of 139-140, **144** (map), 145-149, **147** (engraving)
Cumberland, Duke of
    Command in England 109, 112-113
    Portrait **115**
    Pursuit of Jacobites 116-118
    Carlisle taken 120
    Command in Scotland 131-132
    Arrival in Edinburgh 133-134
    Pursuit of Jacobites in Scotland 134-136
    Camp at Nairn 137-139
    At Culloden 139-140, 145-149
    Aftermath 150, 152
Dalziel, Robert *see* Carnwath, Earl of
Daniel, John 114, 119, 125, 128, 134, 139, 146, 150
D'Eguilles, Marquis 140
Derwentwater, Earl of 28-29, 31, 53, 55-56, **63** (wax impression of head), 72-74, **73** (final speech)
Devon, failure of Jacobites 11
Dickson Sgt 112
Dirks 19, **58, 61**
Divine Right 10
Dormer, Brigadier 53
Douglas's Regiment 120
Dreus Regiment 111
Drummond, James (titular Duke of Perth) 83, 90, 91, 96, 109, 111, 114, 115, 132, 135, 145, 146, 150, 152
Drummond, Lord James (in 1715 rising) 13, 15, 22, 25, 70
Drummond, Lord John 114, 118, **119** (portrait), 125, 126, 127, 128, 130, 136, 137, 146, 148, 150, 152
Duffus, Lord 13
Dumfermline incident 27-28
Durand, Colonel 110-111
Dutch auxiliaries 65-66, 120
Edinburgh 15
    Castle raid (1715) 22-23
    Taken by Jacobites (1745) 93
    Entry of Duke of Cumberland 133

Elcho, Lord 94, 109, 113, **143** (portrait), 149, 151, 152
Errington, Lancelot 30
Errol, Earl of 13
Erskine, John *see* Mar, Earl of
Evans's Dragoons 46, 48, 126
Exeter, Earl of 113
Falkirk, Battle of 124 (map), 127-131
Farquharsons 128, 146
Fitzjames, James *see* Berwick, Duke of
Fitzjames's Regiments 125, 136, 139, 148
Fleming's Regiment 128, 145
Forbes, Duncan (of Culloden) 86, 88, 89, **89** (portrait), 108, 110, 125, 137, 150
Forfar's Regiment, Battalion company sergeant **34**
Forster, Tom 28-31, 32, 41, 43, 51-56, 72-73
Fraser, Donald 134
Fraser, Simon (Master of Lovat) 133, 135
Frasers 16, 28, 44, 125, 128, 129, 135, 146, 152
Gardiner, Colonel 105
Gardiner's Regiment 87, 91, 96, 105, 111, 129
George I 9, **9** (portrait), 10, 11, 12, 13, 67, 68
George II 78, 84, 85, **85** (portrait), 131
Gladsmuir *see* Prestonpans
Glasgow 15
    Occupation 120, 125-126
Glasgow Militia 111
Glasgow Regiment 128, 129
Glenbucket, John Gordon of *see* Gordon, John (of Glenbucket)
Glenbucket's Regiment 146
Glendarule, Laird of 13, 16
Glenfinnan 84
Glengarry, Macdonald of *see* Macdonald of Glengarry
Glengarry Regiment 96, 128
Glenlyon, Laird of 16
Glenmoriston, Grants of *see* Grants of Glenmoriston
Glenshiel, Battle (1719) 77
Glorious Revolution of 1688 5, 10
Gordon, Alexander *see* Huntly, Marquis of
Gordon, General 13, 17, 24, 28, 40, 42, 44, 45, 47, 70-72
Gordon, John (of Glenbucket) 108
Gordon, Lord Lewis 128, 146
Gordon, William *see* Kenmure, Viscount
Gordons 16
Gower's Regiment 120
Granby's Regiment 120
Grants 16, 88, 152
Grants of Glenmoriston 88
Guest, General 91
Guise's Regiment 87, 96
Halifax's Regiment 120
Hall, John 56
Hamilton, General 12, 13, 14, 26, 44, 66
Hamilton's Dragoons 87, 91, 92, 96, 105, 111, 129
Handasyde, General 111
Harrison's Foot 109
Hawley, General 120, 126-132, 136
Hay, Colonel 12, 16
Hay, John 114, 133, 139
Hesse, Prince of 135

Highlanders
    Chieftain's dress 33
    Clansmen 98
    Dress and Equipment 18-20, **38, 58, 59, 60, 61, 64,** 109-110
    Effects of 1745 rising 152-155
    Fighting techniques 45, 105-106
    Government Highlander **103**
    Peasant Dress **37**
    Way of Life 7-8
    Women **102**
Holland, John 22
Home, John 83, 84, 89, 91, 93, 96, 106, 109, 117, 127, 130, 131, 145
Honeywood, Brigadier 53, 54, 55
Horses, Highland 19, 36
Hotham's Foot 30
Howard's Regiment 120, 128, 145
Huntly, Marquis of 13, 14, 17, 19, 41, 44, 46, 65
Huske, General 126
Huske's Foot 109
Inverness, Earl of *see* Hay, Colonel John
Irish picquets 114, 125, 130, 146
Islay, Lord 28
Jacobite (definition) 5
James I of England and VI of Scotland 6
James II of England and VII of Scotland 5, 6, 7, 8-9, 17
Jamie the Rover 75
Johnson, Dr 155
Johnson's Regiment 120
Johnstone, Chevalier de 86, 90, 95, 96, 106, 108, 112, 117, 118, 119, 120, 129, 131, 139, 145, 147, 148, 150
Keith, George *see* Marischal, Earl
Kellie, Earl of 94
Kenmure, Viscount of 13, 31-32, 41, 53, 72-74
Keppoch Macdonald of *see* Macdonald of Keppoch
Keppoch Regiment 96, 128, 135
Ker, Colonel 140
Ker, Lord Mark 133, 145
Kerr's Dragoons 46
Kilsyth, Viscount of 13
Kingston, Viscount of 13
Kingston Light Horse **103** (trooper), 120, 145
Kinlochmoidart, Donald Macdonald of *see* Macdonald, Donald (of Kinlochmoidart)
Lally's Regiment **122** (private)
Lascelle's Regiment 87, 96
Lee's Regiment 87, 96
Leslie's Regiment 120
Ligonier, Colonel Francis 129
Ligonier, Sir John 109, 111, 112
Ligonier's Regiment 109, 111, 120, 128, 129, 130, 145
Linlithgow, Earl of 13, 15
Lochaber axe **38,** 93, **98**
Lochgary 133
Lochiel, Cameron of *see* Cameron of Lochiel
Lochiel's Highlanders 96, 133, 135, 140, 146
Lockhart, George (of Carnwath) 21, 41
Lonsdale, Viscount 50
Lothian Militia 111
Loudon, Earl of 87, 95, 125, 128, 134, 135
Louis XIV 6, 11, 24
Louis XV 66, 79, 86, 140

Lovat, Lord 129, 152
Lowland Scottish Force (1715) 30
Macdonald, Aeneas 81, 82
Macdonald, Alexander (of Boisdale) 82
Macdonald, Alexander (of Glengarry) 13, 45, 47
Macdonald, Alexander (of Sleat) 82
Macdonald, Donald (of Kinloch-moidart) 82
Macdonald, Flora 152, **152** (portrait)
Macdonald of Clanranald 45, 88, 96, 128, 133, 152
Macdonald of Glengarry 88, 128
Macdonald of Keppoch 84, 128, 129, 133, 135, 140, 148, 149
Macdonald of Morar 138, 145
Macdonald of Scothouse 133, 148
Macdonalds 28, 45, 47, 82-83, 84, 88, 96, 117, 118, 129, 134, 135, 145, 146, 148, 152
Macgregors 91, 96, 106, 135
Mackenzie, William *see* Seaforth, Earl of
Mackenzies 28, 128, 135, 152
Mackinnon of Mackinnon 108
Mackintosh, Brigadier William (Old Borlum) 17, 25, 26, 32, 50, 51, 53-56, 72, 73, 76
Mackintosh, Lady 134, 135
Mackintoshes 25, 128, 134, 146
Mackintosh of Mackintosh, Colonel 53
Maclachans 94, 128, 146
Maclean, Sir John 45
Macleans 146
Macleod of Macleod, Norman 86, 134
Macleods 82, 84, 125, 134, 152
Macpherson of Cluny 89, 118, 135, 140, 152
Macphersons 128, 129, 135, 152
Mar, Earl of **12** (portrait)
  Raising the rebellion 11-18
  Tactics 23-25
  Advance from Perth 28
  Awaiting the Pretender 40-41
  At Sherriffmuir 44-49
  Report on Preston 56
  Letter to Pretender 65
  Arrival of Pretender 66-67
  Plans to end rebellion 68-69
  Into exile 70
  Responsibility for failure 74-76
Marischal, Earl 13, 14, 17, 66, 70, **76** (portrait), 77, 79, 86
Mary of Modena 5
Maxwell, James (of Kirkconnell) 152
Maxwell, William *see* Nithsdale, Earl of
McLean, Captain 22-23
Melford, Earl of 70
Moidart, Seven Men of 83
Molesworth's Dragoons 30, 54
Monroes 16, 89
Munro, George (of Culcairn) 89
Munro's Regiment 128, 147, 148
Montague's Regiment 120
Murray, John (of Broughton) 80, 83, 84, 114
Murray, John *see* Atholl, Duke of
Murray, Lord Charles 15, 25, 53, 54
Murray, Lord George 15, 86, 90, 91, 94-95, 96, 105, 106, 109, 110, 112, 113, 115, 117-120,
126-135, 137-140, **143** (portrait), 145, 146, 148, 150, 151, 152
Murray's Regiment 87, 128
Nairn, Lord 13, 15, 25, 72, **73** (portrait)
Nairn, night raid 138-139
Newcastle, defence of (1715) 29, 30
Nithsdale, Earl of 13, 31-32, 53, 72, 73
Norris, Sir John 79-80
Northumberland rising (1715) 28-30
Ogilvy, Lord 108, **143** (portrait)
Ogilvy of Boyne, Brigadier 44, 45
Ogilvy's Regiment **100** (private), 128, 146
Oglethorpe, General 116
Old Borlum *see* Mackintosh, Brigadier William
Old Mr Melancholy 75
Old Pretender *see* Stuart, James Francis Edward
Orléans, Regent 66, 76
Ormonde, Duke of 11, 74, 75
O'Sullivan, Colonel John William 80, 90, 119, 126, 128, 129, 131, 132, 137, 138, 140, 145, 146, 148, 149, 152
Oxburgh, Colonel 54-55
Paisley Militia 111
Panmure, Lord 18
Patten, Robert 13 (Patten's *History* is quoted throughout Chapters 1 and 2)
Pattenson, Thomas 110
Perth, Duke of *see* Drummond, James
Perth
  Events in 1715 16, 40, 43, 44, 69
  Events in 1745 90-91
Philip V of Spain 77
Pipe, small **62**
Piper **101**
Pistols, Highland **60**
Pitsligo, Lord 108
Portmore's Dragoons *see* Royal Scots Greys
Powder flasks **64**
Preston
  Arrival of Jacobites (1715) 52
  Battle 53-56, **57** (map)
Prestonpans, Battle of 95-96, **104** (map), 105-106
Price's Regiment 128, 130, 145
Prince's Life Guard **122**, 146
Princess of Wales Regiment **34** (grenadier)
Pultney's Regiment 128, 145
Radcliffe, Charles 29
Radcliffe, James *see* Derwentwater, Earl of
Rae, Peter 12 (Rae's *History of the Rebellion* is referred to throught Chapters 1 and 2)
Richmond, Duke of 136
Richmond's Regiment 120
Robertsons 91
Rollo, Lord 13
Roper's Regiment 120
Roquefeuille, Admiral 80
Rosses 16
Royal Artillery **123** (uniforms) 145
Royal Ecossais Regiment **100** (private)
Royal Highland Regiment (Black Watch) **101**, 128

Royal Scots Greys **36** (trooper), 46, 48
Royal Scots Regiment 84, 128, 145
St Clair's Foot 109, .128
Saxe, Comte de 79, 80, 83
Scothouse, Macdonald of *see* Macdonald of Scothouse
Scottish Lowlands, definition 7
Scottish Museum of Antiquities 37
Scot's Fusiliers 145
Scott, Sir Walter 11, 32
Seaforth, Earl of 13, 24, 28, 45, 65
Semphill's Regiment 120, 145, 148
Seton, George *see* Wintoun, Earl of
Sheldon, Lt. General 70
Sheridan, Sir Thomas 80, 137, 149, 152
Sherriffmuir, Battle of **39** (map), 45-49
Sinclair, John 15, 17, 23, 26, 44
Sinclair's Regiment 120
Sleat, Alexander Macdonald of *see* Macdonald, Alexander (of Sleat)
Sobieska, Clementina 77
Sophia, Electress of Hanover 6, 9
Southesk, Earl 13, 18
Sowle's Regiment 120
Stair's Dragoons 46, 48
Stapleton, General 146
Stewart, Colonel John Roy 146
Stewarts of Appin 45, 88, 128, 146
Stewarts of Ardshiel 84, 133
Stirling Bridge, strategic importance 15, 25, 27
Stormount, Viscount of 13
Strathallan, Lord 13, 114, 119
Strickland, Francis 80
Stuart, Charles Edward (Bonnie Prince Charlie)
  Birth 77
  From Rome to France 79-80
  Arrival in Scotland 81-85
  Portrait (as a young man) **83**
  Entry into Perth 89-90
  To Edinburgh 91-94
  At Prestonpans 95-96, 105-106
  Advance into England 107-114
  Retreat from Derby 114-115
  Into Scotland 119-120
  In Glasgow 125-126
  At Falkirk 127-131
  Strategic Retreat 132-134
  Shortage of Money 135
  Raid on Nairn 138-139
  Culloden 139-140, 145-149
  Route in Britain **141** (map)
  Temperament 151
  Escape 152
  Old Age 153, **153** (portrait)
Stuart, James Francis Edward (The Old Pretender) 5, 6, 9-10, 11, 12
  Portrait **64**
  In Scotland 66-69
  Departure from Scotland 70-71
  Responsibility for rebellion's failure 75
  Further attempts at his restoration 77
  Farewell to his son 79
Stuart, Lt. Col. (of Edinburgh Castle) 22
Sutherland, Earl of 23

Target 19, **61**, **98**
Tencin, Cardinal de 79
Thomson, James 22
Tory Party 9-10, 11, 16, 52
Traquair, Earl of 13
Treaty of Utrecht 76
Tullibardine, Marquis of 13, 14, 15, 77, **77** (portrait), 80, 84, 89, 109, 150, 152
Volunteer horseman **35**
Wade, George 7-8, 88, 109, 110-111, **111** (portrait), 113, 116, 120, 126, 155
Walpole, Sir Robert 78
Walsh, Antoine 80, 81
Weapons, government **142**
Weapons, Highland 19, **58**, **59**, **60**, **61**, **64**
Whetham, General 47
Whig Party 9-10, 23
White, Alderman (of Newcastle) 30
Whiteford, Colonel 105
Whittel, Ebenezer 15
Widdrington, Lord 72
Wightman, Major-General 15, 48, 49, 77
William III 5-6, 8
Wills, Major-General 51, 52, 53, 54, 55, 56
Wintoun, Earl of 31-32, 42-43, 53, 72-73
Wolfe's Regiment 128, 145
Young Pretender *see* Stuart, Charles Edward